B.F. KEITH'S PALACE THEATRE

SOPHIE TUCKER
EVERYBODY'S PAL

Nazimova
in "India"

Willie West & McGinty

Phil Baker
A Bad Boy From A Good Family

Doyle & Dixon

Judy Garland

PROGRAM
© 1923
M. P. HANAFORD

BOOKS BY MARIAN SPITZER

THE PALACE

I TOOK IT LYING DOWN

A HUNGRY YOUNG LADY

WHO WOULD BE FREE

THE PALACE

THE PALACE

MARIAN SPITZER

With an Introduction by Brooks Atkinson

ATHENEUM

New York

1969

To my children

ERIC, EVA, EVAN *and* JOAN

PROLOGUE

IT WAS THE DAY before Easter, and cold; fair but cold, and the wind whipped the ladies' skirts way up above the tops of their eight-button shoes. The year was 1913 and no nice girl wore slippers on the street. Inside my new Easter coat, however, I felt very, very warm and under my large Easter hat my eyes were bright with excitement.

My father had taken me to a matinee; it was *A Good Little Devil* and it was wonderful, and there was a wonderful girl in it, a great big movie star already. But in that play she looked like a little girl. Her name was Mary Pickford. Another little girl in it played a fairy, and her name was Lillian Gish.

When we came out of the Republic Theatre, it was growing dark and people were streaming out of all the other theaters on the block. Right across the street the New Amsterdam, home of the *Ziegfeld Follies*, housed a musical comedy called *Oh! Oh! Delphine!* And farther down the block was the Eltinge, where Jane Cowl had been making people cry for months in a thrilling melodrama, *Within the Law.* She had made me cry, too, only a little while before, when I'd sneaked away from high school to see it on a Wednesday afternoon. But my father didn't know about that.

Between the New Amsterdam and the Eltinge were other theaters and a handsome restaurant called Murray's Roman Gardens, which I didn't discover until a few years later. We were going to tea at the Knickerbocker Hotel, across Broadway on 42nd Street. We called it tea, but my father had coffee and I had hot chocolate. I was hoping to see Caruso, who lived there, but he was playing a matinee himself that same afternoon, down Broadway at the Metropolitan Opera House. *The Girl of the Golden West* was the opera, with Caruso as the hero and Emmy Destinn as the Girl. Toscanini conducted.

Across the street from the Met you could see the Empire, the foremost legitimate theater of that time. Just then they were celebrating its twentieth birthday with a play called *Liberty Hall;* the star was John Mason. Down Broadway at 39th was the Knickerbocker Theatre and at 38th the Casino, famous houses of the era, both playing musicals. Lights were going on, Broadway was crowded with dressed-up matinee-goers. Everything looked terribly glamorous, only the word hadn't come into the language yet.

In the glimmering dusk we strolled up Broadway after tea at the Knickerbocker, where I had been allowed a peek at the famous King Cole Bar. The air was sharp and I shivered, but as much with delight as with cold. There was so much to look at: the *New York Times* Tower on the famous triangle that made Times Square, directly across 42nd Street from the Knickerbocker; catty-corner from it, Hammerstein's Victoria, with twelve acts of vaudeville; on the next block, Shanley's Restaurant in the Putnam Building, where General Putnam and George Washington had battled the British so many years ago; a block farther on, the beautiful Astor Hotel, only a few years old, and the home of many celebrities of the period. These were all on the left side of Broadway going uptown.

Across Broadway from the Astor stood the famous Rector's, where people like Diamond Jim Brady and Lillian Russell and Weber and Fields and Victor Herbert and *chorus girls* came to eat after the show. My father had tales to tell about them all, whether real or fancied I'll never know and I'm not at all sure he did.

There were other theaters, too, on both sides of Broadway —Cohan's and the Criterion and the Gaiety and the Globe and lots more, their electric lights sparkling in the darkening sky. Neon lights had not yet been invented; it truly was The Great White Way.

When my father said we really ought to be going home now, I begged to walk a little farther; the prosaic purlieus of Washington Heights had never seemed so uninviting. So on we strolled, and there, where Broadway and Seventh Avenue and 47th Street came together, loomed the newest theater in town; a vaudeville theater, much discussed as a possible rival to Mr. Hammerstein's Victoria. It was the Palace, ready and waiting for its opening performance the day after tomorrow —Easter Monday afternoon.

As I look back through the mist of years and romantic legend, it would be lovely to say that the Palace that March afternoon was a thing of fabulous beauty, giving promise of its future glory. Only it wouldn't be true. Compared to the great show places of the day, the Met, the Empire, the New Amsterdam, all gleaming with the patina of tradition, it was not particularly exciting. Tall and narrow for a theater, with a modest marquee, wedged between a pair of low brick buildings housing a cheap café, a pool hall, and a music publisher's office, the Palace that day seemed an object of no spectacular beauty. Still, I turned for one last look as we walked toward the subway. And the last thing I saw was the huge sign painted on the windowless 47th Street wall:

THE PALACE THEATRE

ACKNOWLEDGMENTS

READING ACKNOWLEDGMENTS in other people's books, I have always thought that this must be one of the hardest things to do. And so it is. During the many months of preparation and writing of this book, my help from countless friends and acquaintances, even relatives, was beyond measure. They dug generously into their files and memories and gave me a wealth of material, both factual and anecdotal. What I would like to do is name them all individually. But because of their great number and the limitations of space, I cannot. Nonetheless, every one of them has my gratitude.

I am particularly indebted to the following, however, who gave me access to their archives as well as their personal recollections: Abel Green, editor of *Variety*, and his girl Friday, Norma Nannini; Sam Zolotow of *The New York Times;* old Palace hands William McCaffrey, Arthur Willi, Max Gordon, and John Byram; Sol Schwartz, former President of RKO; Thomas J. Crehan, Vice-President of RKO–Stanley Warner Theatres; the present Palace management–

ACKNOWLEDGMENTS

James Nederlander, Paul Vroom, William Dean, and Ralph
Alswang; Jack Perlman, attorney for the Palace; Louis A.
Rachow, Librarian of the Walter Hampden Memorial Li-
brary at The Players; Paul Myers, Curator of the Theatre
Collection, New York Public Library at Lincoln Center; and
the New York Society Library.

Special thanks are due Sam Pearce, Curator of the
Theatre and Music Collection of the Museum of the City of
New York, who made available to me the resources of that
fine collection; also to Ann Marlowe Straus, who introduced
me to Mr. Pearce and the collection.

And, finally, my deep appreciation goes to Melvin Parks,
not only for his intensive research and wise advice, but also
for his moral support from the day I set down the first word
until I wrote "The End."

M.S.

INTRODUCTION

by Brooks Atkinson

UNTIL THE LATE 1920s and early 1930s it hardly seemed possible that vaudeville would disappear as a form of public entertainment or take fleeting refuge on the television screen. Vaudeville was a civilization—and a good one, too, for its performers were lively people and the acts in which they appeared were crisp and tonic. A theater buff could have a stimulating time by going to vaudeville shows exclusively.

The Palace was built to house vaudeville. For many years its bill changed every week. No matter how good or bad a show might be, something different opened there the next Monday afternoon. After a dismal beginning the Palace became the crowning vaudeville house in North America and retained that distinction until talking pictures and the mammoth film cathedrals changed the nature of show business.

By beginning early, Marian Spitzer became the perfect vaudeville goer. When she saw her first Palace show, escorted

xiii

by her father, she knew that it was acted especially for her, and she has always been susceptible to a well-staged vaudeville turn, whether a hot song ignited by the torrid Sophie Tucker or the hilarious *Dr. Kronkhite* sketch played by Smith and Dale. Or, as far as that goes, the romantic singing of Judy Garland and the comic virtuosity of Danny Kaye, both of whom appeared at the Palace for long runs after the continuity of weekly vaudeville shows had been broken.

But Miss Spitzer had one experience that puts her in the highest category. In the twenties she worked on the publicity staff of the Palace under the direction of Walter Kingsley, a humorous press agent who was also a delightful person. From her first assignment to a desk on the fabulous Sixth Floor, where vaudeville shows were put together, she lived in the midst of chaos and rejoiced in it.

She had other privileges: glimpses of E. F. Albee, grand panjandrum of the whole enterprise, and close association with J. J. Murdock, general manager of the corporation. In her job of composing publicity releases for the Palace, she could and did interview its greatest stars, who were demigods of their day. She could see all the shows without a ticket, sneak in through the back door to attend rehearsals and make use of the theater like a member of the family. During her mature life she has been a part of the entertainment world herself, in New York and in Hollywood. But her experience at the Palace gave her an introduction of the greatest value. She learned that show business consists of human beings—stars of the human comedy.

While reading Miss Spitzer's book it occurred to me that in retrospect any part of show business is comic. Now that

Albee has long been dead, the perspective on his career changes. His ferocity, his assaults on competitors, his pitiless discipline, his sanctimoniousness seem absurd. To read about him today is to realize that nothing was worth that driving energy. And so it goes throughout the whole saga of the Palace: the schoolboy penalties placed on agents who broke the rules, the competition for the star's dressing room, the hysteria incited by the appearance of Sarah Bernhardt, Nora Bayes' unbridled temperament, the craze surrounding the ballroom dancing of Vernon and Irene Castle, the desperate attempts to shake off the competition of talking pictures, the savagery of some of the trade-paper reviews—all these things become part of the human comedy as they recede into history.

Since Miss Spitzer has many happy memories of the Palace, and has done formidable research in the preparation of this chronicle, she is making a notable contribution to the mythology of Broadway. It is a comfort to have the Palace Theatre still in business. But there is something sedate about a theater that books long-run musical shows produced by different managements. What the Palace lacks today is bustle. Miss Spitzer reminds us of the power and personality it had when it was the home of vaudeville.

ILLUSTRATIONS

Follow page 108

All illustrations not otherwise credited are from the Theatre and Music Collection of the Museum of the City of New York

Advertisement of Palace opening in 1913, *The New York Times*

Sarah Bernhardt, drawing by Mortimer Menpes

W. C. Fields, caricature in crayon by Irving Hoffman

Ed Wynn

Bert Williams, caricature by Al Frueh
(The Walter Hampden Memorial Library at The Players, used by courtesy of the family of Al Frueh)

Nora Bayes

The Castles

Ethel Barrymore

Toto

Houdini

Singer's Midgets

Annette Kellerman, caricature by Al Frueh
(The Walter Hampden Memorial Library at The Players, used by courtesy of the family of Al Frueh)

Bert Wheeler, photograph by Bruno

The Dolly Sisters

ILLUSTRATIONS

Eva Tanguay, photograph by Strauss-Peyton
Jimmy Savo
(Theatre and Music Collection, The New York Public Library, Astor, Lenox and Tilden Foundations)
Eddie Cantor, painting by Roberto Gari
Jimmy Durante, photograph by Philippe Halsman
Fanny Brice
Sophie Tucker, photograph by Maurice Seymour
Grace Hayes, photograph by Mitchell
Bill Robinson
Ray Bolger
Ann Pennington
The Marx Brothers
Blossom Seeley
(Courtesy of Miss Seeley)
Weber and Fields, caricature by Al Frueh
(The Walter Hampden Memorial Library at The Players, used by courtesy of the family of Al Frueh)
Clark and McCullough
Frank Fay
William and Madeline Cameron Gaxton, photograph by Strauss-Peyton
(Courtesy of Mrs. Gaxton)
Alan King and Judy Garland
(Courtesy of Mr. King)
Danny Kaye, photograph by Roy Schatt
(Courtesy of Mr. Schatt)
Harry Belafonte, drawing in charcoal and conte crayon by Lisa Rhana
Gwen Verdon, drawing in charcoal and conte crayon by Lisa Rhana
(Courtesy of The Seven Arts Collector's Gallery)

xviii

THE PALACE

CHAPTER ONE

On Easter Monday, March 24, 1913, at two in the afternoon, the Palace opened its doors for the first time. Following a frigid Sunday, which had driven Easter paraders off the Avenue into the churches, the weather remained cold, wet, and disagreeable. The theater itself, living up to advance publicity, was spacious, handsome and lavishly decorated in crimson and gold. But nothing happened that afternoon to suggest the birth of a great theatrical tradition. No bells pealed, no guns roared, no signs appeared in the sky. To those on hand it was just "another op'nin', another show."

And not a notably spectacular show at that. The other important Keith houses in Manhattan—the Colonial and the Alhambra—had far more impressive names on their

3

vaudeville bills that week. Down Broadway at Times Square the undisputed queen of variety theaters, Hammerstein's Victoria, offered sixteen acts topped by Mr. and Mrs. Carter de Haven and the British dramatic star William Hawtry, plus a short film, all for a top price of fifty cents. Up Broadway at Columbus Circle's Park Theatre, the cyclonic Eva Tanguay headed her own vaudeville show. At the Hippodrome on Sixth Avenue the brothers Shubert were presenting a Mammoth New Circus. And at Madison Square Garden the really mammoth circus, Barnum & Bailey's, was turning away customers by the thousands. Pretty stiff competition for a new and untried theater, however handsome, which had the temerity to charge the unheard-of price of a whole dollar for a matinee, and a two-dollar top for evening shows.

There are many conflicting reports about that Palace opening, not any two in complete accord about the first bill. Since apparently no copy of the program survived, the display ad from that morning's *New York Times* must serve. The performers listed there included the Eight London Palace Girls, a dance ensemble; McIntyre and Harty, a comedy team; *The Eternal Waltz*, a condensed version of a Viennese operetta, with music by Leo Fall and a cast of thirty (known as a "flash act"); the Four Vannis, a wire act; La Napierkowska, a pantomimist and interpretive dancer; Ota Gygi, billed as the court violinist of Spain; Hy Mayer, featured cartoonist of *The New York Times*; George Ade's one-act play *Speaking to Father*, starring Milton Pollack; and, finally, Ed Wynn, listed simply as "a comedian," in a sketch called *The King's Jester*. Strange as it

4

may seem today, Wynn was not featured; in fact, he occupied a lowly spot on the bill. Ed's son, Keenan Wynn, explained recently that his father was a late addition to that first Palace bill. One of the acts originally booked was found wanting in rehearsal, and Ed, then appearing in Chicago, was hurriedly summoned as a replacement.

That first Palace performance was attended less by the public than by people in show business, both friends and enemies, though the enemies proved more numerous and more vocal than the friends. Between matinee and night shows word got around Broadway that the new theater was a flop. Indeed, between the two shows one act had been dropped— McIntyre and Harty—to be replaced by Taylor Holmes. Mr. Holmes was a versatile actor who had begun in vaudeville, then graduated to the legitimate stage, where he had played in everything from bedroom farce to *Hamlet*. Now, back in vaudeville, he did a monologue.

Next day the *Times* carried a mild review, describing the theater as a copy of a London music hall, and speaking with amused indifference of the program. About La Napierkowska, who had top billing, the reviewer wrote: "She danced with feet and arms bare and wore several veils, which she gradually took off as she Duncanized and Saintdenised." *The Eternal Waltz* won the most space and the highest praise. As for Ed Wynn, he was barely mentioned as an also-ran. Most of the other dailies politely turned thumbs down and indicated that the new theater had a dim future. When *Variety*, already the bible of show business, came out later in the week, its notice was more like a delighted funeral oration than a review, with a murderous attack on everything and everybody connected with the theater.

PALACE $2 VAUDEVILLE A JOKE, trumpeted the headline, while the subhead declared "No Praise and No Attendance." The story itself denounced the theater's prices, program, management. It was a blithely malicious account of poor attendance, high expenses, low grosses, and a hopeless future. "The fate of '$2 Vaudeville' at the new Palace was sealed before the house opened Monday," ran the first sentence, introducing two columns of undiluted venom. Singled out for special disdain was Ed Wynn, his act labeled as small-time speed. "Wynn, the jester, told jokes to the king. If the king failed to laugh, the jester would die. Fortunately the audience did not play the king." Happily for Ed Wynn and for future audiences who loved The Perfect Fool, he did not heed *Variety*'s advice to drop the act.

According to *Variety*, bets were being made up and down Broadway that the Palace would die before the season's end. William Hammerstein, the enormously successful manager of his father Oscar's Victoria Theatre (himself the father of Oscar 2nd, the great lyric writer), danced with glee and took a whole day off to celebrate the imminent demise of the presumptuous upstart. Admittedly, there was no reason to believe that a fabulous legend had just been born.

Like so many legends, the Palace had been the realization of one man's dream. That man was Martin Beck, who had come to this country at the age of sixteen with a troupe of Middle European actors. Failing to win an American public, the company broke up and scattered. Like other unemployed actors, past or present, Beck turned to anything that would

6

keep him alive. He sold pictures door to door, did all sorts of odd jobs, and finally turned up as a waiter in a Chicago music hall. That was in 1893, the year of the World's Fair. With his theatrical experience he soon found uses for his talents as part-time stage manager, house manager, and bookkeeper. But sometimes he even tended bar.

It was not long before he got a better job at a rival music hall. There he worked his way up to a partnership and eventually opened still another hall. Things went well for a while; then a sudden collapse, and back on the road went Martin Beck. He joined an outfit called Schiller's Vaudeville Company, then starting a west-bound tour.

Although strolling players who sang and danced and joked for their supper were known in ancient Greece and Rome, the actual word *vaudeville* seems to have originated in fifteenth-century France. There, in the province of Normandy, is a spot called Val (or Vau) de Vire—the valley of the river Vire—where the inhabitants entertained one another nightly with ballads and satirical folk songs. Presently their fame spread beyond their own valley, and they traveled to other parts of France. In the course of time, *vau de vire* was corrupted to *vaudeville*.

Some scholars maintain that the word first occurred in Paris with the singing of revolutionary songs, and that the phrase *voix de ville* (voice of the city) eventually became *vaudeville*. The earlier explanation is more commonly accepted, however. Regardless of its source, the word became international in character, and was first used in the United States during the mid-1800s. Some early American showmen found it too fancy for their taste, preferring the word *variety*, but it caught on, and by the time Martin Beck arrived in this country, *vaudeville* had entered the language.

During the Schiller troupe's San Francisco engagement, Beck met Gustave Walters, owner of the Orpheum Theatre. The Orpheum was a combined saloon and music hall, and because Walters knew more about buying liquor than buying talent, Beck soon became house manager and booking agent for the theater. Shortly he attracted the attention of some San Francisco tycoons who took over the Orpheum for unpaid debts. These tycoons were businessmen but not show-businessmen, so Martin Beck continued to run the Orpheum for them.

Combining a shrewd business sense with artistic awareness, Beck made the Orpheum a great success. Acquiring a pair of show-wise partners, he picked up theaters in other parts of California, and so the Orpheum Circuit was born. Later he formed an alliance with the ruling powers of vaudeville in Chicago and surrounding territory. The corporate name was Western Vaudeville Association, which along with the Orpheum Circuit controlled most vaudeville bookings from Chicago to the Pacific Coast.

Just as the Western Vaudeville Association dominated the Orpheum Circuit in the West, so did its New York counterpart, the United Booking Office (UBO), dominate the Keith Circuit, which included most vaudeville theaters, big-time and small-, in the East. Years later the name UBO was changed to Keith Vaudeville Exchange. No matter what it was called, this organization ruled the lives of thousands of vaudeville performers. Its nominal head was B. F. Keith of

Boston; its active head his long-time partner and aide, Edward F. Albee.

There were competitors, of course. One of them was Percy Williams, who rose from boy actor to millionaire theater owner and is now immortalized by the Percy Williams Home for retired actors in East Islip, Long Island. Another was William Morris, an immigrant boy who became the world's foremost theatrical agent and personal manager, and founder of the giant talent agency that bears his name. The formidable third was Oscar Hammerstein, mentioned earlier, the onetime cigar maker and inventor who became an opera impresario and vaudeville manager. For years he remained a thorn in the flesh of the Keith Circuit with his Victoria Theater and Roof Garden at the corner of 42nd Street and Broadway.

Despite an imposing array of rivals and adversaries of the circuit in general and of E. F. Albee in particular, the Keith Circuit maintained its stranglehold on vaudeville from the beginning of the twentieth century until the early 1930s.

Martin Beck had long dreamed of invading New York, and the success of his Orpheum Circuit only intensified that desire. As a start he took offices in the building that housed the UBO. From there he made plans: to build a vaudeville theater that would surpass every other vaudeville theater in the country, not only in physical beauty but also in the caliber and importance of its performers.

Exactly how long it took Beck to turn his vision into reality nobody now alive can accurately say. Of the many

9

accounts given, the most convincing is the one told by George Rector, who owned jointly with his father the famous theatrical restaurant at Broadway and 44th Street. According to him, the project originated in the restaurant when a young Philadelphia real-estate man, Felix Isman, joined Beck in whispered conclave, dragged him out in the middle of his meal, and came back half an hour later with Beck on his arm, a Cheshire Cat grin on his face, and a deal in his pocket.

Maybe that's the way it happened; maybe not. One thing is certain: shortly thereafter Martin Beck acquired property at Broadway and 47th Street. The lease was signed on October 21, 1911. Isman's role in all this is not quite clear, but somewhere in the lease his name is mentioned in connection with a $300,000 mortgage. And George Rector contended that Isman made something like $800,000 from the transaction.

The original lease still exists. It is an agreement between The Palace Theatre & Realty Company, lessee, and George H. Earle, Jr., of Philadelphia, lessor. The latter was the father of Governor Earle of Pennsylvania. Interesting to note is the absence of the name Martin Beck anywhere in the lease or among the signatories. The document was signed by Mr. Earle and—for the Palace Theatre Company—by Herman Fehr, President. Since Mr. Beck knew that his moving in on the New York territory would be looked upon by Albee and his cohorts as a declaration of war, the absence of his name can hardly be construed as modesty or an oversight.

The lease covered property on the east side of Broadway from the corner of 47th Street southward to the center of the

10

block, and five buildings on the south side of 47th Street. It became effective on January 1, 1912, providing for a ground rent of $41,000 a year for the first year, with escalations of several thousand dollars over a period of twenty-one years. After this the lessee had the right to exercise the first of a series of twenty-one-year options, the last to end on the 31st day of December 2017. The proposed theater, which of course would be owned by the Palace company, was guaranteed to be fireproof, and its office space to be at least six stories high.

One term of the lease, the demolition of all buildings included in the property, was not carried out to the letter; photographs of the Palace in 1915 show it flanked by a group of two- or three-story brick or brownstone buildings, scruffy-looking even then. To the north, now the site of Whelan's drugstore, were a cheap eating place called the Palace Café, where Leo Lindy got his start as a waiter (according to Max Gordon), and the music-publishing firm of Maurice Abrams, later the husband of a great Palace star, Belle Baker. To the south were a pool parlor and a United Cigar store.

Ask anybody in New York, or a lot of other places, where the Palace Theatre stands. Invariably the answer is "the corner of Broadway and 47th Street." As a matter of strict fact, it does not. The theater itself is one door south of the corner, though the office building extends to and around the corner of 47th Street. And if anyone wants to be even more meticulous, it is a moot point whether the theater stands on Broadway or Seventh Avenue, because that particular spot is where Broadway and Seventh Avenue merge to form the

11

northern end of Times (formerly Longacre) Square. Today that area is called Duffy Square, in honor of Father Francis Duffy, famous chaplain of New York's "Fighting 69th" Regiment. Directly opposite the Palace on the little triangle that joins Broadway and Seventh Avenue is a statue of Father Duffy.

On the first of January 1912, Martin Beck's long dream began to take visible form. And so did a long nightmare. If there is anyone still alive who knows exactly what happened between Beck's announcement about the Palace and the completion of the theater, he cannot or will not tell. The bare facts are simple: none of the vaudeville magnates was going to stand still for Beck's control of the newest, grandest and most widely heralded vaudeville house in New York. Separately or in combination they were determined to freeze him out.

By the time the Palace opened on March 24, 1913, Beck's opponents had worked out a devious plan to reduce his financial interest in the theater he had built and give the controlling interest to E. F. Albee, now supreme boss of the Keith Circuit. Some time earlier Albee had made a deal giving Oscar Hammerstein the exclusive rights to book Keith acts in the theatrical district as far north as 59th Street. Now Hammerstein was threatening to bring an injunction which, if successful, would prevent any Keith act from appearing at the Palace and, in effect, would keep the Palace from opening.

But Albee knew that Hammerstein was in financial straits and in desperate need of cash. So he bought back the rights at a price quoted variously between $200,000 and $250,000. This move accomplished three things: first, it gave Albee access to the acts he needed; second, it weakened Hammerstein's position; and, third, it gave Albee the leverage to wrest financial control of the Palace from Martin Beck. Though he still had his theater, Beck could book no acts except on Albee's terms.

At any rate, when the bloodless coup was over, Albee controlled the Palace and Beck retained only 25 percent of the stock. He did have an office in the Palace Building, and at the beginning the booking was done through him. He also had the knowledge that he had created the theater, for whatever that was worth to him. And he had two other invaluable assets—enterprise and taste.

Typically, some weeks before the Palace opened he sailed for France, called on Sarah Bernhardt in Paris and persuaded her to come to the United States for a tour of the Orpheum Circuit with excerpts from plays she had done successfully in this country. Beck suggested that she start on the West Coast, work her way east to Chicago and on through the Keith houses, with a Palace engagement as the grand climax. Mme. Bernhardt agreed, but it would take some time to complete arrangements.

Meanwhile Mr. Albee, having solved the problem of the invader Martin Beck and the rival Oscar Hammerstein in one stroke, had other vexing matters to contend with. For years he had been conducting a feud with the independent William Morris, basically because Albee couldn't tolerate the idea that anyone could get along without him, and Morris had been doing just that rather well. Having failed to lick

Morris, he tried to join him by offering him a managerial job with the UBO. Honest as well as independent, Morris refused the offer for several reasons, but especially because it would have meant splitting agents' commissions and taking kickbacks from actors he engaged.

Now enraged, Albee took out after Morris with everything he had. The edict went out: no act under the management of William Morris, no act that played any theater that Morris controlled, directly or indirectly, could work for the UBO, which meant the Keith Circuit. Though this was a severe blow to Morris, he managed to overcome it, partly by acquiring an empty theater, the American, on 42nd Street and Eighth Avenue; partly by signing up Harry Lauder, the Scottish singing comedian, whose tour throughout the country he arranged with great success, largely aided by his friend Sime Silverman, founder and publisher of *Variety*.

Sime Silverman was a young New Yorker with a passion for vaudeville and a compulsion to speak the truth as he saw it. In the early 1900s he wangled a part-time job on the *Morning Telegraph* at a salary of five dollars a week. One of his tasks was covering vaudeville, and his scathing reviews of acts he disliked cost the paper a good deal of advertising. It also cost Sime his job. He decided the only way to speak his mind independently was to have his own theatrical paper. So, on December 16, 1905, after much toil and trouble, he launched *Variety*, a weekly with emphasis on vaudeville. Its publisher's credo, needless to say, was: "Get the most, get it first, get it straight, and tell the facts."

The toil and trouble continued, but with his own guts and the help of loyal friends, Sime kept his paper alive. Because he always insisted on speaking frankly, he made a number of enemies, chief among them E. F. Albee. From the beginning of *Variety*, Silverman and Albee had been at war, and Sime's stepped-up attacks on Albee in behalf of William Morris only intensified the vendetta. A series of derogatory news stories about the Palace and bitter editorials from Sime's acid pen marred the image of the new theater even before it opened.

Variety was damaged, too—not in reputation so much as in its cash drawer. Sime's attacks naturally infuriated Mr. Albee further, and early in 1913, shortly before the Palace opened, he issued another edict, banning from work on the Keith Circuit any act that advertised in *Variety* or was seen reading it. This blacklist makes the one of the Joe McCarthy era pale by comparison. Bad as it was, the political blacklist of the 1950s affected, however unjustly, only a fraction of people in the movie, radio and TV industries. Albee's boycott, vigorously enforced, included everyone in vaudeville who had the effrontery to disobey him.

The Albee ban did not apply only to performers. Managers and other employees of the Keith theaters were warned that anyone known to have a copy of *Variety* in his possession would be summarily fired. Naturally, there were very few copies of the weekly to be seen around the Keith theaters, and *Variety*'s advertising fell off alarmingly. Albee had also warned music publishers not to advertise there if they wanted their songs to be played and sung in the Keith theaters. This ban extended to the Orpheum Circuit, which gives some idea of its punishing effect on entertainers throughout the country. Despite all this, *Variety* managed to survive, and rumor had it that a few brave souls smuggled it into their homes or hotel rooms between the pages of their daily papers.

To quote a Jimmy Durante byword of a later day, them was the conditions that prevailed when the Palace opened on that rainy Easter Monday of 1913.

CHAPTER TWO

IT WOULD BE dramatic but untrue to say that the Palace leaped from its disastrous first week to a sudden success. Business continued to be poor and the onslaughts of the theater's enemies lost none of their vigor or venom. The second week's bill, featuring the singer Elizabeth Murray, was not much better than the first. Three acts of the original bill had been held over—the London Palace Girls, Ota Gygi, and La Napierkowska. Also featured was the legitimate star Frank Keenan, father-in-law of Ed Wynn and grandfather of Keenan Wynn. The third week was distinguished by the presence of dancer Ruth St. Denis and Florence Roberts, a top film star of the period.

The theater struggled along for another couple of weeks, with a few acts then or later well known to the public: for example, José Collins, a popular musical-comedy actress; Cecil Lean, also from the musical stage; Miss Juliet, gifted impersonator; and the standard vaudeville comedy team of Whiting and Burt. But the position of the Palace remained precarious. Bets on its impending demise were still being made, foes were still gleeful, everyone connected with the enterprise blamed everyone else for the coming debacle.

And then, on the 28th of April, in the sixth week of its existence, Palace business took an upturn. The bill was much the best so far, including as it did the popular dancer Bessie Clayton; the well-liked comedy team of Dooley and Sales; the harmonizing Courtney Sisters, one of whom—Florence —later married George Jessel; Nat Wills, the comic tramp; and, to cap it all, the First Lady of the American Theater, Miss Ethel Barrymore.

It is no news to theater buffs that Ethel Barrymore played the Palace. But not many people realize that she played there so early in its life, and that she was at least partially responsible for saving it from certain failure and launching it on the road to success. Nearly everyone, even the most theater-minded, associates her Palace appearances with a famed one-act play by Sir James M. Barrie, *The Twelve Pound Look* (considerately translated in program notes as *The $60 Look*), but that came later. Miss Barrymore's Palace debut was made in a one-act play by Richard Harding Davis, *Miss Civilization*. Reviews were favorable, if not ecstatic, and business improved that week.

Not until May 5, however, did the Palace really turn the corner, as a result of Martin Beck's recent trip to Paris.

18

History was made that day, and the Palace began its climb toward the pinnacle it occupied for virtually two decades as the royal house of vaudeville. It is a point worth noting that this feat of magic was not achieved by a vaudevillian, any more than the upswing of the previous week had been. It was accomplished by another star of the legitimate stage. Not just the First Lady of the American Theater, not just the First Lady of the French Theater, but the First Lady of the Theater the whole world over: Sarah Bernhardt. The one, the only, the Divine Sarah.

Bernhardt had brought several classic and semi-classic plays to Broadway, and she had twice toured the Orpheum Circuit for Martin Beck with great success. This, however, was her first appearance in New York vaudeville. Advance publicity had been tremendous, aided by a backlog from years past. Tales of her temperament, eccentricities such as her habit of sleeping in a coffin, a legion of lovers, all vied with her unquestioned genius to attract audiences who wanted to see the legend as much as they wanted to see the actress. Prices were raised for her engagement, and people gladly paid.

Bernhardt brought with her several members of her company from the Théâtre Sarah Bernhardt in Paris, including a handsome young leading man named Lou Tellegen, who later became an idol of American theater and films, and husband for some time of Geraldine Farrar. She also brought a considerable repertoire, changing programs several times a week. Her opening performance was a one-act play co-authored by her son, Maurice, entitled *Une Nuit de*

19

Noël sous la Terreur, tactfully subtitled "A Christmas Night Under the Terror" for Palace spectators who might not know French.

With her arrival, too, came news of a benefit performance by Mme. Bernhardt while appearing in San Francisco a few weeks earlier. It had been a special performance for a very special audience. She took her company to San Quentin, that grim prison overlooking San Francisco Bay, and gave a performance of *Une Nuit de Noël* for the inmates. The prisoners and their keepers alike were overwhelmed by her eloquence, whether or not they understood her language; and even more impressed by her entrance to the prison in an automobile, the first one ever seen within those gates.

Other items in her Palace repertoire were an abbreviated version of Sardou's *Théodora;* two scenes from Racine's *Phèdre;* an act from *Lucrezia Borgia* by Victor Hugo; and as *pièce de résistance*, the last act of *The Lady of the Camellias,* the Dumas play known colloquially and incorrectly as *Camille.* Since the last act of that drama, with its heart-rending, cough-racked death scene is probably the greatest tearjerker in theatrical annals, and since it has been said that the Divine Sarah could reduce an audience to a sodden mass merely by reading the telephone book, it is easy to imagine what happened at the Palace whenever *The Lady of the Camellias* was performed. Business boomed. The public stormed the Palace doors as if attacking the Bastille. One venerable man I know, who boasts of having seen everything in the Bernhardt repertoire as well as every other "Camille" in his lifetime, claims there has never been anything like Sarah's performance before or since.

20

If that sounds like extravagant praise, I can confirm it personally. My father had a birthday during Bernhardt's engagement, which ran through May, and on that afternoon he took me to the Palace to see her. I've done my share of weeping over that old soap opera, but I cannot remember any performance, not even when Ethel Barrymore expired in the embrace of Conway Tearle at the Empire, or when Garbo breathed her last in the arms of Robert Taylor, that reduced me to such a pulp. It took the rest of the program, including "Edison's Moving-Talking Pictures" about the cabinet of New York's Mayor Gaynor, to get me dried out and calmed down enough to leave the theater. Even then I was so overcome that I refused a chocolate soda. They talk about four-handkerchief shows. That one could have used a baker's dozen! Years later I can only think what agony it must have been for the hapless performer who had to follow that lachrymose experience. Poor little Bessie Wynn, "The Lady Dainty of Vaudeville"! She must have shed tears, too, but they were no doubt tears of rage and frustration.

Although Bernhardt had originally been booked for only two weeks, the run was extended—truly by popular demand —for a third, and she stayed for the first half of another, leaving on the Thursday of the fourth week because of prior commitments in France. That third week was the most lucrative in the theater's brief existence. *Variety,* no great friend of the Palace, gave the week's gross as $22,000, which meant a profit of $6,000. But *The New York Times* listed the gross at a very healthy $27,000.

Probably the most repeated legend about Bernhardt involved her monetary demands. It is on record that her salary was $7,000 a week, but various chroniclers offer slightly varying details. Some say she would not go on stage for a performance until she had been paid $500 in gold. Others claim that payment was made after each performance, and not necessarily in gold but in folding money. Still others maintain that she was trusting enough to wait until after the evening show. But that she did receive $1,000 every day seems to be the basic truth. Another story given much currency described a bearskin carpet leading from her dressing room to the stage, placed there to muffle the sound of her wooden leg. That did happen during a return engagement; in 1913 both legs were her own.

Imperious as she was, however, her attitude toward other players demonstrated sympathy and kindness. Having enjoyed one of the turns on her bill, a "living statue" act called *Poems in Marble*, she summoned its creator, Paul Selden, to her dressing room. After congratulating him, she wrote him a letter of praise and granted him permission to use it in advertising. This he did, in a fairly gaudy full-page ad on the back cover of *Variety*. Apparently Mr. Selden was not afraid of Albee's boycott.

Before she returned to France, Mme. Sarah was greatly honored. At one matinee three worshipful young American stars paid homage to her by doing walk-ons during one of the plays. They were Laurette Taylor, Jane Cowl, and Elsie Janis, all appearing in hits of their own that season: *Peg O' My Heart, Within the Law* and *The Lady of the Slipper*, respectively. (According to an unpublished manuscript by Laurette Taylor, it was Marguerite Clark, not Elsie Janis, who was one of the trio. Also, Miss Taylor recalled, Jane

Cowl, dismayed at the costume she would have to wear, walked out, and a Palace secretary was hurriedly impressed to impersonate her.) During one show toward the end of her run a large group of top theatrical people, headed by David Belasco and Charles Frohman, assembled on stage and presented her with a laurel wreath made of silver and gold.

Bernhardt may have overshadowed other performers, but May 1913 marked some important beginnings at the Palace. Early in the show during the week of the 10th a man appeared with baggy pants, a tattered cutaway, a battered top hat, and a large red nose. He was billed as "The Silent Humorist," a comic juggler who did not speak. He convulsed the audience, and even *Variety* gave him a rave notice. He was W. C. Fields. Contrary to one of the most enduring myths of show business, that Fields never spoke a word on stage until much later in his career—notably as Eustace McGargle in *Poppy*—he did play a speaking role as early as 1905 in *The Ham Tree*, supporting the blackface team of McIntyre and Heath.

Another one-man show on that same Bernhardt bill was the protean actor Owen McGiveney, a vaudeville favorite then and for many years thereafter. McGiveney was the oustanding quick-change artist of them all; in split seconds he could do several scenes from *Oliver Twist*, playing Bill Sykes, Nancy, and the villainous Fagin, making his changes in lightning time to the bewilderment and appreciation of his audience. Owen, Jr., his son and heir to his talent, repeated the same show on television while this was being written.

Bernhardt sailed for France on the 16th of May, and after the evening show of that date the Palace went dark for the summer. Today it would seem folly to close a theater that had only just climbed out of the red after three precarious months. But air-conditioning was not even a dream in 1913, and all big-time vaudeville houses closed till after Labor Day.

The Palace stayed dark until September 1, but the magic of Bernhardt and clever publicity for upcoming programs kept the public as well as the Broadway boys on the alert. Rumors of internecine warfare also piqued the curiosity of the entertainment world. It is part of the mystery of show business that, though it was his signing of Sarah Bernhardt which rescued the Palace from early oblivion, Martin Beck got little or no credit for that feat. He was attacked from within the organization and jeered at from without. Once, when he booked the concert baritone David Bispham into the Palace, *Variety* twitted him: "Oh you, Mr. Beck, would you rather have a Beethoven Sonata yourself than a Berlin rag? Honest now, Martin Beck?" And later: "The Palace lost $5,000 last week, probably under Keith management, although Martin Beck is allowed to pose for a short while longer as 'Metropolitan Impresario.'" Whatever such gibes may have done to his innermost soul, he stuck it out and gave no sign of suffering. It may be that his personal profits from the Bernhardt engagement did much to soothe his wounded pride. In any event, when the Palace reopened, Martin Beck was still booking the shows.

The headliner of the opening autumn bill was Fritzi Scheff, the musical-comedy star with the enchanting Viennese accent, who had captured all New York some years back in *Mlle. Modiste* when she sang Victor Herbert's all-time classic, "Kiss Me Again." Though she did capacity business the first day, her act was not too well received, largely because Miss Scheff disappointed women in the audience by wearing only one gown throughout. It was noted that at the Wednesday matinee Mme. Schumann-Heink, massive contralto of the Metropolitan Opera, sat in a box with Martin Beck, giving rise to speculation that he was trying to lure her into doing a turn at the Palace.

Supporting acts, big names already or not long after, were Laddie Cliff, a song-and-dance man from England, and Julius Tannen, for years one of the most brilliant monologists in vaudeville and revue. Although technically a stand-up comic, he was not a one-line jokester or a clown. His humor was based on ideas, not gags. He was a witty comedian, brilliant and kind. And he had those most invaluable qualities for a vaudevillian, a quick mind and an economy of effort. Once, in the middle of his act, the theater's great black tomcat strolled across the stage and settled down comfortably at his feet. He glanced down at the creature. "This is a monologue," he said, without missing a beat, "not a catalogue."

His career reached a peak, where it stayed for a long time. Then, in the inexplicable way of some actors, he began to slip. For a while he left show business and tried selling furniture. But he couldn't take it, and went back to the stage. He never made it back all the way, and eventually landed in Hollywood, where he had roles in a few pictures before dropping out of sight.

Other supporting people on that first fall bill were Minnie

Dupree, a legitimate actress in a one-act play; and Horace Golden, the magician. Golden and Miss Scheff were held over for a second week. Also on that bill appeared two of vaudeville's strongest attractions: Joe Jackson, the tramp cyclist whose antics delighted audiences until the day he died (and whose son Joe, Jr., is doing the same act on television); and Victor Moore, with his wife, Emma Littlefield. Their hilarious *Change Your Act or Go Back to the Woods* drew roars of laughter from at least two generations of vaudeville audiences. It need hardly be said that Moore won even greater fame on the legitimate stage as the befuddled Alexander Throttlebottom in the Pulitzer Prize musical *Of Thee I Sing.*

Business was good that first fall week, though it fell off during the second, *Variety* claiming that the house lost $5,000 those seven days. But as the season progressed, both business and reputation began to build. It was during that season of 1913–14 that the detractors grew less vehement, the prophets of doom almost imperceptibly moved from gleeful hope to reluctant acceptance, and the tradition of Monday-afternoon-at-the-Palace began. The bill always changed with the Monday matinee, and a special excitement filled the air. The audience was largely professional: other performers, vaudevillians with an open week, legitimate and musical-comedy stars and near-stars with an eye to future gold. Broadway producers or their scouts got into the habit of coming, to see which acts were good and who might be worth tempting away from vaudeville for the greater prestige of the legitimate theater. And of course there were the rival vaudeville magnates.

26

After Fritzi Scheff's second week the Palace bill was topped by two important women. One was the handsome Nora Bayes, formerly of the *Ziegfeld Follies*, with her crystal-cool voice and her flawless enunciation, singing the never-waning "Shine On, Harvest Moon." Nora didn't strain, she didn't move around, she didn't shout. Yet you could hear her in the last row of the gallery, and a microphone would have been as necessary to her as a fur coat to a Bantu. Though this was true of all singers those days, Bayes made it seem effortless. The other headliner was a leading light of the heavy drama, Nance O'Neill—she too had coughed and wept her way through *The Lady of the Camellias*—in a one-act play called *The Second Ash Tray*.

There was only one star dressing room at the Palace, not very large as dressing rooms go, and which of these rather imperious and high-strung ladies got it, no one now remembers. It must have caused a spot of trouble. At any rate, both stars got good reviews, and shared the bill with a family of acrobats and a troupe of monkeys.

After that came the Stan Stanley Trio, a team of hilarious trampoline comics; the aforementioned David Bispham; and the Gus Edwards Revue, a kid act including assorted small fry who got around a lot as time went by— among them a sweet little girl called Cuddles, later to become the film star Lila Lee; and a collection of boys—two Georgies, Price and Jessel, and another boy named Eddie Cantor. Walter Winchell also was an early Gus Edwards kid.

Any attempt to list all the people who played the Palace through the years would read like *Who's Who in the Theatre*, but a sampling of those one could see and hear just from the close of September 1913 till the year's end must include: Marie Dressler; Henry E. Dixey; Maurice and Walton, who vied with the Castles for the honor of starting the ballroom-dancing craze; Bert Melrose, who drew gasps and giggles by climbing precariously up a seemingly topless pile of chairs, swaying dangerously back and forth until he finally landed gracefully unharmed on his feet; Olga Nethersole, whose daring production of Daudet's *Sapho*, adapted by Clyde Fitch, had so shocked the public back in 1900 that she was arrested and Wallack's Theatre closed after twenty-nine performances. Miss Nethersole was tried and acquitted, the play reopened, and her reputation was made forever.

Marie Lloyd, the London music-hall star, also played the Palace that season after a bit of a dust-up. On her arrival she had been detained at Ellis Island because she was traveling openly with a man not her husband. Moreover, she forthrightly used four-letter words in a time when that just wasn't done. For this and her personal life, she became known as "the female Rabelais." After what was criticized as too long a delay, Keith and Beck came to her rescue and she scored a great success at the Palace and elsewhere.

A story is told of her on the occasion of a London theatrical benefit. After a number of turns had appeared, the master of ceremonies announced: "Now, ladies and gentlemen, Miss Marie Lloyd will entertain." At which a voice from the gallery shouted: "Marie Lloyd's nothing but a dirty whore." "Nevertheless," interrupted the unruffled announcer, "Miss Lloyd will entertain."

Another singing star who played the Palace during Miss

Lloyd's second week also came from England, where she was a great favorite "on the halls," as the British put it, and in revue. She was Ethel Levey, American by birth and the divorced wife of George M. Cohan, with whom she had appeared in a number of shows on this side of the Atlantic. Years later, when Jimmy Cagney made *Yankee Doodle Dandy,* the award-winning movie of Cohan's life, Ethel Levey sued the producers, Warner Brothers, for a huge sum on the grounds that she had been misrepresented by the character portrayed as Cohan's wife, and that her right of privacy had been invaded, although another name had been used in the film.

Ethel Levey scored a big hit at the Palace and came back several times in later years. Contrary to widely held belief, the fabulous George M. never played the Palace himself, though his statue at the 46th Street base of Duffy Square is only a pigeon's flutter from the theater. The only reason ever offered for this omission, and not by him, was fear of facing that Monday matinee mob. Since fear and modesty were not among his outstanding characteristics, this seems hard to believe; some old vaudevillians claim that Cohan had had a tremendous quarrel with Palace booker Eddie Darling over a potential booking, and that neither man ever forgave the other. Vicariously Cohan reached the Palace in 1968 in the person of Joel Grey, star of *George M!,* the musical based on Cohan's life.

Two other great names in the entertainment world are automatically but incorrectly assumed to have played the Palace: Al Jolson and Sir Harry Lauder. Al Jolson couldn't because he was under contract to the Shuberts, mortal enemies of the Keith Circuit and all its personnel. (Al's brother, Harry Jolson—an unreasonable facsimile—did appear there.) Lauder couldn't because he was under contract to William Morris, whose enmity was even more intense than the Shuberts', if that were possible. His absence in the flesh, however, did not prevent the Palace from running a short sound movie of him, in which the name LAUDER appeared in extra-large type and the subject matter was almost invisible.

A handful of other notables who played the Palace that year were beautiful Lilian Lorraine from the *Ziegfeld Follies;* May Wirth, the equestrienne; Adelaide and Hughes, a stunning pair of ballroom dancers; Bernard Granville, comedian and father of Bonita, child movie star; and Cissie Loftus, the impersonator. Others included Cressy and Dayne; Bert Williams, the great Negro comedian and singer; plus a mixed bag of acrobats, jugglers, dog acts, "living pictures," and magicians.

Two notable women stars emerged that season. One was Belle Baker, of "Eli Eli" fame, who introduced a couple of Irving Berlin's songs—the popular "Michigan" and a comedy number called "Cohen Owes Me 97 Dollars." "You could do songs like that in those days," Mr. Berlin told me recently "without offending anybody."

The other newcomer was Blossom Seeley, already known on the musical-comedy stage. She did an act with the baseball player Rube Marquard, who was then her husband. Miss Seeley, pert and blonde today as she was half a century ago, later worked with her second husband, Benny Fields, and remained, like Miss Baker, a favorite Palace regular.

Although control of the Palace had already been seized

30

from Martin Beck, word did not get out until the theater had been operating for more than six months. *Variety* broke the story in a manner sympathetic to Mr. Beck, pointing out that Palace business "under Martin Beck is surpassing business in the other New York Keith houses." *Variety* also predicted that the Keith name would soon go up outside the theater. On November 10 it did, despite Beck's statement a few days earlier that there was no friction and that the various interests were coming closer together.

During the first week of January 1914 the bill boasted an outstanding list of names: Louis Mann, the dramatic star; Jack Norworth, singer, songwriter, and sometime husband of Nora Bayes; and Will Rogers. That same month Vernon and Irene Castle first played the Palace. Joe Laurie, Jr., reports in his book *Vaudeville* that the Castles were doing their act at Hammerstein's that same week. This is a little hard to understand, considering the rivalry between the two managements, but it seems to be a matter of record. Later it became a fairly frequent practice for a popular act to play two theaters during the same week, dashing back and forth by car to make deadlines. But this was always for the Keith theaters. The Castle doubling in rival houses was unique at that time. Laurie also says that they were accompanied by a twelve-piece Negro orchestra, which the Hammersteins would not allow in the pit. Whereupon Vernon Castle put the orchestra on stage.

Along with the Castles were Maggie Cline, the legit comedienne; Sam Bernard, the "Dutch" comic; Cross and Josephine, a standard vaudeville act for many years; and, in the animal department, both horse and dog acts.

For the rest of that month and through February to the middle of March the Palace bills contained such then and future stars as singer Adele Ritchie; Hyams and McIntyre, the parents of movie star Leila Hyams; and Clark and Bergman, another standard vaudeville team. There was also a revue entitled *Jesse Lasky's Redheads*. This same Lasky, formerly a young man with a horn, became head of Famous Players–Lasky, which in turn became Paramount Pictures. A couple of Blanches, Walsh and Bates—both dramatic actresses—appeared. For variety there were the bouncing beauty Trixie Friganza; Joan Sawyer, the dancer, with Art Jarrett as her partner; and an amusing act called Howard's Ponies.

It was in February 1914 that Fanny Brice made her debut. Eddie Foy was there too with his Seven Little Foys. Others included the Avon Comedy Four; Claude Gillingwater, who became a well-known character actor in the movies; Anna Held, the charming French girl once married to Florenz Ziegfeld (Luise Rainer's portrayal of Anna in MGM's *The Great Ziegfeld* was so moving that it won an Academy Award); the team of Lambert and Ball; Mae Murray, the silent-movie star with the bee-stung lips, and *her* partner, Clifton Webb; Swor and Mack, an indigenous vaudeville team; Gus Edwards' *Kid Kabaret* (that's the way he spelled it) ; and George White, then a young dancer, later the producer of *George White's Scandals*. Among White's several dancing partners was the beautiful Lucille Cavanagh, with whom he had a long run in 1916.

On the theater's first anniversary bill, March 23, with holdovers Mae Murray and Clifton Webb, appeared William Faversham, a great legitimate star, in a one-act play; and Yancsi (later Jennie) Dolly, with her current husband and partner, Harry Fox.

When summer came around, the Palace broke with tradition and stayed open despite the heat. Some of the great names in vaudeville, then and later, played there through the summer. Among them were Rooney and Bent—Pat and Marion, beloved characters on and off stage. Pat came from a long line of dancers, and anyone lucky enough to have been around at the time remembers his famous waltz clog and other specialties. And, leaping ahead almost four decades, anyone lucky enough to have seen *Guys and Dolls* in the early 1950's remembers with delight his endearing performance as the wise and gentle missionary, especially his touching rendition of the song "More I Cannot Wish You."

A few other standard names of vaudeville played the Palace that summer, among them Morton and Glass; Grace LaRue of the sweet voice and the huge red cartwheel hat; Joseph Santley; Valerie Bergere in a sketch called *Judgment;* the team of Riggs and Witchie; Mr. and Mrs. Carter de Haven (parents of Gloria, of film and television fame); and James and Bonnie Thornton. Ruth Roye, an attractive and enormously popular singer, introduced a silly song that was a hit of the era, "Abba Dabba Honeymoon." There were also the zany Arnaut Brothers with their bird imitations (their sons are doing it now on TV); the Empire City Quartette; Rae Samuels, "The Blue Streak of Vaudeville"; and a host of others, including the usual Noah's Ark assortment of animal acts.

An impressive array of legitimate stars picked up some

sizable spare change that summer. Ethel Barrymore played a return engagement, and half a dozen famous names, fresh from Broadway engagements, lent their luster to the Palace, either in one-act plays written specially for them, or sections of past plays. Such figures as Amelia Bingham, Douglas Fairbanks, Wilton Lackaye, and Mary Nash were among them; also the distinguished actor Arnold Daly, who had been arrested some ten years earlier when he brought Shaw's play *Mrs. Warren's Profession* to the New York stage after it had been banned in England. Mitzi Hajos and Lina Abarbanell each took a turn at the Palace, too; they came from the Broadway musical stage.

That summer was notable for the vaudeville debut of one person whose name was, and still is, practically synonymous with vaudeville in general and the Palace in particular. That person was Sophie Tucker, later billed as "The Last of the Red Hot Mamas." Trying to explain Sophie is like trying to explain a force of nature. Besides, it is hardly necessary. Although she died in 1966, she still remains a living presence.

It was like that from the start. When she opened at the Palace on July 24, 1914, she had to compete with the outbreak of the First World War. As far as show business was concerned, Sophie won. Hot from Hammerstein's and a successful season of night-clubbing, she sang a group of new songs, ranging from the saccharine "There's a Girl in the Heart of Maryland" through Irving Berlin's "International Rag" to the sizzling "Who Paid the Rent for Mrs. Rip Van Winkle (When Rip Van Winkle Was Away)?"

Bill McCaffrey, a booker there at the time, says that Miss

Tucker was canceled right after her first Monday matinee because of the Rip Van Winkle song. She made no mention of that incident in her autobiography, *Some of These Days,* but did quote from one unidentified reviewer: "She just walked out and owned the place, putting over eight songs so quick and great that at five o'clock she stopped the show dead until she made a speech. . . . Sophie made the biggest hit ever made in this house by a single woman." On the bill with her was the scatologically comical Chic Sale, whose outhouse humor apparently did not offend Mr. Albee's well-known standards for public performance.

Albee, from the beginning of his career in Boston, when he cleaned up the tiny store that antedated the B. F. Keith Theatre there, was determined that vaudeville—and that included the Palace—must be scrupulously pure, a form of entertainment for the entire family.

"The old variety houses," he said in one of his edicts, "used to be filthy places, but we changed all that. We believed in soap and water, and in a strict censorship of the stage." This rule applied to the entire circuit, but the Palace, as star of the chain, had to set a perfect example, though Palace audiences were probably more sophisticated and worldly than those of smaller cities.

Though some "blue" material occasionally got by a small-town manager (maybe because he didn't recognize it?), this couldn't happen at the Palace because Mr. Albee was on the spot, with his eagle eye and his eagle scouts to detect the smallest infraction of the bulletin he had posted backstage where no one could fail to see it. "Remember this theater caters to ladies and gentlemen and children," it read.

"Vulgarity will not be tolerated. Check with the manager if you have any doubt about it. Don't use the words hell, damn, devil, cockroach, spit, etc. . . ." Anything objectionable in an act was ordered cut. If the order was defied, then the act was o-u-t. And that was that. With one exception.

During the early days at the Palace, Frank Keenan was playing a dramatic sketch called *Vindication.* He portrayed an old Confederate soldier whose son had been convicted of murdering a Northerner. Pleading with the governor to spare his son's life, he ended with the ringing words: "Governor, don't hang my boy. I don't think you know how it happened. This man, this man, he *spit* on the picture of Robert E. Lee, and *God damn* him—my boy shot him!" GOD DAMN HIM! That blasphemy in a theater where *hell* was banned and even the word *devil* frowned upon. The audience gasped in horrified fascination, and the wise boys knew Frank Keenan was doomed. But so effective was his bravura performance that Mr. Albee suspended his iron rule and let the offending expletive stay in. Amazed people up and down Broadway and on "the beach" in front of the Palace couldn't figure out why.

The "beach" was that strip of pavement just outside the Palace entrance. There it became the habit of vaudeville performers, some but not all of them unemployed, to lounge about, exchanging gossip, trading gags, looking for tips on the job market, or just showing off.

Apropos gags, there is one story attributed to Joe Frisco, as well known for his stuttering as for his comic gifts. Frisco was standing outside the Palace in the humid heat of a summer afternoon. The asphalt was melting, the sidewalk was boarded up, and sweating workmen were drilling holes in the street, even as today. Another actor, identity unknown, strolled by. "What's going on here?" he asked Frisco, over the din of the drills. "I'm nnnnnnot sure," Frisco answered. "I ggggguess Albee's kkkkkid llllllost his ball."

Not only profanity did Mr. Albee ban. Anything he regarded as vulgarity—and that was sometimes hard to understand—was taboo. No female performers could appear unless wearing stockings. One act was firmly requested to alter the line "Give us this day our daily bread, yo ho ho and a bottle of rum." In justice it should be said that any reference to religious differences, physical deformities like lameness or blindness, or serious mental defects was also strictly forbidden.

The worst offense of all was the slightest hint of immorality. Ladies of easy virtue were regarded as completely unsuitable for the family trade so cherished by Mr. Albee. One clever little sketch came to the Palace with a fairly well-known legitimate actress making her vaudeville debut. In it the heroine was accused of being a scarlet woman. Denying it vehemently, she did concede that she might be "a little pink." And she wasn't talking politics. The act was canceled.

Probably the best-known and most costly example of Mr. Albee's insistence upon purity at the Palace involved the famous dramatic star Mme. Alla Nazimova. Having worked her way east in a one-act play by George Middleton, *The Unknown Woman*, she opened at the Palace to tremendous advance publicity. In the sketch Nazimova portrayed a fallen angel hired by a rich man to supply false evidence in his wife's divorce action. A fairly obvious piece of propaganda against New York's hypocritical divorce laws, the play was received by the Monday-afternoon audience with unanimous enthusiasm—well, almost unanimous. As it turned out, there was one spectator who reacted differently. That spectator was an engaging, personable, and high-minded young priest who, among other things, served as a watchdog for the Archdiocese and was known in some irreverent quarters as "Cardinal Hayes' yes man."

Incensed at the Nazimova sketch, the young priest dashed up to Mr. Albee's sanctum on the sixth floor and made known his outrage. Mr. Albee was shocked at his revelation. It seems that somehow or other, despite the long cross-country trek, Mr. Albee had never been informed of the contents of the Middleton play. That was Monday afternoon. Monday night Mme. Nazimova did not go on. Nor did she go on at all during the next five weeks, for which she had been contracted. Canceled or no, the contract stood and Madame received $15,000 in full.

An odd sidelight on this episode: when the Nazimova play was dropped, it was replaced by an old and popular sketch called *The Cherry Tree*, written by Aaron Hoffman and starring comedian Harry Green. It related the troubles of one George Washington Cohen, who could not tell a lie. A few years earlier Mr. Green and his act had been canceled after one performance for showing George Washington Cohen at the gates of heaven, conversing amiably with St. Peter.

Somehow the cancelation of Nazimova because she played a lady of easy virtue makes one wonder how Sarah Bernhardt got away with *Camille* and the rest of her more than

somewhat soiled heroines. Maybe since her plays were all in
French they didn't count. And what about Sophie Tucker?
Sophie, as the world knows, was a great entertainer and a
wonderful woman with a heart of gold. But Elsie Dinsmore
she was not. How did she get away with that Rip Van Winkle
song, as eventually she did, or the uninhibited "Mama Goes
Where Papa Goes or Papa Don't Go Out Tonight"? After a
time, it would seem, she had become a law unto herself, and
her forthright earthiness was so disarming that nobody, not
even the strict Mr. Albee, cared.

There are other examples of the rules that were made only
to be broken, and those that were enforced, but these will do
for the moment. The over-all picture must have been one of
great propriety, and Mr. Albee frequently received com-
mendatory letters from the public. One was from an old lady,
not necessarily from Dubuque, thanking him for providing a
place of amusement where she could safely take her grand-
children on Sunday.

As a matter of fact, the Palace frequently lent its facilities
to religious, philanthropic, and patriotic organizations on
Sunday mornings for special services and fund-raising activities. It was even the setting for a funeral service once, on
the death of Sam K. Hodgdon, a Keith executive with a
reputation as a friend of actors.

CHAPTER THREE

H AVING CAST its ominous shadow for a long time, World War I began officially on the 3rd of August 1914, when England entered the conflict against Germany. To the theater in general, the war seemed far more remote than the current week's grosses. A few British actors rushed home to enlist, a few American performers were trapped abroad, but, on the whole, nothing much changed. An act called The Meistersingers played the Palace that August—obviously German, but nobody seemed to object.

The guns of August at the Palace included some pretty big ones. Among them were dancer Laddie Cliff; Sylvester Schaffer, the magician; Adelaide and Hughes; Cecil Lean & Cleo Mayfield from musical comedy; Robert Edeson of the legitimate theater; W. C. Fields again; monologist Joe

Welch; Kitty Gordon, the musical-comedy star famous for her beautiful back; and Ethel Barrymore in a return engagement.

Some interesting firsts hit the Palace that season. One was Irene Franklin, the charming redhead, with her husband, Burton Green, at the piano. Another was Tom Lewis, a very funny monologist who never finished a sentence. A third was Louise Dresser, romantic actress and later a featured player in films. Throughout most of her career Miss Dresser was believed to be the sister of two illustrious men, Theodore Dreiser, the novelist, and his brother Paul Dresser, composer of the American classic "On the Banks of the Wabash." W. A. Swanberg, Dreiser's biographer, finally revealed her true identity, however. She was not their sister, he explained; her real name happened to be Louise Kerlin, but Paul Dresser had liked her, believed in her talent, and introduced her as his sister so she could have the advantage of his famous name and thus be helped in her profession.

Joe Cook, with his insane talk about why he would not imitate four "Hawiiiiiiyans," became a Palace regular. Dave Chasen, Cook's mute and marvelous stooge of later years—the little man with the wild hair and the wild gesture—was not with him then. But he did appear in vaudeville with an act called *Currents of Fun.* "It was a comedy electrical act," Dave told me recently, "and we did play the Palace, but I didn't go with Joe Cook till later, when he did *Rain or Shine.*" For many years, of course, Dave has run the famous Chasen's Restaurant on the border of Beverly Hills.

Blanche Ring, who had set the whole country singing "Rings on My Fingers, Bells on My Toes," appeared that season. So did Adeline Genée, the ballerina; Hugh Herbert, who can still be seen on the late shows in old Warner Brothers comedies; Doyle and Dixon, a marvelous pair of hoofers, precise and gracefully elegant in their white ties and tails. Of all the things lost when vaudeville died, that special kind of dancing is the most greatly to be mourned. Nobody does it any more, not Fred Astaire, not Gene Kelly, not Ray Bolger until recently in the Empire Room.

Others came on before the year's end: Bobby North, the monologist; and Harry Houdini, certainly the most publicized if not necessarily the greatest magician of them all. He was, of course, more than a magician. He was the escape artist, a gadfly to the practitioners of spiritualism, and a man who yielded to nobody in his admiration of Harry Houdini.

Annette Kellerman, the champion diver and swimmer, arrived at the Palace, too. She scandalized the nation with her one-piece black tank suit, a slinky figure-hugging garment that revolutionized women's bathing attire. If you wonder why she was allowed to appear that way at the Palace, remember that the suit covered her legs all the way down to her feet. She was not violating the no-stocking dictum.

Harry Carroll, whose song "I'm Always Chasing Rainbows" introduced Chopin to a lot of people, made his first Palace appearance that year. And, to end it with a great big bang and see 1915 in with appropriate noise and excitement, there was the one and only Eva Tanguay, the "I Don't Care Girl," with her manic manner, mad attire, and mop of blond hair. Eva had the fizz and taste of a not very good brand of champagne, but she gave people a vicarious release from their inhibitions (a word scarcely known way back then) and she was admired by many. Oddly enough, she also sang that most maudlin of period songs, "Put Them All Together, They Spell M-o-t-h-e-r."

The Palace, unlike Hammerstein's, very seldom booked the acts of people more valuable for their notoriety than for their talent. But one of the first acts booked in 1915 was Evelyn Nesbit, the glorious girl in the red velvet swing. She had achieved fame as the wife of Harry K. Thaw, who killed the great architect Stanford White for his alleged seduction of Evelyn years before. The Thaw-White-Nesbit story has been told too many times to need recounting here, but the recent death of the ineffable Evelyn, an obscure woman in her eighties, recalls a cynical reporter's story about an incident at a fashionable men's club the evening of White's death. A member came rushing into the club before the murder, crying: "My God, Harry Thaw's threatening to kill the man who ruined Evelyn." And by eight o'clock half the members present had left town.

Miss Nesbit's main attractions were her beautiful face and her notoriety, but she did have some dancing ability. She remained in the news for years and, teamed up with a professional dancer named Jack Clifford, did rather well in vaudeville for some time. According to booker Bill McCaffrey, the act was well worth its $2,000 a week. And Evelyn apparently had a well-developed sense of her own value. Arriving with her partner in Mr. Albee's antechamber one day, she was asked to wait. "Wait for him!" she exclaimed with some hauteur. "You'd think he was a king or an emperor instead of a mere theatrical manager!"

On the bill with Evelyn Nesbit was another team, playing its first Palace date—the Cameron Sisters. These two lovely girls, blonde Madeline and brunette Dorothy, were both beautiful dancers. Before turning to vaudeville they had trained and worked for three years in the *corps de ballet* at the Metropolitan Opera. They were a great success in vaudeville and furnished the front office with a potent threat to the Dolly Sisters. Madeline's later marriage to actor William Gaxton was a long, happy union until his death in 1963.

Despite the contretemps of the year before, Alla Nazimova returned to the Palace in 1915—not, of course, in the offensive *Unknown Woman,* but in a highly dramatic one-acter based on the plight of women left behind when their men went off to battle. *War Brides,* it was called, and she played it on and off throughout World War I, always to great acclaim. Sharing these bills were Ina Claire, the enchanting comedienne, making her Palace debut; Charlotte Walker, also from the legitimate theater; and Nan Halperin, a singing comedienne later to score a hit in *Little Jessie James.*

After years of struggle the Marx Brothers broke into the big time; they had their first Palace booking in the 1915 season. It is impossible to think of Groucho and Harpo as anything but Groucho and Harpo, but as late as March 1921, in a *Variety* story, Groucho was referred to as Julius and Harpo as Arthur. The Marx Brothers were nephews of Al Shean, of Gallagher-and-Shean fame; their mother was Shean's sister. Together on and off since early burlesque days, Gallagher and Shean struck it rich with the song that became their trademark, "Oh Mr. Gallagher, Oh Mr.

44

Shean." That endless and endlessly imitated number was written for them by Bryan Foy, motion-picture producer and one of Eddie Foy's seven children.

The perennially popular Van and Schenck, an integral part of the Palace throughout its years of glory, had their first turn there that year, too. Gus Van, ruggedly attractive, played the piano while Joe Schenck (no relation to the MGM magnate of the same name, erstwhile husband of Norma Talmadge), dapper and handsome, stood facing the audience. Together they sang some of the top songs of the era, among them "That Old Gang of Mine" and "I Wonder What's Become of Sally." They were among the most copied acts in vaudeville, but no other singing team ever approached them.

According to one story, they had been motorman and conductor, respectively, on a trolley car, and had sung in harmony to beguile the passengers on trips through darkest Brooklyn. Later Gus Van denied this as a fiction their press agent had dreamed up. After Joe Schenck died in June 1930, Gus Van went on alone. In fact, he played a solo week at the Palace as late as the 1950s. He was still playing occasional night-club dates in Florida, where he lived, until his recent death at the age of eighty.

The year 1915 was also noteworthy for the first appearance of the Cansinos. There were four of them—three brothers and a sister. They were magnificent Spanish dancers and tremendously popular with Palace audiences for years to come. One of the brothers, Eduardo, had a baby daughter, Margarita. Later, when the Palace and all vaudeville had come to its melancholy end, he built a dance act around

himself and his daughter, a graceful, raven-haired teenage
beauty. Appearing at a hotel in Agua Caliente, Mexico, the
girl was seen and admired by a movie executive. In the course
of time the beautiful raven-haired teenager emerged as the
beautiful, tawny-haired love goddess Rita Hayworth.

As the Palace climbed upward, its chief rival, Hammerstein's Victoria, slid downward. In 1914 Willie Hammerstein, who had mocked the Palace during its parlous early
days, died, and the theater he loved so dearly succumbed a
year or so later. The Victoria closed its doors forever on
April 26, 1915.

For those who are too young to remember the Palace in its
heyday, it is hard to convey its magic. The truth is that
never in theatrical history was so much offered to so many at
so little cost to them. There may be those who cite today's
television variety shows, which are theoretically free, but
they are really not the same, though even on TV the name of
the theater has recently been invoked to draw viewers by the
millions to a weekly show called *Hollywood Palace*.

When the theater was being restored in 1965, Michael
Stern wrote in the now-defunct *World-Telegram* that the
Palace was to vaudeville what La Scala is to opera. That
may sound a bit far-fetched, but actually it is a good comparison. The richness of Palace bills at their best was a mar-
vel, a feast for eyes and ears, drawing forth immeasurable
laughter and occasional tears. Take the year 1915, for instance. Among the hundreds of performers from all branches
of the entertainment world were Orville Harrold, the concert
star; Mrs. Leslie Carter, the flaming redhead who had swung

from a bell in *The Heart of Maryland;* Edith Taliaferro, the star of *Rebecca of Sunnybrook Farm;* Long Tack Sam, the Chinese magician (who taught Orson Welles the art of magic) ; Fiske O'Hara, the Irish tenor; Dainty Marie, an extraordinary acrobat; Trixie Friganza, the hit from the halls; and Mme. Emma Calvé, former star of the Metropolitan Opera (the latter two on the same bill) ; Frank Tinney, one of the great funny men, sharing top honors with William Morris (not the agent, but an actor and the father of movie star Chester Morris) ; the Metropolitan Opera Ballet; and Joe Jackson.

One of the most successful turns at the Palace that year was a one-act play starring Blanche Walsh, a temporary refugee from the legitimate theater. By that time people in New York were beginning to be aware of the conflict in Europe, and Miss Walsh's play concerned itself with that. Called *The Spoils of War,* it was set in the general's headquarters in a captured city. A program note, to maintain neutrality, said: *"The Spoils of War* is to be considered as pure drama, the events being those that might happen in any country, in any way, when 'woe to the vanquished' is the battle cry."

On that same bill was Helen Rook, who modestly proclaimed herself as a "Beautiful Genius of Song"; Bessie Clayton, in her own words "The Darling of Terpsichore—America's Premiere Danseuse"; and the aforementioned team of Doyle and Dixon, that pair of high-style hoofers.

Among the assorted delights of that period were Amelia Bingham from the dramatic stage; a Gilbert-and-Sullivan company sharing the bill with Vernon and Irene Castle; and

Winsor McCay, the cartoonist—creator of *Little Nemo*, a favorite comic strip of grownups as well as children. *Little Nemo*, like *Li'l Abner* of a later day, had been converted into a highly successful show, with music by Victor Herbert.

Also appearing were the incredibly brilliant dancer Jack Donahue; the great comedy team of Weber and Fields; Eddie Leonard, the blackface singer, with his "Roly-Boly Eyes"; Lew Hearn, the Jewish comedian; Gertrude Hoffman, the interpretive dancer; Lydia Lopokova, the Russian ballerina. And Herb Williams, a very funny man who climbed to vaudeville fame on the strength of a single word: "Spotliiiiiiight," wailed plaintively up to the electrician in the balcony. His wife, Hilda Wolfus, was his patient partner.

Not to be omitted was Lillian Russell, still in the prime of her buxom beauty, sharing the bill with Whiting and Burt, a team indigenous to vaudeville, as were the Watson Sisters; a version of the Passion Play, done by the newly formed Washington Square Players; Lew Dockstader, the minstrel; and Lillie Langtry, who had been the great and good friend of England's King Edward VII. Only a random sampling, this should give some idea of what could be seen at the Palace for as little as a quarter and no more than two dollars, unless you wanted to be very fancy and sit in a box for two-fifty.

The year 1916 was ushered in at the Palace by Elsie Janis, the great impersonator and musical-comedy star. Elsie's billing at that time was "International Star & Darling of Queens." Old-timers say that this bit of hyperbole was the creation of Ma Janis—Elsie's mother, Mrs. Bierbower, known throughout show business as the first and fiercest of the Stage Mothers. It is true that a couple of years later, when she returned to the Palace, Miss Janis billed herself simply as the "Queen of Make-Believe."

It might be pointed out here that most vaudeville people showed no tendency to be reticent or modest about their talents. In that same January show, for instance, was an act called the Two Tom Boys, who made the puzzling claim that they were the "Only Ladies Presenting a Bumsti-Bumsti Act." To date, no one has been found to explain what a bumsti-bumsti act was, though it sounds rather onomatopoeic. A few other self-descriptions of the period would amuse today's sophisticated audiences.

Miss Robbie Gordone: "Classic Reproductions of Famous Statues"

Billy B. Van and "The Clever, Fascinating Beaumont Sisters"

Dorothy Toye: "The Girl with Two Grand Opera Voices"

Wm. Rock and Frances White in a "Dansant Characteristique"

Doraldina: "The World's Most Versatile Dancer"

Armand Kalisz: "He with the *Savoir Faire*"

Rooney and Bent, however, were content simply to say "Twenty Minutes with Pat and Marion."

It was in 1916 that the Dolly Sisters made their first appearance as a team at the Palace. Jenny, as already mentioned, had been seen there earlier with her then husband, Harry Fox.

Another famous pair making its Palace debut that year was the great and glorious team of Savoy and Brennan. Jay

Brennan was universally regarded as the most gifted "straight" man in show business—and for those who know the word only in its current usage or not at all, it means the man who feeds the lines to the comedian: the one who asks the questions and gets the answers.

Of all the people who ever played the Palace, one of the very funniest, off as well as on, was Bert Savoy. Oversized, overblown, overexaggerated, with his flaming red wig, curvaceous costumes and enormous picture hats, this great female impersonator seems in retrospect to have been a travesty on Mae West as a sex symbol even before Mae West *became* a sex symbol. But there is a theory in some quarters that Miss West modeled her Diamond Lil and future characters on the extravagances of Savoy. In any case, Bert Savoy was funny —outrageously funny. And outrageous. In an era when the mores did not include open recognition of the homosexual, let alone admission of being one, Bert was an outspoken example, yet so funny about it that nobody seemed to mind.

On stage his act consisted of dishing the dirt to his partner, Jay Brennan, about his experiences with his girl friend Margie. Margie was never actually seen, but so graphic and trenchant were Bert's comments about her that she became perfectly visible to the audiences. Each season the adventures of Margie changed, and each season provided a catch line that became a sort of trademark, like Mae West's "Come up and see me some time" in a later day.

One year as Jay Brennan adroitly questioned him about his adventures with Margie, Bert replied: "I'm glad you asked me . . . I'm *glad* you asked me." Pretty soon everyone

50

was saying it. Another year, discussing the garbage in Margie's kitchen after a party, Bert complained about the fact that nobody came to collect it. "What happened to it?" asked Jay. "Oh," said Bert, "we kicked it around till it got lost." And pretty soon everybody was saying *that*. Just as memorable was his plaintive cry when in distress: "My nerves is all unstrung."

Off stage, Bert more often than not referred to himself, mockingly, as if he were in truth a woman. One day, driving up Fifth Avenue with some friends, he stopped the car to inspect the framework of an imposing new building going up between 49th and 50th Streets, a building soon to emerge as that luxurious landmark, Saks Fifth Avenue. "Look at that thing," exclaimed Bert, standing up in the car and pointing to the elegant structure. "It's just too much. I don't care if he *is* building it for me . . . I'll never live in it!"

Bert talked freely of his homosexual friends, often referring to them by the feminine pronoun. There were many such incidents, the last of which may be regarded as blasphemous but a perfect and frightening example of a cautionary tale.

One sultry midsummer's afternoon, when they had a week's unexpected layoff, Bert and Jay with a couple of their friends went down to Long Beach for a swim. As they were strolling along the water's edge, a sudden thunderstorm came up. At one especially violent clap of thunder, Bert looked up at the sky. "Mercy," he said to his companions, "ain't Miss God cutting up something awful!" A split second later a terrifying flash of lightning streaked across the heavens. And a split second after that, Bert Savoy lay dead on the Long Beach sand.

By way of contrast, 1916 unveiled such personalities as Mrs. Thomas Whiffen, the venerable English star; Irene Bordoni, the flirtatious French actress; Florence Nash, the American comedienne and sister of the dramatic actress Mary; the Three Keatons, the youngest of whom was the well-remembered Buster; and Rock and White. Frances White was the girl who sang "M-i-s-s-i-s-s-i-p-p-i."

Among the one-act plays that year was Edward Everett Hale's classic, *The Man Without a Country*, dramatized by William Anthony McGuire. Agitation for the United States to enter the war had been growing steadily, and this patriotic appeal undoubtedly was intended to fan public enthusiasm.

Despite the fact that Woodrow Wilson had been re-elected President on the slogan "He Kept Us Out of War," the sinking of several American ships and Germany's declaration of unrestricted submarine warfare brought war fever to a climax, and on April 6, 1917, Congress declared war on Germany and joined the Allies. A large number of American actors hastened to join the armed forces, and far greater numbers involved themselves in the war effort in important if less dangerous ways. All of which was reflected at the Palace through its personnel and its programs.

The theater was the scene of an enormous mass meeting, encompassing all branches of show business, for the purpose of organizing units to entertain the troops overseas, at hospitals and camps. George M. Cohan presided. According to

Joe Laurie's *Vaudeville*, the idea had originated with actor E. H. Sothern and producer Winthrop Ames, but Cohan evidently spoke with such fervor that when he asked for volunteers the entire audience rose. A forerunner of the USO of World War II, this organization was called the Over There Theatre, in honor of Cohan's classic call to arms. The units were sent out by the YMCA, and that gave rise to another song, not by Cohan but by Irving Berlin—"I Can Always Find a Little Sunshine in the YMCA." Concerning the Palace, it should be noted that E. F. Albee headed a subcommittee, representing vaudeville people, which sold more than $27,000,000 worth of Liberty Bonds.

Anything like a complete account of what the Palace and its people did during the war would be impossible, since there are great gaps in the old programs. But some few interesting items have come to light. Elsie Janis, for instance, began a two-week engagement before going to London and then to the front. In a special flyer announcing the limited engagement, the Palace announced that her "new act will be a timely, topical, war-time surprise," and that "already Pershing's men have asked that she visit their camp and entertain them before they charge the breakers of grey-coat Huns and face the steel sleet." The fact is, Miss Janis did a remarkable job in every aspect of war work and won great acclaim from all the Allied nations.

Later that year Maurice and Walton, back at the Palace "from France on a short furlough," performed, among other things, the Chasseurs' Foxtrot, "as danced by them at the front for French and English soldiers." Florence Walton, the program proudly proclaimed, was the first American artist to entertain in the war zone and had received "the distinction of the Berry of the Chasseurs." (The Chasseurs wore berets; whether the word Berry was a joke or a mistake is not clear.)

Doing a new act at the Palace before going out to entertain the troops, Nora Bayes introduced a new song and a new composer. The song was "Black Eyed Susan" and the composer Lewis Gensler, there to hear her sing it. Miss Bayes asked him to stand up and take a bow. The spotlight picked out a slender, very young man in the uniform of the U.S. Navy. Proud but embarrassed, he rose, bowed modestly, and got a standing ovation from the audience. Not too many years later—in 1922, to be exact—Gensler's first Broadway show was produced. Its name was *Queen O' Hearts*, it contained one of the classic show tunes, "Cross My Heart," and its star was Nora Bayes.

Another service-inspired turn was that of the 72nd Regiment, composed of actors and including Bernard Granville, who had played the Palace before. With the act came Earl Carroll, who later built a theater named for himself and produced a series of *Vanities*. In the 1920s he won notoriety with his nude girl in the champagne bath.

Vernon Castle had some time since gone off to join the Royal Flying Corps. Mrs. Castle, having created a national furor by bobbing her hair, played the title role in a wartime film serial called *Patria*, which closed the Palace bill for many weeks. Vernon was killed in a plane crash while serving as a flying instructor in Texas.

Palace playbills provided excellent media for recruiting pitches, propaganda pieces, and the like. One program as

late as July 1917 included a broadside addressed to BRITISH-
ERS, reminding them that they were needed by the British
and Canadian armies and urging them to apply at the British recruiting mission. On the same page was an ad from the
"Our Boys in France Tobacco Fund," pleading for contributions so it could send cigarettes overseas. "GUN SMOKE
EVERYWHERE," read the heading, "but not a Whiff of Tobacco Smoke to Cheer a Soldier Up. Tobacco cheers them,"
it went on, "home and friends loom up in the fragrant
smoke; they can fight like the devil after a smoke."

One program carried a column admonishing audiences to
"stop spoken sedition" and report to the authorities any
disloyal comments heard or overheard. Another ran a dramatized discussion between two soldiers about to go overseas,
urging votes for women (then looming on the horizon), so
their interests would be protected by their wives and mothers
while they were at the front. Still another ran, in large
boldface type, the lyrics of "The Star-Spangled Banner."

And the program of November 12, 1917, carried the first
announcement of the war tax on theater tickets, a tax originally intended to end when the war itself ended, but which, as
every theatergoer knows, did not.

With it all, the show went on. Through enlistment, draft,
or other wartime service, the Palace continued to put on
splendid bills, and war-worried people flocked to the theater
despite Heatless Tuesdays and the abandoning of the intermission "in order to conserve fuel."

Among the acts playing there toward the end of 1917 were
Carmela and Rosa Ponzille, "The Italian Girls," who later
changed the spelling to Ponselle. Rosa was discovered at the

Palace by scouts from the Metropolitan Opera, where she sang leading roles for many years. "The Live Wire"—Ray Dooley—and her brother Gordon, the standing, sliding, slipping comedian, were on the same bill. Ray Dooley is married to Eddie Dowling, the actor-producer, who also played the Palace.

L. Wolfe Gilbert—later an ASCAP executive—and his partner, Anatole Friedland, writers of a clutch of very popular songs including "Waiting for the Robert E. Lee," did a week at the Palace in one of those "and-then-we-wrote" routines. So did another popular songwriter: Ernest R. Ball (of Lambert and Ball) was the author of "Mother Machree," "Goodbye, Good Luck, God Bless You," and a host of others. Lady Duff-Gordon, more commonly known as Lucile, the couturière, presented what she described as a pantomimic musical fashion revue for the benefit of French-American Aid to Devastated France. How entertaining it was remains a question, but it certainly brought added chic to the Palace. For contrast, there was Doraldina, the hula dancer.

December saw Sarah Bernhardt returning in triumph to the Palace, older, war-ravaged, stumping from dressing room to stage over her bearskin carpet, one leg gone, but as compelling as ever. For three weeks, till the year's end, she thrilled Palace audiences with her impassioned portrayal of Joan of Arc in the great trial scene. One person who still recalls the excitement of that performance is Madeline Cameron Gaxton, who was on the bill with Madame.

Mrs. Gaxton remembers Bernhardt, raddled with age and handicapped by her infirmity but brilliant and gallant as ever, signing autographs for the other people on the bill, who, entranced, watched her from the wings. "She was too busy holding court to pay much attention to the rest of us," Madeline recalls. "She was constantly surrounded by a train of adoring young men. She must have been deep in her seventies by then, but she was ageless. And her acting was as great as ever."

1918 proved a big year for the Palace, by now unquestionably established as *the* great variety theater of the world. War or no, performers came from near and far for a chance to be seen there. For once seen—if liked—their future was assured. The fifth-anniversary bill, headed by Eva Tanguay, presented the Three Dooleys, another Gus Edwards revue, and a playlet called *Submarine F-7*.

So richly varied was the fare that the programs carried the following note: "The position which an act is allotted on the program does not in the least affect its merit. When a bill is made up almost exclusively of headliners—a state of affairs not unusual at the Palace—every number is frequently worthy of the 'star spot' on ordinary vaudeville bills. It is only fair to the artist, therefore, to judge his work solely on its merits." True enough, as witness some of the names on bills through that season and on into the new decade. To name a few: Julian Eltinge, the great female impersonator, and certainly the only one to have a theater named for him; Valeska Suratt, one of the early vamps; the Mosconi Brothers, Louis and Charles, long-time Palace favorites; Hobart Bosworth in a new one-act play based on Jack London's *The Sea Wolf*.

Lou Holtz, who could switch from Yiddish to British dialect in the wink of an eye, made his Palace debut one of those days. Others appearing were Olga Petrova, from the legitimate stage; Marguerita Sylva from opera; Moran and Mack, later famous as the Two Black Crows; Karyl Norman, the Creole Fashion Plate, another female impersonator; Ted Lewis, a great Palace institution as time went by; J. C. Nugent, actor, playwright, and father of Elliott; Toto the Clown; Sissle and Blake, the team who later won fame in *Shuffle Along*.

Noble Sissle and Eubie Blake had been with Jim Europe's great Army band overseas. When they returned after Europe was killed, they formed a songwriting team, producing such popular classics as "I'm Just Wild About Harry," and performing them at private parties. (Many years later "I'm Just Wild About Harry" became President Truman's campaign song, and just recently it found a permanent place in the Truman Library at Independence, Missouri.) Pat Casey, the genial, rotund talent agent and labor-relations man (today he'd be called a mediator), heard them play and sing their numbers and got them booked into the Palace after a brief tryout in a suburban theater. They were the first Negro entertainers to do their act straight—no levee sets, no torn overalls, and no Uncle Tom accent. They just came out in dinner jackets, played and sang their songs— this, to his credit, at the insistence of Pat Casey—and were an immediate hit.

They played the Palace often in the next couple of years, and then wrote, produced, and performed in revues. Blake was the composer and Sissle the lyricist for numbers made popular by others, including "You Were Meant for Me"

58

(not to be mistaken for the Arthur Freed–Nacio Herb Brown song of the same name) sung deliciously by Gertrude Lawrence and Jack Buchanan in *Charlot's Revue of 1924*, on the occasion of their New York debut with that later Palace player, Beatrice Lillie.

Others were A. Robins, the musical clown; Demarest and Collette—Bill Demarest later became a favorite movie character actor; Walter C. Kelly, "The Virginia Judge," whose brother George became a famous playwright, and whose niece is Her Serene Highness Princess Grace of Monaco.

Toward the end of the war and after, there were numerous acts that came from the armed services. For instance, Lieutenant Pat O'Brien, from the British Army (not to be confused with our own Irish Pat O'Brien); Lieutenant Gitz Rice, who teamed with Irene Bordoni and wrote two popular war songs, "Keep Your Head Down, Fritzie Boy" and "Dear Old Pal O' Mine"; the U.S. Navy Band and Glee Club; and the Yip Yip Yaphankers, a troupe of acrobats from Irving Berlin's great wartime revue, *Yip Yip Yaphank*. The big hit from that show was "Oh, How I Hate to Get Up in the Morning," sung in a small, troubled voice by Irving himself. Joe Frisco once said, "Irving can sing all right, but you have to hug him to hear him."

Later that year Irving Berlin played the Palace for one week as a single, doing some of his own songs. He remembers singing "Mandy," "You'd Be Surprised," and "Nobody Knows and Nobody Seems to Care." By that time he must have been pretty tired of "Oh, How I Hate to Get Up in the Morning," but the audience wouldn't let him off the stage without hearing it again.

59

On the bill with **Mr. Berlin** were Bee Palmer, Gilda Gray's chief rival as a shimmy exponent; Joe Laurie; Kitty Doner, conceded to be the greatest male impersonator on the American stage; and the comedy team of Moss and Frye.

The news toward the end of 1919 bore an almost startling resemblance to the news of today. In fact, a sampling of headlines during the last two weeks of December that year might sound like yesterday's paper—or tomorrow's. For example: "Congress a House Divided" . . . "President [Wilson] Under Attack" . . . "No Peace Without Religion, Says Pope" . . . "Interest Rates Rising as Strikes Flare." These were national. In New York a glance should prove the validity of the old saw that the more things change, the more they remain the same. For instance: "City Crime Causes Rise in Insurance Rates" . . . "Tie-Up on New Haven R.R." . . . "Delay in Teachers' Pay a Public Scandal" . . . "Nixon Calls Meeting to Protest Transit Conditions." *That* Nixon's first name was Lewis, and he was New York's Public Service Commissioner.

As 1920 drew near, Prohibition was on everybody's mind. Although officially it would not go into effect until January 16, predictions were made that December 31, 1919, the last "wet" New York's Eve in the foreseeable future, would be "a tribute to John Barleycorn to be remembered as long as there was a thirst." The predictions were accurate.

In the world of the theater, significant things were happening, too. Actors' Equity Association, having won its fight for a union, celebrated the victory with a gigantic ball at the beautiful Hotel Astor. Thus encouraged, the nation's playwrights established the Dramatists' Guild and won a con-

60

tract from the producing managers. Another achievement was the formation of the Theatre Guild, a new and strong voice in the American theater.

At Madison Square Garden, Walter Hampden, who had played a triumphant *Hamlet* the season before, was starring in an American version of the Passion Play, *The Wayfarer*, with Blanche Yurka as his co-star. At the Lexington Opera House, which Oscar Hammerstein had built and eventually lost, the Friars were frolicking for their favorite charity. At the Hippodrome a favorite Palace performer, Poodles Hanneford, the equestrian clown, starred with his family in an extravaganza called *Happy Days*. Another Palace pet, Elsie Janis, was doing great business at the George M. Cohan Theatre, with Her Gang in a revue based on shows they had given for the troops overseas.

Up and down Broadway, past and future Palace headliners were starring in their own vehicles; among them William Courtenay, Charlotte Greenwood, McIntyre and Heath, Ina Claire, the team of Santley and Sawyer, and Ethel Barrymore. At the Palace itself the New Year's Eve bill was headed by Leon Errol, the rubber-legged comic who specialized in playing drunks, an appropriate way of ushering in the Roaring Twenties.

CHAPTER FOUR

THE TWENTIES, the decade of a lost generation, with its flappers, bootleg liquor, and brownstone speakeasies where hard-faced men guarded the doors and looked through peepholes at would-be entrants—that decade has come down in song and story as a golden age. It certainly was the golden age of the Palace, which more than ever was the "in" place to go, especially on Monday afternoons. Many people bought annual subscriptions for the same seats every week of the year, just as those on a theoretically higher cultural level annually subscribed to the Metropolitan Opera.

The early twenties have many memories for me. One was a simple problem in economy. My father, never exactly affluent, now found himself in serious difficulties. So if I wanted to finish college—and I did—I would have to work my way through the last two years. By a series of maneuvers I got a job as cub reporter on the *Evening Globe,* now long defunct. Then fate further obliged by causing the entertainment editor of the paper to fall ill or have a baby or something, and a kindly city editor sent me on a Palace interview in her place.

The subject was that same W. C. Fields I had so enjoyed back in 1913 when my father took me to see Sarah Bernhardt. Having become a Palace fan, I had seen Fields several times since, but going backstage with the Palace press agent, I had qualms of nervousness along with my excitement.

Fields made me very comfortable, however. Surrounded by admirers—mostly girls—he gave me my interview in that curious voice, something between a whine and a snarl; also words of advice, to go at once and read Mark Twain's "The Man That Corrupted Hadleyburg." That brilliant and bitter tale, the comedian said, was the greatest short story ever written. An opinion which tells a good deal about the character of W. C. Fields.

He also gave me a drink. It was bourbon, and it came out of a theatrical trunk fitted up as a bar, which even included a brass footrail. Liquor backstage was strictly forbidden, but W. C. Fields, then and always, made his own rules. The interview must have been all right because I did several more and became well acquainted with Walter Kingsley, a legendary figure along Broadway.

That was lucky, too, because the time came when I needed a job. Love had entered my life and occasionally I would skip an assignment, assuming by a process of wishful thinking that it was based on a false tip, and go riding on the

Staten Island ferry with the object of my affections, a man
named Harlan Thompson. He was a reporter on the *World*,
and sometimes wrote one-act plays, one of which played the
Palace. Twice I got away with my wrong guesses, but the
third time I muffed what turned out to be a big story and
thus lost the *Globe* a clean twelve-hour beat.

Next day the city editor, still kindly, told me I was guilty
of the worst crime a reporter could commit. He was sorry,
but he had to let me go. He was also right. I deserved to be
fired, but it meant a crisis for me. I had to have a new job,
and fast. So I went to see Walter Kingsley and my luck held.
It just happened that because the Shuberts were introducing
something called Advanced Vaudeville, the Keith moguls had
decided to expand their publicity department. Walter had
an assistant named Carroll Pierce, but he could use one
more. He sent me, with a recommendation, to see Mr. J. J.
Murdock, Mr. Albee's second in command.

Mr. Murdock's office was on the sixth—the executive—
floor. The office was big. Mr. Murdock himself was small. He
couldn't have been terribly old then, but to me he looked old.
He had lots of white hair and a large white mustache in a
benign pink face. With his innocent manner and slightly
rustic turn of speech, he seemed like an ingenuous man from
the country, the kind who could be sold a gold brick, or even
the Brooklyn Bridge. Needless to say, he was not. He
greeted me amiably, asked a few questions, listened to my
answers, and discussed the job, all the while snipping away at
a piece of folded newspaper. The whole interview lasted ten
minutes. When it was over he dropped the scissors, unfolding
a string of little dancing figures—like a line of Rockettes—

and told me to start the next day. That's how I became a member of the Palace guard—at twice the salary, incidentally, I had been getting at the *Globe*. This was one instance when crime paid.

When I reported next morning I was sent back to the Sixth Floor. The use of upper-case letters here is not a typographical error. That floor was the heart and brain of the Palace—indeed, of the entire circuit—and whenever insiders spoke of it you could hear the capital letters in their voices, as if they were talking about something sacred. Not only was Mr. Murdock's office on the Sixth Floor, but so was Mr. Albee's. And Eddie Darling, chief booker of the Palace, had his office there, too.

There was no office for me. Either I didn't rate one or none was available. All I had was a desk and a typewriter, in a wide corridor outside what was called the Booking Office (also in upper case), although it wasn't an office at all, just a huge open space surrounded by a wooden railing. Inside the railing operated the bookers for the Palace and the rest of Keith big-time vaudeville. (Small-time was booked on the fifth floor.) The bookers, after the bosses, were the most important people in the chain of command. Their area was strictly forbidden to anyone selling talent. Outside the rail, in a struggling, noisy, gesticulating mass, flourished the agents and the few, the very few, performers who represented themselves.

Among the better-known bookers were George Gottlieb, (later Godfrey), Arthur Willi, and the aforementioned William McCaffrey. Godfrey, after a long career in vaudeville, eventually became a casting director in Hollywood. Arthur

Willi is now semi-retired and engaged in part-time executive duties with an advertising agency. Bill McCaffrey today is an important figure in television as eastern representative of several top-flight film and stage stars. McCaffrey, who started his Palace career as a uniformed page boy when the theater opened, soon became Mr. Albee's secretary and worked his way up to the booking department. Two other page boys, Ben Thau and the late Charles Morrison, also reached important positions in the world of entertainment.

My desk, just outside the railing separating the bookers from the agents, proved an ideal listening post. Between batting out press releases on upcoming Palace shows and interviewing current performers, I would watch the excited bargaining with puzzled amazement.

What was it like on that booking floor? Well, it has been called an auction room with the performers as merchandise; or a slave market. Small wonder that actors' agents have been dubbed flesh peddlers. It has also been likened to the floor of the New York Stock Exchange on a very busy day—there was the same frenzied activity.

Beyond the physical resemblance there was one definite similarity between the Stock Exchange and the booking floor: the matter of franchise. Just as brokers cannot do business on the trading floor without owning a seat or working for a firm that owns one, so talent agents couldn't do business on the booking floor without a franchise. That franchise was official permission to offer their human merchandise for sale. It was not, however, automatically obtainable. It couldn't be bought for money, theoretically at any rate. It was granted, like political patronage, at the discretion or whim of the management. And, like political patronage, it could be withdrawn suddenly—sometimes permanently, sometimes just temporarily—as punishment for some real or fancied misbehavior. A terrible punishment, for an agent without a franchise was likely to become an agent without clients.

Naturally I did not glean all this on the first day or even in the first weeks of my new job. Most of my time was spent learning and carrying out my duties as Mr. Murdock had outlined them to me. These duties were rather special. Though I was to turn out a certain amount of routine press material for the regular Palace bills, my main assignment was to concentrate on a group of top-flight stars and write special feature stories about them. These included Sophie Tucker, Frank Fay, Irene Franklin, John Steel, Singer's Midgets, and Vera Gordon. Miss Gordon, who was doing a sudsy sketch entitled *Lullaby*, had scored a great success in a movie based on Fannie Hurst's novel *Humoresque*. Vera was the archetypal Jewish mother, off stage as well as on, and her great heart knew no bounds when it came to helping people.

Once when I shepherded a group of Palace players up the river to perform for the inmates of Sing Sing, she became interested in one of the prisoners. He was serving a life sentence for the murder of his wife, whom he had found with another man. He was handsome, intellectual—he had taught school—and "a nice Jewish boy." Vera kept in touch with him and later, with the help of a young woman reporter on the same expedition, managed to get him paroled. Vera's

interest was strictly maternal. The reporter's interest must
have been something else. When he got out, she married him.

Naturally, not all my special charges appeared at the
Palace simultaneously, but when they were not there they
often played the outlying Keith houses, such as the Colonial,
the Riverside, the Alhambra, or the Royal in the Bronx. So
frequently I would travel to these outposts and do my interviewing there. Occasionally I would buy my way into a Shubert vaudeville show and check on how things were going in
the enemy camp. That particular activity was reported to
Mr. Murdock directly, but the copy I wrote was turned in to
Walter Kingsley, whom I saw at least once every day, sometimes two or three times. My encounters with him were both
instructive and entertaining.

Walter, resembling a college professor with a sense of
humor, whose eyes twinkled behind owlish glasses, was one of
the most interesting and picturesque figures on the Broadway scene, far more so than many of the people he helped to
fame. Before going to work at the Palace he had been,
among many other things, a reporter covering the Boer War
and press representative for such celebrated characters as
Kaiser Wilhelm of Germany, Queen Marie of Rumania, and
George M. Cohan, king of Broadway.

Along with a brilliant mind and a generous heart, he had
an extraordinary eye for beauty. As an avocation he helped
Florenz Ziegfeld find some of his glorified girls, among them
Justine Johnstone, Leonora Hughes, Jessie Reed, and
Peggy Hopkins Joyce. The only decoration I remember in
his office was a framed sign bearing a quotation from

Nietzsche: "Be Hard; Live Dangerously." He did live dangerously, no doubt of that, but hard he was not. He was a good man, gentle, kind, and endlessly amusing.

I know it was Earl Carroll who invented the slogan "Through these portals pass the most beautiful girls in the world," but I can state unequivocally that many of them also passed through Walter Kingsley's office door. Sometimes, while I waited in his anteroom to see him, they would come out looking a little disheveled but never unhappy. By the time I got in, Mr. Kingsley, with a slightly Cheshire Cat smile on his kindly countenance, was ready to talk business.

After he left the Palace some years later, Walter went to work officially for Ziegfeld, doing publicity for those lovely girls he had discovered. In February 1929 he collapsed on the sidewalk outside Ziegfeld's New Amsterdam Theatre, and a few days later he died. In an appreciation of him for the Sunday *New York Times*, his friend and Palace colleague John Pollock wrote: "It has been said that he never grew up—that he was a Peter Pan, or as he liked to be called, 'The Playboy of Broadway.' That was true. He worked hard and he played hard and enjoyed the one as much as the other. . . . Kingsley was a man everybody knew—rich man, poor man, beggar man, thief—and everybody liked." At his request, he was cremated and his ashes were scattered from a plane over the Broadway he loved.

It is impossible to explain how the Palace operated without relating it to the monolithic structure that governed not only that house but also a huge sprawling collection of theaters between the Eastern Seaboard and Chicago. All functioned under the total domination of one man, the omnipresent, omniscient, omnipotent E. F. Albee, whose czardom must be understood in terms of the many thousand performers whose lives he dominated.

There had been sporadic attempts to protect the economic rights of these far-flung professionals. In the early days of the twentieth century, under the fiery but somewhat eccentric leadership of Harry Mountford, an English music-hall performer who had migrated to the United States, vaudevillians had founded an amorphous organization named the White Rats, so called after a British actors' group called the Water Rats. *Rats* was *star* spelled backward; what the words *water* and *white* stood for remains a mystery.

The purpose of the White Rats was to gain some measure of independence from the powerful Vaudeville Managers Protective Association, of which E. F. Albee was the moving spirit. The idea of organizing vaudevillians had originated even earlier in the mind of a monologist, George Fuller Golden, who had prophetically forecast a vaudeville trust. Early meetings were attended by many successful actors of the era, among them Eddie Foy, Dave Montgomery, Fred Stone, DeWolf Hopper, Joe Weber, Lew Fields, J. C. Nugent, and even George M. Cohan, who later had far different ideas about actors' unions. Nothing really came of their high hopes until Harry Mountford, a persuasive personality and clever organizer, entered the picture. His combination of qualities and the spirit of the times created the right climate for the White Rats, and for a while this early actors' union had the backing of Sime Silverman, whose *Variety* was already a power in the vaudeville world. Silverman never trusted Mountford, but he supported the organization because he disliked Mountford less than he hated Albee and because he believed in fair play for performers. By some malicious whim of fate, there came a time when Sime and Albee lived in the same apartment building and glared at each other when they passed in the lobby or were trapped in the same elevator.

Despite all efforts, the White Rats never accomplished much for its members. The managers were too strong. When a deputation from the White Rats called on Albee to remind him of a promise the managers had made but broken, his customary poker face remained unchanged as he allegedly replied: "Businessmen don't keep promises." It has also been said of Albee that he originated what later became the slogan of W. C. Fields: "Never give a sucker an even break."

In 1916 a strike called by Mountford failed dismally, due partly to mismanagement and partly to the individual actors' lack of staying power. After all, few vaudevillians had much money in their "grouch bags." It wasn't long before the strike was broken, and eventually the White Rats.

Through the help of a few performers and under the guidance of Mr. Albee, who also gave financial aid, a new organization formed. Called the National Vaudeville Artists —NVA—it operated strictly as a company union, if indeed it was a union at all. Later, again with the help of Mr. Albee, this pseudo-union took over the old White Rats clubhouse on West 46th Street.

Joe Schoenfeld, a former *Variety* reporter writing in its 1956 Golden Jubilee issue, summed things up this way: "Thus the actors got or regained some of the clubhouse creature comforts, but placed themselves completely at the mercy of the managers. From that day (1917) until the middle thirties, when the American Federation of Actors came into being, the vaudevillians were represented by a company union, which meant they weren't represented at all, so far as collective bargaining was concerned."

All through the twenties the NVA still exercised complete control. During that period it had an active membership of twelve thousand and its own magazine, the *Vaudeville News*, on whose staff was a bright, ambitious young ex-hoofer named Walter Winchell. As time passed, the Palace became more than ever the Seventh Heaven of the vaudevillians' dream, but except for illustrious visitors from the legitimate theater or the music world and a few aristocrats of pure vaudeville, the road to the Palace was long and hard.

The Palace, for all its greatness, was merely the brightest star in a whole galaxy of vaudeville houses throughout the country. The theater was glamour personified, but as part of the Keith Circuit it was also big business. So, to understand how the Palace worked, it is necessary to understand the business practices of the circuit as a whole.

Every theater on the circuit was a separate corporation, and each act had to sign an individual contract with each house it played. The house manager would pay the act, but before he did so he would deduct 5 percent from the total and send it to the B. F. Keith Vaudeville Exchange in the Palace Theatre Building. In other words, the employer charged the employee 5 percent for the privilege of working. And 5 percent of the aggregate salaries added up to quite a tidy sum for the home office.

Also, the performer's agent had to be paid, and the legal

rate those days was 5 percent. But the agent was not allowed by the circuit to collect his commission directly from the act. That 5 percent, too, was taken out of the act's salary and sent by the house manager to the home office, where a department called the Keith Collection Agency then doled it out to the agent. Any agent who tried to collect his own commission soon found himself in trouble. For this infraction he could be deprived of his franchise and banned from the booking floor.

The Collection Agency claimed that its operating costs were heavy. To meet those costs a clever system was devised —clever and beautifully simple. The Collection Agency charged the agent 50 percent of his legitimate commission. This left him with only 2.5 percent of his client's salary. Small wonder that some of the agents got around that by becoming personal representatives or managers and rendering real or pretended services above and beyond getting work for their clients.

The "cut week" house was another profitable stratagem devised by the home office. Certain theaters on the circuit arbitrarily paid the acts considerably less than the salaries their contracts called for. The reasons varied: it was a poor show town, or the weather was too hot or too cold or too rainy. Of course, the act had a choice. It could choose to take the cut or it could choose not to work for the circuit. And if it didn't work for the Keith Circuit (which also meant not working for the Orpheum Circuit), it couldn't work for any of the smaller circuits, which were afraid to buck the big bosses.

So, naturally, most of the acts took the cut. That meant working for a quarter or sometimes as much as a third less than the contractual salary. Though every theater was not a cut-week house—the Palace, for instance, wasn't—hidden costs always conspired against the performer.

How did the system work? Take a hypothetical song-and-dance act composed of a man and two girls, an act that worked regularly and maybe played the Palace once a year: Rolly Madden and Company, Songs, Dances and Funny Sayings. Rolly Madden naturally headed the act. The contract was signed by him, and the salary, when it finally reached its destination, was paid to him. The contract called for $1,000 a week. But playing a cut-week house at a reduction of 25 percent brought the salary down to $750. Out of that, Madden had to pay the Keith Vaudeville Exchange its 5 percent for the boon of working for the Keith Circuit. That reduced the salary to $712.50. The agent's 5 percent cut another $37.50 from the paycheck, leaving Madden a total of $675. From that was subtracted what he had to pay the two girls in his act, transportation, sets, costumes, and incidental expenses, which didn't leave much profit.

The contract, still reading $1,000 per week, fooled nobody in the business and was soothing only to Madden's pride. But anything could be endured if it led to the Palace. An engagement there could lead to others in Broadway shows and night clubs, which in turn might lead to an enhanced position and more money next time around at the Palace. For the less successful, those inevitable "little people" who opened or closed the bill or played some other lowly spot, the Palace was the final accolade and worth any sacrifice. Such people were glad to take a pay cut if they had to. Many of them would have worked for nothing, maybe even paid for the chance to be seen in the holy of holies.

But even though the Palace meant the fulfillment of a lifelong dream, it could be a performer's nightmare as well. An act might open there on a Monday afternoon, and if it met with a cold reception from the hard-boiled professional audience or failed to please the watchdogs from the Sixth Floor, it could be off the bill before the night show. (That precedent was set, it may be recalled, on the very first day in the life of the Palace, when an act was dropped after the matinee.) To call this a fate worse than death is hardly exaggerating. It was about as disgraceful as being drummed out of the army for dishonorable conduct. If you flopped at the Palace, there was nowhere to go but down.

The bliss of really making it is shown in the story of one small-time performer for whom that glorious chance had finally arrived. On a frigid Monday afternoon the matinee had opened with an animal act—Fink's Mules, if memory serves. Two men stood in the wings. One was a popular singing comedian, the week's headliner, who enjoyed watching the show. The other was a virtually unknown monologist, only recently graduated from the minor circuits. In his cheap striped suit with slanting pockets and sharp lapels, he typified the vaudevillian made famous at the time by George M. Cohan's *Song and Dance Man,* and much later by Laurence Olivier in John Osborne's harrowing play *The Entertainer.* His clothes were shabby, but his eyes shone, and, waiting to go on next, he just couldn't contain his ecstasy.

"Gee," he said to the headliner, "it's a small world, ain't it? I been in show business almost twenty years and this is the first time I ever played the Palace. Last time I was back

home—that's Hannibal, Missouri, you know, where Mark
Twain comes from—my brother-in-law, he's in hardware,
wanted me to quit show business and go to work for him. I
told him I'd never quit till I'd played the Palace. And he
says to me, 'Joe,' he says, laughing kinda mean, 'Joe, it'll be
a cold day when you play the Palace.' And this is the coldest
day in the last ten years, and I'm playin' the Palace. Some
co-instance. Wait till I tell that to my brother-in-law!"

One interesting routine I was privileged to observe was the
weekly audition. Every Thursday morning the theater was
thrown open to aspiring performers who wanted to market
their wares, meaning themselves. Small-time acts with big-
time hopes would bring their music and props onto the vast,
cold stage before a small, cold audience of bookers and other
executives and put themselves on display.

The aspirants were not limited to professionals, even the
most lowly ones. Occasionally the stage was taken over by
amateurs who would have been given the hook at the smallest
of small-time amateur nights.

Two auditions remain in my memory after all these years.
One involved a team of highly untalented hoofers, doing an
obvious but hopeless imitation of the marvelous Mosconi
Brothers, Louis and Charlie. They had once been on a bill
somewhere with the Mosconis and were convinced that these
scions of a long line of dancers had "borrowed" their famous
skating waltz from them. It was an occupational disease of
vaudevillians that, whatever they did, they *knew* they did it
better than anyone else, and that if they weren't at the top of
their profession it was a matter of bad luck, lack of pull, or

some such external cause, never a matter of their being less than perfect. If they had not felt that way, life with its series of rejections would have been past endurance.

The other audition was even sadder. A single woman, obviously a stranger to the profession, showed up one morning in a flaming orange chiffon gown, with hair to match. She went into a series of writhing contortions which she called a snake dance. Since she must have weighed in at two hundred, and since her snake consisted of several stockings sewn together and stuffed with lumpy paper, it was an acutely embarrassing few minutes for everyone but the lady herself. Needless to say, she didn't get the job, but in an exhibition of unusual gallantry the bookers allowed her to finish before saying those fatal words, so well and painfully known to most performers, even those who have risen to the top: "Thank you very much."

A certain amount of talent must have been unearthed at these Thursday-morning auditions, otherwise they would have been dropped. But so far as anyone then active can remember, only one important act got started that way. That was the team of Buck and Bubbles, the Negro dancers who became headliners and played the Palace in the twenties. John Bubbles later won considerable fame and some fortune as Sportin' Life in *Porgy and Bess.* His partner, Ford L. Buck, had a role in the same production.

Apropos the Mosconis, not only were they among the most gifted people ever to play the Palace, but also among the most popular with critics and audiences alike. A dancing family whose skill passed from generation to generation, they varied their offerings from time to time. Louis and

Charlie were the basic team and often appeared *à deux*. But sometimes the other members of the family would join the act —little sister Verna and younger brother Willie.

Once they appeared on a bill whose other top-liners were Bessie Clayton, the toe dancer; the Avon Comedy Four; and the great Paul Whiteman with his Palais Royale Band.

So tremendous was this bill that at the Monday matinee the Mosconis didn't even make their entrance till five-thirty, an hour when the audience was usually on its way up the aisles toward the exit. But when the name Mosconi flashed on the announcement cards that flanked the stage, the audience remained seated and a great roar went up, a roar exceeded in volume only at the finish of the act, some time after six. Occasions like these gave the Palace its constantly growing reputation as the greatest variety theater in the world, and explained why performers were willing to stand for any kind of high-bindery in order to play there.

Speaking of the Mosconis, it is pleasant to know that the two brothers are still flourishing, even though they no longer perform. Louis has a dancing school in Hollywood, and Charlie owns a theater-ticket brokerage on West 44th Street, just across the street from the old Claridge, a glamour hotel for theater people in the twenties. The Mosconis, incidentally, are cousins of the billiard champion Willie Mosconi.

As for the Avon Comedy Four, two of that quartet, Smith and Dale ("I'm Kronkhite," "I'm dubious," "How are you, Mr. Dubious?") are also still around, occasionally appearing on TV. Only recently they were honored by a show at the Lambs Club, celebrating their seventy-year association as partners and friends. They started life as Joseph Seltzer and Charles Marks, but were renamed by the owner of a little vaudeville house who couldn't resist a bargain. It seems that a printer was stuck with show cards for a team named Smith and Dale, who had changed their names, and the theater owner bought a hundred of them for twenty-five cents. So Seltzer and Marks became Smith and Dale.

After a few months at my desk outside the pale on the Sixth Floor, I was moved to a real office—a small thing but mine own. It should have delighted me, yet I missed my former spot in the open. Gregarious by nature, I enjoyed the sight and sound of so many people. And being a reporter by instinct and training, I had found that desk most useful. There I had picked up much information about the business. Most of it just drifted my way, but some was volunteered by disgruntled agents or Palace employees not always as careful as they should have been. Maybe such talk was deliberate. Where there's an absolute monarch who imposes his will on his minions, the loyalty of those minions is not always as absolute as the monarch believes. Mainly I missed the breezy, if hectic atmosphere of the booking floor, where something was constantly going on. The agents were a mixed crew of tough in-fighters, fiercely competing with one another for the best bookings and the most money for their clients. They had to be tough; they were up against a tough situation. After all, with a maximum of nine acts at the Palace or any of the other top-flight vaudeville houses, and approximately twenty thousand acts to place, competition had to be fierce. If the agents didn't get good routes and good pay for their

clients, they soon lost them to others with a better sales pitch
or a better entree, real or invented, to the booking office.

Among the agents with a real "in" was a young man
named Max Gordon. Max, who later became a highly successful producer of dramatic and musical shows, was the younger
brother of Cliff Gordon, a vaudeville star of the 'teens,
known as "The German Senator." Cliff, to whom Max was
greatly attached, died in Chicago while playing on a bill
with Sarah Bernhardt during one of her perennial farewell
tours. In his autobiography Max quotes what may well have
been his brother's last words—certainly prophetic ones—
spoken to the theater manager after a matinee. "I couldn't
get 'em," Cliff said, walking off stage to a stunning lack of
applause. "Any comedian who tries to follow Bernhardt is
bound to die." Felled by a heart attack, he never made it to
the next show.

Max, an exuberant, brash young man whose inelegant
language and bold exterior hid a sensitive soul, had formed a
partnership some years before with Al Lewis, a quiet, soft-
spoken ex-actor, stage manager, and burlesque comic.
Though neither of them had had more than a minimal education, both had aspirations far beyond the ordinary business
of flesh peddling. Max, for all his tough talk, would quote
Shakespeare to make a point. I remember how he startled me
once by reciting, quite eloquently, the entire garden scene
between Lorenzo and Jessica from *The Merchant of Venice*.
And Al Lewis had been involved with the newly formed
Washington Square Players, where Katharine Cornell made
her professional debut, and from which the Theatre Guild
later emerged. Lewis and Gordon functioned not only as a

firm of agents, but also as producers of one-act plays which they sold to vaudeville. These plays earned money and heightened their prestige.

One-act plays, or cut-down versions of full-length plays, had long been used as vehicles for legitimate stars taking their occasional flyers in the two-a-day. One of the best and most enduring was a comedy called *Kisses,* which served William Gaxton for many years. It was written by S. Jay Kaufman of the *Globe,* one of the first Broadway columnists. Another was *The Valiant,* in which Bert Lytell starred for countless seasons. Later it became a favorite play for high-school dramatic societies throughout the country.

Lewis and Gordon, along with another firm of agents headed by Rosalie Stewart, concentrated on the one-acters and became enormously successful with them. After one disastrous experience with an English comedy called *The London Fire Brigade,* they acquired a short drama, *Straight,* by Aaron Hoffman, one of the most prolific and successful authors of this genre. Many of their one-act plays, including that durable comedy *The Cherry Tree,* which served Harry Green for many years, were written by Hoffman.

Other writers of one-act plays came under the Lewis and Gordon management, and for years there was hardly a month without some Lewis-and-Gordon plays on the Palace bill. Among these writers were Edgar Allan Woolf, Edwin Burke, and John B. Hymer. The latter two had been vaudeville actors themselves, so knew the need for economy of speech and good timing. Later they proceeded to write full-length plays and motion pictures.

The list of stage stars who appeared under the L&G management was quite impressive, including such names as Henry Hull, Judith Anderson, Roland Young, and Mary Nash. From the movies came Francis X. Bushman and Beverly Bayne, the great lovers of the silent screen.

Jean Adair, still remembered as one of the adorable and murderous old ladies in *Arsenic and Old Lace*, had two successes in Lewis-and-Gordon one-act plays, both of which played the Palace.

One acquisition that Lewis and Gordon were particularly proud of was a drama of World War I by a struggling playwright totally unknown north of Greenwich Village. The play was *In the Zone* and the playwright Eugene O'Neill. Through their success with that, Max and Al were able to get the rights to the whole Washington Square Players catalogue.

Apart from their production chores, Lewis and Gordon continued as agents for individual acts. They brought together two young men who already had been modestly successful. One was Phil Baker, an accordion player; the other, Ben Bernie, a violinist. Neither started out as a comedian, but in combination they developed a comedy routine along with their music and appeared together successfully before going their separate and enormously prosperous ways. They played the Palace frequently, and still later each became an outstanding radio figure, Bernie as a band leader and Baker, the "bad boy from a good family," as M.C. of the popular quiz show *Take It or Leave It*.

Among other Lewis-and-Gordon clients who played the Palace were Lew Dockstader, the minstrel man, and Raymond Hitchcock, the comedian. There was also George Jessel. George, who had entered vaudeville as one of Gus Edwards' child prodigies and later worked as partner to Eddie Cantor when they were still very young, came to the Palace in 1920 in a miniature revue, *George Jessel's Troubles of 1920*, produced and sold by Lewis and Gordon.

Considering that year, it is noteworthy that one of the most successful people ever to play the Palace was a woman who could not be called a star in the usual theatrical meaning of the word, but who was a star of worldwide renown. That woman was Helen Keller, the blind and deaf girl whose triumph over her handicaps was later to be immortalized by William Gibson's play *The Miracle Worker*.

How Helen Keller happened to come to the Palace and whose idea it was is still a matter of conjecture. But there she was. Covering the Palace bill on February 2 of that year, *The New York Times* wrote of Miss Keller: "Before she had been on the stage ten minutes Helen Keller had conquered again . . . the Monday afternoon audience—one of the most critical and cynical in the world—was hers."

Her voice, the *Times* review went on, was clear and distinct, and her act—if it could be called an act—entranced both the audience and the other people on the bill. There had been some misgivings about her booking, understandably, but so successful was her appearance that she and her teacher, Anne Sullivan Macy, were held over for a second week. The other headliner for the second week was that somewhat different personality, Sophie Tucker. Sophie was greatly affected by Miss Keller and, openhearted as always, took the time to help her put on her make-up, going so far—according to legend—as to teach the blind woman how to apply it herself.

Another outstanding agent was Rosalie Stewart, who with her partner Bert French produced a number of one-act plays. One of the most successful was *The Flattering Word*, written by and starring the young actor George Kelly. Rosalie also put on another of George Kelly's one-act plays which was later expanded into the full-length production of *The Show-Off*, making an overnight star of Louis Jean Bartels, giving Lee Tracy his first Broadway role, and providing an award role for Helen Hayes in the recent APA repertory revival.

Still another Rosalie Stewart coup was a third George Kelly play, *The Torchbearers*, that wild farce about the little-theater movement so pervasive at the time. After its Broadway run, the excerpted second act played the Palace with its two original stars, Mary Boland and Alison Skipworth. Not long after that, Kelly won the Pulitzer Prize with his harrowing drama of the obsessive *Craig's Wife*. Rosalie also represented Yorke and King, a simon-pure vaudeville act, very popular at the Palace. Other agents who helped make Palace history were Louis Shurr; H. B. Marinelli, once a famous contortionist; the firm of Rose and Curtis; and Max Hart.

Pat Casey, a delightful pink-faced giant of a man, had his own agency and very strong connections with E. F. Albee. Oddly enough, he also had strong connections with Sime Silverman and with William Morris. So great were his powers of persuasion that he brought about the uneasy truce that finally came to pass between Albee and *Variety,* and he poured an ample supply of oil on the troubled waters of vaudeville labor relations. According to Bill McCaffrey, Casey got William Morris re-enfranchised so that his acts could be booked into the Palace and on the circuit in general.

One of the most colorful of the agents was Billy Grady, a good-looking Irishman, who represented W. C. Fields and shared his rugged individualism and independent spirit. Neither of these qualities was looked upon with approval on the Sixth Floor and Grady was always in trouble.

"I was continually on the carpet," he told me. "When Murdock's office was built, there was a cup base for a fire extinguisher that was never installed. It resembled a holy water font. When I was called on the carpet, before entering the presence I'd dip my fingers in the base as though it were filled with the blessed water, bless myself, and enter the little man's private office.

" 'Grady,' he'd say, 'you're in trouble, serious trouble. Did you book that act in opposition to our theaters, changing the name of the act to avoid detection?' I would admit my foul deed and be barred from the floor for a week.

"My longest 'off the floor' period was for a month. That was punishment for booking a private party, in opposition to the booking-office private-party gal. A month on the street did the penance.

"I'll say this for J.J.," Grady continued, "he was a maverick himself in the old Chicago days, and he knew I was emulating him. In later years out here"—out here being

85

Hollywood, where Billy Grady was for many years head casting director for MGM—"J.J. and I used to have many laughs over my actions."

From all accounts, Mr. Murdock was quite as much of a tyrant as Mr. Albee. Yet everyone who reminisces about Murdock does it with a laugh and a philosophical attitude, while scarcely anyone mentions E. F. Albee without intense bitterness. Maybe it is because Mr. Murdock had a sense of humor, never forgot his lowly origins, and looked so innocent while perpetrating his iniquities. Whereas Mr. Albee, with his relentless air of holiness, was totally without humor and grim of visage as he wielded his destructive power.

Here and there one runs into kind words about Mr. Albee, and it seems only fair to mention them. Mostly they had to do with his showmanship. Bill McCaffrey tells of the time an English comedian named Wilkie Bard opened at the Palace on Monday afternoon with a monologue so entirely British in tone and anecdote that he was an abysmal failure. Humiliated, he didn't even show up for the evening show. Contrary to the usual procedure, he wasn't canceled or docked. Albee caught Bard just as he was packing to go back to England and told him not to quit. He explained what was wrong with the act, asked for and listened to Bard's repertoire of stories. He then picked a few that he was sure would do well with the Palace audiences and re-routined the entire act. Three days later Bard went back to the Palace with his new act, scored a big hit, and became a favorite with American audiences from that moment on.

There is another story, told by Max Gordon, that presents

Mr. Albee as a good samaritan. After considerable difficulty with the big boss, Max finally won his way—with J. J. Murdock's help—into the old man's good graces. And it was Albee who was responsible for one of Max's most gratifying achievements. It happened in connection with Eddie Foy. As his children grew up, they were the Seven Little Foys no longer, and for some reason the senior Foy couldn't seem to make good on his own. Albee heard of his plight, called Gordon in, and told him to have his writers fashion a script that would bring out Foy's best points.

The script, as Max describes it, had Foy portraying an ex-hoofer, now a stage doorman, who saves a quarreling boy-and-girl team from ruining their professional and personal lives by telling them the story of his own downfall. For a finish he went into a dance—"just like the one the boy does in the act." It sounds like the quintessence of corn, but corn can be very effective, and this was. In Max's words, "The dance, of course, was the famous old Foy soft-shoe. . . ." After a break-in at a small-time theater, where Max took Albee to see the act, the old man immediately booked it into the Palace.

"The Monday afternoon Foy opened at the Palace and went into his dance," Max goes on, "the regulars, along with the rest of the crowd, were stamping and whistling and cheering. To use an old show-business term, they were tearing the house down. I went backstage to Foy's dressing room when it was over. Tears were streaming from his eyes.

" 'Max,' he said, 'they didn't talk to me at the Astor yesterday; they hardly knew me. But they'll talk to me now. Max, you'll go to heaven for this.' "

87

It may be that E. F. Albee's greatest contribution to the theater was one he never knew about. He had a son, Reed Albee, who used to be around the Palace in some capacity. Reed married, and in the course of time he and his wife adopted a son. The little boy, named for his adoptive grandfather, turned out to be Edward Albee, one of the most brilliant and controversial playwrights of our time.

Very few performers acted as their own agents or managers, partly because they were not good at business and partly because the booking office didn't encourage it. The ones who did were known as "office acts." One of them was Bert Williams. Bill McCaffrey tells of Williams' visits to Mr. Albee's office, where he would be closeted for a couple of hours and, having performed the almost impossible task of rousing the normally poker-faced boss to roars of laughter, would emerge with a new and advantageous contract.

Another star who handled his own business was Houdini —not, however, by the use of laughter. Houdini was no more inclined toward merriment than Albee was. But he was a hard-headed businessman, well aware of his own worth.

Once during a gab session at the NVA Clubhouse there was an argument about astrology. Houdini, disdainful of anything remotely occult, was naturally skeptical. Men make their own destiny, he maintained. "Now you take E. F. Albee and me, for example," he said. "There must be at least a hundred men in New York who were born on the same day we were. And who's ever heard of them?" Challengingly: "Where, I ask you, are they now?" "I can guess," answered one of the group, Ballard MacDonald, the lyric writer.

"Probably in Dannemora."

In justice to Houdini it must be said that he accomplished much good with his dedicated campaign to expose and discredit fraudulent spiritualists who made fortunes preying upon the bereaved and gullible by promising to bring them into contact with their lost "loved ones." When he died in November 1926 *The New York Times,* in an editorial, wrote: "He did not deny that communication with spirits was possible; all he asked was that in any given case of alleged communication he be allowed to reproduce the phenomenon by natural methods. The result was often appalling. Mediums who had baffled Harvard professors went crashing down to ruin through his demonstrations; apparently there was not one bit of occult hokum which he could not reproduce to the delight of audiences who watched. A man who devotes himself to such a pursuit does a real public service."

While learning something about the business side of vaudeville during my tenure on the Sixth Floor, I was also getting to know what went on in the theater, and about the vaudevillians themselves. As a reporter and part-time interviewer, I had become somewhat aware of this special world, but it wasn't the same as belonging. Now I was in a constant state of exhilaration. To be a modest part of this wonderful, magical Palace, to drop into the theater without being asked for a ticket, to be greeted by the ushers, to walk through that secret door from a box to the back of the house or down the 47th Street alley to the stage door without being challenged by the stage doorman (grumpy and severe, even as in the movies), to stand in the wings and watch the acts, or sit in performers' dressing rooms and get their stories—all that was the headiest kind of excitement.

One of the privileges that gave me the most fun and the strongest feeling of being on the inside was attending the Monday-morning rehearsals. Each Monday the acts would gather backstage, renew old friendships, swap gossip and information, tell jokes—but not ones they intended to use— hand their music to the orchestra leader, and rehearse their acts. The bookers were always there to time the acts, plan the order of their appearances, and relay instructions from on high. Often there would be a little jockeying for position among the acts, but unless there was an unbreakable clause in the contract, it was the bookers who had the last word, because they had made a fine art of scheduling programs.

Once set on Monday morning, the routining didn't necessarily stay that way. Frequently after the Monday matinee the bill would be rearranged, and sometimes that happened two or three times before the result was right. One week the bill was changed almost daily. Luckily, the headliner was Irene Franklin, a delightful and untemperamental lady, so there was no serious trouble.

Everyone loved Irene. She was pretty, clever, amiable, and she knew her business thoroughly. Her marriage to Burton Green, whom she had met when he was a pianist at Tony Pastor's and she sang there, was a happy one. He became her accompanist and they had a highly successful life together, both on and off the stage. During World War I they went overseas to entertain the troops, and upon their return they were more popular than ever. Unhappily, Burton Green died a comparatively young man. Irene, left with two daughters, kept on with her career, teaming up with the pianist Jerry Jarnagin, who had been John Steel's accompanist. Later she married him, but it ended in tragedy when Jerry took his own life.

The greatest excitement of all was the Monday matinee. A lot of clichés have been written about the quiver of expectancy that ripples through an audience on a play's opening night as the house lights dim and the curtain starts its slow rise. At the Palace, opening night occurred every Monday afternoon. Just being there was a thrill, and the greatest thrill was standing at the back of the orchestra, leaning on the rail, watching the show like a real pro, surrounded by the really real pros, down from the Sixth Floor to judge the bill and decide the fate of the people on stage.

It was fun, too, dropping into the St. Regis Café next door and catching some of the acts in their off-stage moments. Even more fun was the little eating place around the corner, a few steps from the stage door on 47th Street. Known then as the Somerset Coffee House, it had been started by a Greek immigrant, Andrew Ponaras, who had first set up shop outside the stage-door alley, selling fruit to the performers on their way into the theater.

Later when his two sons, Gus and Andy, joined their father in the business, it was renamed Gus and Andy's and became a favorite eating place for most of the Palace people. New routines were tried out there and many a gag line grew out of the ad-lib exchanges of the comics. There is a legend that Dr. Rockwell's banana stalks, used in his monologue on the human anatomy, were supplied by Gus and Andy.

Their landlord was St. Mary's Episcopal Church, up the

block toward Sixth Avenue. Many a time during the Depression the church had to wait for its rent. But somehow Gus and Andy managed to hang on, and even continue feeding actors on the cuff when necessary, which unfortunately was all too often. The brothers never forgot their father's credo: "Be nice to actors."

The true vaudevillian was unlike anybody else in the world. Not only unlike what actors call civilians, but not —with the rarest exceptions—like other denizens of the entertainment world: the actors and actresses from the legitimate stage or the opera and concert people who came in from time to time to fatten their purses. The vaudevillians seemed to regard these visitors from another planet with a mixture of awe and superiority.

The true vaudevillian even had his own language. Most of it has long since entered into our common speech, but during the heyday of the Palace this language would have been quite bewildering to what actors call a private person. Walter Kingsley maintained that if such a person suddenly found himself backstage at the Palace, he would understand just about as much as if he were cast ashore in some strange foreign land. To amuse himself, he compiled a dictionary of vaudeville speech. Omitting words that are now part of the American language, here is a sampling of Kingsley's lexicon:

HANDCUFFED   an audience which won't applaud
A FISH   a poor act
A BRODIE   a complete, humiliating flop
THE GRAND JURY   the gallery mob
DOUGHDY   the week's salary

EXCESS BAGGAGE   a non-pro wife who travels with her
    husband
DOING A HOUDINI   getting out of a tight spot
A CHOOSER   a performer who lifts material from other
    acts

Speaking of Choosers, one can't help being reminded of
Milton Berle, proclaimed by all entertainers, including himself, as the champion Chooser of them all. And speaking of
Berle, who had his first real success at the Palace many years
later, brings to mind an early *Variety* comment on him when
he was doing a juvenile act with a girl named Kennedy.
"The boy," said *Variety* succinctly, "borders on the precocious."

CHAPTER FIVE

A PALACE BILL was chosen with tremendous care by the bookers, not only on the basis of the talent and popularity of the acts involved, but also to assure the proper balance, the greatest possible variety, and the maneuverability of the acts.

Many of them used the full stage—the flash acts, one-act plays, many acrobatic and animal acts, and big bands, for instance. Others, like monologists, singers who did single turns, some dancers, most comedy acts, concert and opera stars, appeared "in one"—that is, on the front section of the stage with a backdrop behind them. Obviously two full-stage acts couldn't be scheduled back to back; the stage wait between would be too long. A full-stage act would have to be followed by an act in one, so that the next full-stage set could be put up during the performance. Sometimes an act would open in one and go to full stage, and this, too, would affect the routining of the program.

The usual vaudeville bill had only one headliner, but at the Palace there were never less than two, often three or even four. Incidentally, no headline names were up in lights on the marquee. The Palace remained the stellar attraction for many years.

Most Palace bills consisted of nine acts, not counting a newsreel or two. Occasionally, if one act was unusually long, there would be only seven. Once in a great while there would be ten. Theoretically, the best spot on the bill was next to closing; that is, the attraction that came on just before the "dumb act" that usually ended the show. *Dumb* in this usage meant silent, although some players chose to think it also meant stupid. At least, that's what the dumb acts thought the other acts thought, despite the fact that many of them were highly skilled, highly paid, and highly popular, and not infrequently had good billing. Among them were May Wirth, a great equestrienne; Poodles Hanneford, the clown rider, recently dead; and Lillian Leitzel, generally regarded as the greatest aerialist of them all. She fell to her death during a circus performance in Copenhagen.

An equally prestigious spot on the bill was the one just preceding intermission. For some illogical reason, that was always referred to as "closing intermission."

A typical Palace bill might be something like this:

1. An animal act—full stage
2. A song-and-dance team—in one

3. A flash act—revue, mini-musical—full stage
4. A concert singer with accompanist—in one
5. A name band—full stage with effects

INTERMISSION

6. A good monologist—in one
7. A one-act play with legit stars—full stage
8. A favorite jazz singer—in one
9. An acrobatic act—full stage

And following is an actual Palace program from the spring of 1923:

1. 3 Whirlwinds (acrobatic skaters)
2. Bill Robinson, "The Dark Cloud of Joy"
3. *World of Make-Believe* (a revue)
4. Gracie Deagon and Jack Mack (a clever comedy team)
5. Harland Dixon—with Marie Callahan and 16 Sunshine Girls

INTERMISSION

6. Ruby Norton (a popular singer)
7. *The Torchbearers*, with Mary Boland and Alison Skipworth
8. Rae Samuels, "The Blue Streak of Vaudeville"
9. Juggling Nelsons

But it wasn't all that simple. With two or more top-liners on every bill, there was a never-ending struggle over billing and routining, a struggle that taxed the patience and ingenuity of chief booker Eddie Darling. One of the thorniest problems concerned dressing rooms. There was only one star dressing room, on the main floor. How to satisfy two stars with one dressing room would have puzzled King Solomon, but the resourceful Mr. Darling, according to one of the hardiest of all Palace legends, solved it.

As an example—but only that—let's say that Eva Tanguay and Fanny Brice were on the same bill. Both would expect—and it was probably written into their contracts—the star dressing room. The story goes that Darling had a ladder placed against the dressing-room wall, a canvas spread on the floor and a bucket or two of paint set down on the canvas. Then he would explain, apologetically, that he'd been having the room redecorated and the painters were so slow that the room couldn't be used. Thus spared the need for hand-to-hand combat for possession of the star room, both gals would settle for dressing rooms upstairs.

Fanny Brice was one of the really great ones, not only as an entertainer but as a person. Since her career and her devotion to her husband Nicky Arnstein have been celebrated in the press, on the screen in *Rose of Washington Square*, and on both stage and screen in *Funny Girl*, most people are familiar with the general outline.

Around the theater, at least, no one ever saw anything but the funny girl, funny off as well as on, often at her own expense and usually with the Jewish flavor that was, until Baby Snooks came along, her trademark. Her unspoken motto was "anything for a laugh." Occasionally she carried it too far, as when she took an ad in a trade paper announcing that she could be seen at the Palace "twice daily, including Yom Kippur." This created quite a furor in the Jewish community, and Mr. Albee asked her, more in sorrow than in anger, "Fanny, Fanny, why did you do such a terrible thing?" She looked at him in amazement. "I thought it was funny."

But if there was ever a living example of the laugh-clown-laugh syndrome, it was Fanny Brice. After numbers like "I'm an Indian" (by Blanche Merrill, who wrote much of Fanny's special material) and her marvelous burlesque of both classical and modern dancing, which were Palace favorites for years, it came as a surprise to many that she could so convincingly portray the tragic prostitute singing "My Man." But long before that there were signs of a deep strain of sadness in her nature. One brief incident in her dressing room gave a striking glimpse of the vulnerable woman beneath the comic exterior.

A young woman reporter, Viola Brothers Shore, was doing a feature on a murder case in progress on Long Island, in which a beautiful and socially prominent young matron was on trial for killing her husband after finding him with another woman. Possibly because of rumors that gambling wasn't Nicky's only fault, Viola came to interview Fanny on the subject.

We were waiting in her dressing room when Fanny came offstage, grinning with pleasure at her well-earned triumph. After a few preliminaries Viola asked her question. Fanny's mobile face changed in a flash from the mask of comedy to the mask of tragedy.

"What do I think the verdict should be?" Fanny repeated the question without a trace of her Yiddish inflection. "Not guilty. *Not guilty!*" There was a beat of silence, then as she

98

pounded her fist hard down on the dressing table, she said, "Any man who cheats on his wife deserves to be killed. Shooting's too good for him. If I were on the jury, that poor girl would get a vote of thanks."

She shook her head violently, as if to banish an unwelcome image. Then, aware that she had revealed too much of herself, she abruptly resumed her clown's image. "Nu," she said, "look who's talking."

One thing about Fanny that never became public, because she didn't want it to, was her generosity, especially to old colleagues who had fallen upon hard times. During her life, and maybe after, she supported unnumbered and unnamed ex-vaudevillians who were never able to make the switch to another form of entertainment when vaudeville came to its melancholy end. Fanny had two children by Nicky Arnstein and she loved them dearly, but she didn't make a production of her mother love.

Some of the other stars were considerably more extroverted about their children. Once Belle Baker was going on tour to break in a new act, and since she'd been out of circulation for some time, I was sent along to do a special publicity campaign. We shared a compartment on the train to Cleveland and Belle, a sweet and highly emotional woman, kept me awake most of the night moaning over the enforced parting from her little Herbie, then six months old. She so doted on the child that she even had a song written about him to use in her act.

That boy, Herbert Baker, is today a successful writer and producer of TV and movies. Recently he told me about his parents' romance. Maurice Abrams, before he became a music publisher, was a song plugger and, as such, was in and out of the Palace a good deal. Belle had seen him several times and apparently was smitten, though they had never met. Fanny Brice somehow found out about Belle's crush. At this time Abrams tried to sell Fanny one of his songs—a song with the improbable title, "Put It On, Take It Off, Wrap It Up, Take It Home, Good Night, Call Again." Fanny, ever a fixer, said she couldn't use the song but thought her friend Belle Baker might be interested. She arranged for them to meet. Pretty soon Belle acquired the song and not too much later acquired the song plugger as well. It was a long and happy marriage.

Apropos Belle Baker, a less sentimental anecdote tells how one day as Roscoe Ails, the comic, was walking down Broadway near the Palace, a friend across the street called out, "Ailey, Ailey," and Belle, in a passing taxi, stood up and took a bow.

No discussion of mothers can omit Sophie Tucker. This uninhibitedly earthy woman with her bawdy songs and her "red-hot mama" speech had another side. When she talked about her son, Bert, which she did a good deal, she nearly turned into a madonna. It was touching to listen to her accounts of his progress in military school, his popularity with his classmates, his marvelous good looks. I never got to know him—she kept him away from the Palace, as far as I could see—but on one count she was unquestionably right. A handsome boy in military uniform looked seriously out of a gold frame on her dressing table.

It may come as a surprise to learn that many vaudevillians, despite the gypsy sort of life they had to lead most of

100

the time, were very strong family people, had about the same proportion of children as other people, and gave them a full measure of love and care. It may not have been of a conventional nature, though even that is open to question, but it was strong. And next to their desire to play the Palace, their one great ambition in life was to own their own home, which many of them did.

There can hardly be anyone who hasn't heard of Eddie Foy's Seven Little Foys and Eddie Cantor's five daughters. There were many others, the lowly and the great, who had real family instincts. Pat Rooney and Marion Bent had Pat the Third, who followed in the family footsteps. Irene Franklin had two daughters, who didn't. Ray Dooley and Eddie Dowling were proud parents, and Yvette Rugel, popular Palace regular, had a couple of kids who sometimes were allowed to come to the theater to hear Mama sing. Joe Cook used to say that he developed his superbly insane storytelling skill by inventing fairy tales for a house full of young Cooks in Lake Hopatcong, New Jersey.

All of which does not mean that every vaudevillian was a model of domestic decorum. A few legendary gentlemen would never have qualified as Father of the Year—even if they had children. Their exploits were widely known and are still recalled by those few who are still around to remember.

One of the most popular standard acts in vaudeville, particularly at the Palace, was the team of Duffy and Sweeney. Known in the trade as a "nut act," these two—companions off stage as well as on—were famous for their zany antics and their drinking capacity. The word *incorrigible* has often been applied to them, but everyone who mentions their names seems to do so with great affection. It may well be that their irreverence for the front office had something to do with this.

Once, when playing in a Southern city and meeting with a frigid reception, they thanked the audience with what has become a classic vaudeville story. At the finish, Duffy bowed and said: "Thank you, ladies and gentlemen, for the way you received our act. To show our appreciation, my partner will now pass among you with a baseball bat and beat the bejesus out of you!" This, along with other misdemeanors, was reported to the home office, and after a few more such episodes the act didn't work for a long time.

One day, according to Bill McCaffrey, Duffy managed to work his way into Mr. Albee's office. Clinging to his hand was an appealing little boy. "Look at this kid, boss," he said. "You don't want him to grow up thinking you're a sonofabitch, do you?" Startled, Albee said no, of course not. "Well, then," Duffy proceeded, "put me and Sweeney back to work." And he did.

A great many show-biz stories, some real, some apocryphal, are attributed to a variety of people. The episode of "Albee's kid lost his ball," originally credited to Joe Frisco, has also been attributed to Jimmy Duffy by John Byram, a former member of the Palace publicity department, later associate drama editor of *The New York Times*, and still later an executive in Paramount's story department. According to John, this was one more incident leading to the act's cancelation.

One of the funniest men ever to play the Palace was Jim Thornton, monologist, songwriter, and wit. He, too, was an off-stage comic and also famous for his way with a bottle.

His first wife, Bonnie, who acted as his partner for several years, used every known device to keep him from drinking. But he outwitted her every time. Apparently he didn't show his drinking until a very advanced stage, but there was one sure sign that he was loaded. At a certain point in his act he would suddenly start to sing one of his most popular songs, "Sweet Sixteen." When that happened, it was every man for himself.

Those who remember him agree that he was the undisputed champion drinker of Broadway (and he had some pretty stiff competition), but he carried it off with such a comic flair that it was never held against him. The saga of his alcoholic antics is endless, and one in particular is repeated whenever the dwindling group of old-timers get together.

It seems, according to the legend, that he was booked into a theater in Bethlehem, Pennsylvania, on his way to the Palace. He arrived at the theater, found the billing not to his liking, and objected to his spot on the bill. He told the house manager he refused to go on, he was quitting. The manager, outraged, said, "You can't do that. You can't walk out!" Thornton fixed him with a stony alcoholic stare and said, "Christ walked out of Bethlehem. So can James Thornton." And he walked. Just what happened on the Sixth Floor when the manager's report came in is not recorded. In any event, he survived to play the Palace and, according to some versions, even stopped drinking.

It is impossible to talk about funny men—and drinking men—without talking about Frank Fay. That man was unique. He was not a monologist in the accepted sense of the word. He was not a stand-up comic, though he stood up. He didn't tell jokes. He was a storyteller, a weaver of engagingly daft yarns. He casually walked out on the stage in a dinner jacket, handsome, saturnine, and brilliantly redheaded, looking like a young version of Chet Huntley. He then proceeded to hold his audience enraptured with his long, slow, soft-voiced accounts of people who didn't fit into any known category, like the boy who wouldn't get down off'n the wagon, and the family with a passion for saving string.

Fay was brilliant, sardonic, and contemptuous of most of mankind. He had a spectacular career at the Palace and elsewhere for many years before his triumph on the legitimate stage in *Harvey*. But his Palace bookings were spotted with "off the bill because of illness" or "replaced by so-and-so." He had a demon in him which won out in the end. Despite his brilliance and his inventiveness, the demon got control and ultimately his career was destroyed, but that didn't happen for a long time.

Just about the time I was getting settled nicely into my little hole in the wall, I was moved again. To add steam to the fight against Shubert vaudeville, Mr. Albee had brought into the organization Mark Luescher, a well-known publicity man and onetime producer of musicals. Luescher, a slender man of serious, even solemn mien, transformed a fairly sizable empty space on the second floor into a miniature city room, where half a dozen sub-press agents knocked out their stories and turned them in to him. Luescher then handed them over to John Pollock, a charming man in charge of disseminating stories and pictures to all the theaters on the Keith Circuit.

In that little city room were John Byram; a pair of sisters, Dorothy Ogden and Ruth Rustling; also Charles Welsh, Johnny Cassidy, Pat Grasso, and Harry Mandel. Pat Grasso is still with RKO and Harry Mandel stayed with the company long enough to become its president during the early 1960s. Charlie Welsh produces commercials for television.

It was Mark Luescher who turned me over to Singer's Midgets. Or vice versa. And until you've spent half your waking hours for a whole season in daily communion with twenty midgets (or, to be exact, nineteen midgets and one dwarf), you haven't really lived. The troupe had several Palace bookings and enough work in nearby theaters to keep them in New York for many months.

They all lived together in a brownstone house in the West Seventies, under the guidance and chaperonage of their entrepreneur, Mr. Singer, and his wife. Since only two of them were married, the sleeping quarters were broken up into dormitories, two for girls and two for boys. The married couple had a room of their own. The beds and all the furniture in the house were built to scale, most of it by members of the troupe themselves. In fact, everything connected with their lives was done by their own hands—the cooking, the housework, the costumes, everything. Even their shoes were made by John, the lone dwarf, who had been a bootmaker in the Black Forest of Germany before Mr. Singer discovered him.

They were an agreeable enough collection of little people, apparently well adjusted to their peculiar station in life, and maybe grateful for it. If they had all grown to full size, the chances are they would have had a much harder life. As entertainers they earned far more than they would have in the ordinary course of events. They had a privileged position in the world of show business, like a tiny autonomous duchy —Liechtenstein, for example—occupying favored-nation status among the giant countries of the outside world. Despite their external cordiality, it was hard to get to know them in any real sense. Spending a lot of time with them that season, I remained an outsider to be treated politely, even graciously, but never allowed inside.

They were very co-operative about publicity. Once, by prior arrangement and a certain amount of collusion, I planted ten of them in a taxi for a ride down Fifth Avenue. On cue, a traffic cop stopped the cab to arrest the driver and the ten midgets for violating the law prohibiting more than five passengers to a cab. Protesting that ten midgets equaled not more than five full-sized people, they failed to convince the policeman, who herded them to a magistrate's court, where they were arraigned on misdemeanor charges and bundled into cells. After being interviewed and photographed by all the papers, they were bailed out and the charges dropped. Such were the uses of press-agentry in the 1920s.

What with doing their show, rehearsing, and working around the house, they didn't have much time for dating; but when they did, it was seldom with other members of the troupe. I have distinct recollections of the girls being called for by fully grown young men, and one of the girls broke down enough to confide to me that she would never marry a midget.

From midgets to a giant seems a logical leap, and a giant of the era was soon bestowed upon me. Mr. Murdock called me in one day and announced that he had signed Babe Ruth for a tour of the circuit to begin as soon as the baseball season was over. I was to have the honor of handling his publicity campaign.

There were only two things wrong with this honor. One: I knew absolutely nothing about baseball. The other: there was absolutely nothing to say about Babe Ruth that had not already been said. His private life was unimpeachable; everyone knew what he ate for breakfast; his philanthropies and kindnesses to small boys certainly were known all over the country, if not the world. No use trying to make a Shakespearean scholar out of him, as Gene Tunney later became.

Prize ring, prize ring—the words rang a faint bell. After a bit of pondering I recalled that some time back, just before the Dempsey-Carpentier title fight, Carpentier—the Orchid Man—had garnered worldwide publicity. He had been picked to win by no less an authority than another George, the one better known as Bernard Shaw. Carpentier, Shaw had proclaimed, was the superman of boxing.

Armed with this valuable bit of ammunition, plus an idea, I went down to Walter Kingsley's office. I outlined a plan, not for a whole campaign but for a one-shot which, if it worked at all, would work big. But it needed the help of somebody important in the sports world, and that's where Walter came in. He knew everyone in every world, big or little. He made a telephone call to Madison Square Garden and had a brief conversation with Tex Rickard, the eminent sports promoter and general manager of Madison Square Garden.

That night Rickard cabled a question to Bernard Shaw in London. Knowing Shaw's parsimoniousness, he made clear that the answer was prepaid up to a thousand words. Rickard's cable was fairly short: "You claim Georges Carpentier is the superman of boxing. Would you call Babe Ruth the superman of baseball?" Shaw's speedy answer was even shorter. "Never heard of Ruth," he cabled. "Whose baby is she?"

The years between the wars are still looked back upon with sentimental sighs by most people who lived through them. And of those years the decade of the twenties shines in legend with a lovely light. Never mind the battle, murder, and sudden death of the Prohibition era, the gang wars, the political and private scandals, Teapot Dome, the mysterious death of Warren Harding, the rise of Hitler, the burgeoning Ku Klux Klan, the Depression.

It's easy to forget those things when memory lingers on the surging excitement, the money and talent pouring in a seemingly endless stream from a giant cornucopia. Those were the days of emancipation, of Freud and freedom, shingled hair and garter flasks, the gushing oil wells of Signal Hill, the Charleston and the Black Bottom; of Clara Bow and Valentino, John Held, Jr., and *Gentlemen Prefer Blondes;* Heywood Broun and F.P.A., Lardner and Lindbergh, Texas Guinan and Jimmy Walker, Lou Gehrig and

ABOVE: *Advertisement of Palace opening in* The New York Times *of March 23, 1913* BELOW: *Sarah Bernhardt, whose much-heralded appearance at the Palace saved the theater from financial ruin*

W. C. Fields, first billed as
"The Silent Humorist"

Ed Wynn, obscure jester
of the first matinee, who
became a national idol

Fruch

Bert Williams, one of the comic greats

*The matchless Nora
Bayes, famous for "Shine
On, Harvest Moon," in
World War I costume*

*Irene and Vernon Castle, whose grace
and style made ballroom dancing
an international pastime*

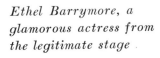

*Ethel Barrymore, a
glamorous actress from
the legitimate stage*

Toto, the immortal clown

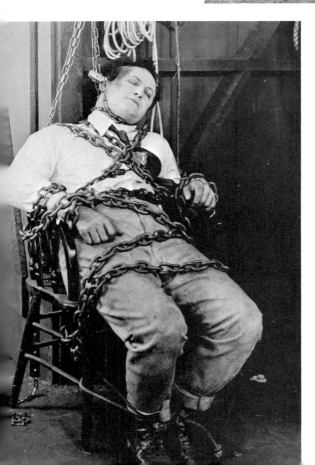

*Houdini, the magician,
performing a typically
daring feat*

Singer's Midgets, the author's most unusual publicity subjects

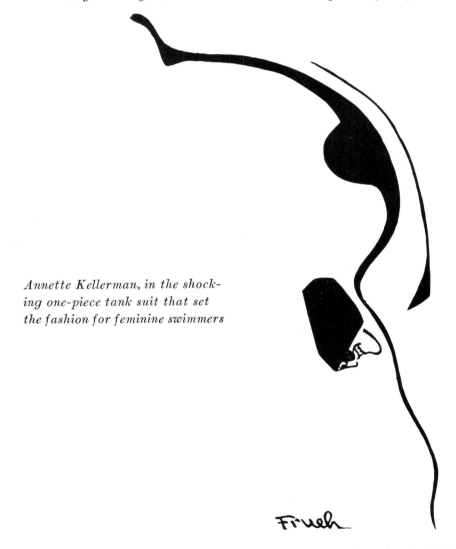

Annette Kellerman, in the shocking one-piece tank suit that set the fashion for feminine swimmers

LEFT: *Bert Wheeler, whose droll delivery and beguiling face made him an all-time favorite* BELOW: *The Dolly Sisters, toast of two continents*

LEFT: *Eva Tanguay, the "I Don't Care" girl*
BELOW: *Jimmy Savo in one of his puckish moods*

ABOVE: *Eddie Cantor of the banjo eyes* BELOW: *Jimmy Durante:*
"The nose knows"

Three Ladies of Special Talent: Above left: *Fanny Brice as she appeared when she sang "My Man"* Above right: *the incendiary Sophie Tucker* Below: *Grace Hayes at the peak of her fame*

A Trio of Great Dancers: Right:
Bill "Bojangles" Robinson Above
left: *Ray "Rubberlegs" Bolger*
Above right: *Ann Pennington of
the dimpled knees*

ABOVE: *The irrepressible Marx Brothers: Chico, Zeppo, Groucho, and Harpo* LEFT: *Versatile Blossom Seeley*

Two outstanding comedy teams:
LEFT: *Weber and Fields*
BELOW: *Clark and McCullough*

LEFT: *Frank Fay, the sardonic master of monologue* BELOW: *A well-loved Palace pair, William Gaxton and his wife, Madeline Cameron*

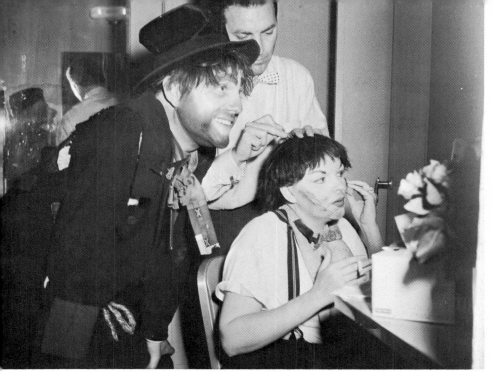

Making-up backstage: ABOVE: *Alan King and Judy Garland* BELOW:
Danny Kaye with photographer Roy Schatt

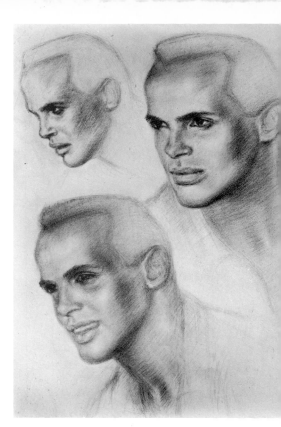

*The incomparable
Harry Belafonte*

*Gwen Verdon, musical-
comedy star of the new
Palace*

Bobby Jones, Red Grange and Johnny Weissmuller, Jack
Dempsey and Benny Leonard.

It was the heydey of *Smart Set* and the start of *The New
Yorker;* Mencken and Nathan, Dorothy Parker and Edna
St. Vincent Millay; *Vogue* and *Vanity Fair;* Hemingway
and the golden boy of those years, Scott Fitzgerald.

It was great to be alive and in New York those years.
Everything was wonderful fun, especially at the Palace,
where that same cornucopia of money and talent was spilling
its treasures on the broad stage for all New York to see.

The Palace management, never inclined to hide its light
under a bushel, published in its program of January 8,
1923, a manifesto of its plan for the upcoming season. In
part, it said: "At the Palace the bills already prepared for
the coming weeks are by far the best in the eventful history
of this, the world's greatest music hall. They are all remarkable for great and diverse excellence. The whole field of
entertainment on both sides of the ocean will be represented
by its most distinguished and interesting exponents."

A glance at some of the names on the programs will prove
that the announcement, though not conspicuous for its modesty, was quite accurate. For example: Ann Pennington, the
dimple-kneed dancer from the *Ziegfeld Follies;* Brooke
Johns, the jazz banjoist; William Faversham, great star of
the legitimate theater in a one-act play; Moss and Frye, a
highly popular pair of true vaudeville comics; the Duncan
Sisters, best known for their *Topsy and Eva* specialty; and
Van Hoven, "The Mad Magician."

Van Hoven had a burlesque magic act with two stooges.
Midway in the act he announced a trick involving two heavy

cakes of ice, each held by one of the stooges. Pretending uncertainty about what he was going to do with the ice, he solemnly asked the audience to be patient while he went off stage to think it over. Then he would descend from the stage to the front of the house, walk partway up the aisle and out a side door leading to 47th Street. Leaving the audience to speculate and amuse itself watching the two stooges suffering under their burden of ice, he'd go to a nearby speakeasy and have a few. After slaking his thirst, he'd come back through the front of the house, walk down the aisle, and return to the stage just as the ice was melting down the trouser legs of his patient stooges. Since few things seem to amuse people more than witnessing the discomfiture of other people, this zany routine was a great audience favorite.

One matinee day Mr. Albee came down to the theater in his private elevator. He watched the beginning of Van Hoven's act and then went into the lobby to talk to the house manager, Elmer Rogers. A few minutes later he was astonished to see Van Hoven enter the lobby from the street, a scuttle of beer in his hands and a rim of foam on his lips.

Albee, understandably, was furious at this breach of professional ethics. "How dare you leave the stage," he thundered, "and come into this theater with that beer!" Van Hoven looked him straight in the eye. "Look, Bud," he said, perfectly deadpan, "if you don't like it, just go to the box office and get your money back. Then you can get the hell out of this theater."

The fact that Van Hoven wasn't canceled immediately for this *lèse majesté* is probably attributable to one thing. He had been booked for a thirty-week tour across the country, and some time earlier a new policy had been formulated by the management—that is to say, Mr. Albee. It was called the play-or-pay policy, and it meant exactly what it said. If an act was canceled, for whatever reason, its salary was paid. This was part of a general improvement in working conditions for the performers; although the basic situation remained the same, some palliating actions had been taken.

These occurred, so the actors felt at the time, as the result of the legitimate actors' successful formation of a real union, Actors' Equity, which vaudeville performers would one day emulate. To stop, or at least postpone, such a development, management exhibited a bit of enlightened self-interest, softening its harsh conditions with a touch of kindly paternalism.

It was during this period that the NVA Clubhouse was completely rebuilt and redecorated, at a cost quoted as half a million dollars. So lavish was the place that one comic said the acrobats had to walk in on their hands.* Another aspect of this benevolent attitude was the institution of the NVA benefit. The proceeds of one matinee a year at each of some two hundred theaters were contributed to the NVA. This windfall added up to about $200,000, part of which went into insurance policies for needy performers. It was the patrons who made these contributions.

Another and more lasting achievement was the founding of a tuberculosis sanatorium at Saranac Lake, New York,

---

* The NVA Clubhouse, pillars and pediment intact, is still doing business at the same old stand—but a very different kind of business. Now called the New York Center, it houses the public-relations department of the Seventh-Day Adventists.

where members of the profession could live and be treated free of charge. William Morris had the inspiration for this haven, which was built on property donated by him. First called the Adirondack Tubercular Fund Northwood Home, its name was later changed to the NVA Sanatorium, with E. F. Albee as president. Mr. Morris was vice-president and remained active in its affairs until his sudden death in 1932. When the NVA—and vaudeville—went the way of all flesh, the name was changed again, to the Will Rogers Memorial Hospital, with support by film and other theatrical people. Today it is a leading treatment and research center for all pulmonary, respiratory, and chest ailments. Anyone connected with show business can avail himself of its services, still without paying a penny.

Life was definitely a bit better for the vaudevillians, but the NVA remained a company union. It had its uses, though. It offered a repository for actors' material, which was guarded both zealously and jealously, especially by the comedians. A line of dialogue or a bit of business that the audience might not find conspicuously noteworthy was often of vital importance to the performer. Sometimes there would be bitter exchanges of letters in the trade papers over which of two people had originated a line no more striking than "beautiful but dumb."

This sort of thing wasn't limited to minor performers. In his autobiography, *I Love Her, That's Why*, George Burns tells about a joke given him by Joe Frisco just before he and Gracie Allen opened at the Palace. He used the joke at the Monday matinee and got a big laugh. That very night he received a wire from Fred Allen saying that the joke was his and would they please drop it. Burns liked the joke so much that he offered Allen $500 for it, but Allen refused, so out it went.

And Bob Hope tells about a joke he'd been using success-fully since 1928. One night in the 1950s he heard Sid Caesar do it on his television show. "I sent him a letter," Hope says in *Have Tux, Will Travel*, "to tell him that if he ever sees me doing it, I'm not stealing it from him. For that matter," he adds with a refreshing touch of realism, "I wonder if I was the first to use it twenty-six years ago?"

Apropos borrowed jokes, Fred Allen—one of the few co-medians who wrote his own material—stated unequivocally in his autobiography that he originated a crack that has been used so often and by so many people that it has become part of the American language. After his first solid Palace engagement, he and his partner, Bert Yorke (this was before he married Portland Hoffa), toured the Keith Circuit. At one of the houses the orchestra leader behaved very rudely, almost disappearing from view as he conducted their en-trance music. After a few days of this, Allen leaned over the orchestra pit and in his acidulous drawl asked: "How much would you charge to haunt a house?"

Fred Allen was one of the most brilliant men on and off the stage. Recalling his great career in all branches of show business, it is hard to realize what a tough struggle he had to reach the top. Though he spent years in vaudeville, he didn't make it to the Palace until 1918, and that turned out to be a disaster. He was doing a single then, playing Proctor's The-atre in Yonkers, when summoned by a telephone call from Mr. Albee, asking him to come to New York next day to replace the opening act at the Palace, a team of acrobats. This was during the time acrobats were forbidden by law to play in theaters on Sunday.

To quote Allen: "Mr. Albee, head of the Keith circuit, sachem of the great vaudeville tribe, was calling me: it was like God bending from His empyrean throne and summoning an ant into His presence. I had no choice. If I turned Mr. Albee down, I might as well have started pricing brine and gone into the pickle business."

So the following afternoon Allen opened the show at the Palace. The theater was almost empty when he started, but by the time he finished the act the house had half-filled, and the applause was heartening. His agent came rushing backstage, full of enthusiasm. The long hard pull was over. This time, after many disappointments, Fred Allen was really *in*.

Except that he wasn't. He wasn't even held over for the evening show. If anyone told him why, he doesn't explain it. And it was eight years before he got to the Palace again. This time he really did make it. The act went over big with the audience, was reviewed very favorably, held over for a second week, and rewarded with thirty-five straight weeks on the circuit. The following spring it played a return engagement at the Palace. Later that year the act split up. Fred married Portland Hoffa and wrote a new act for them which they broke in out of town and then brought to the Palace with great success.

There was another theory to account for the new policy of qualified sweetness and light. Mr. Albee was getting on in years. He had grown weary of fighting, they said; had be-

come increasingly religious, was tired of what today would
be called his image—that of a hard, whip-cracking overseer,
a modern Simon Legree. In their book *Show Biz*, Abel Green
and Joe Laurie wrote: "Albee had apparently decided to call
it a day and wind up his career by winning the good will of
those who had once regarded him as their worst enemy."

The play-or-pay policy worked both ways. For example,
Bert Wheeler, an exceedingly funny, cherubic little man
with the face of a mischievous choir boy and a plaintive
voice, was playing the Palace with his pretty wife, Betty,
when Ziegfeld came to catch the show. Watching Bert sit in
the footlight trough, apparently devouring little powder
puffs under the impression they were marshmallows, and
listening to him dolefully singing "That Dear Ol' Mammy
of Mine" with glycerine tears streaming down his cheeks as
he munched on a ham sandwich, Ziegfeld was entranced.
Shortly thereafter Bert got a bid for that season's *Follies*.

He had several more weeks booked, at the Palace and
elsewhere on the Keith circuit. But the Ziegfeld offer was too
good to pass up, so he canceled the remaining weeks and sent
the booking office his check in full payment of the broken
dates. One story, circulated at the time and later confirmed
by Bert, had the money returned to him with Mr. Albee's
congratulations on his *Follies* opportunity. But Wheeler,
determined to live up to the play-or-pay policy, sent it back
again. This time the office kept it.

The move proved a good one for Bert. That season's
Follies—which included an imposing array of other Palace
favorites, among them Fanny Brice, Harland Dixon, and
Paul Whiteman—was one of the best of the series and had a

long run. Wheeler scored a personal triumph which won him
a five-year contract with Ziegfeld. And when the new Ziegfeld Theatre opened uptown at 54th Street and Sixth Avenue, Bert was the top comedian in the musical *Rio Rita*.
Later, following a few return engagements at the Palace, he
went to Hollywood to make a movie of that show. After that
he and Robert Woolsey, another comic from *Rio Rita*,
teamed up and made more than two dozen pictures during
the 1930s.

The last few years of Bert's life were spent commuting
between New York and the Will Rogers Hospital in Saranac. He died recently at the age of seventy, greatly
mourned by his colleagues. Honorary president of the Cath-
olic Actors Guild, and a much-loved member of the Lambs
Club, he was the only true vaudevillian to have a theater
named for him. The attractive little 225-seat playhouse in
the Dixie Hotel—a stone's throw from the Palace—is the
Bert Wheeler Theatre.

Having a theater named for an actor may seem like the
crowning honor, but one thing that pleased Bert even more
was being named as part of an all-time, all-star Palace bill
by two well-qualified authorities. The first was Bill McCaffrey, who not only included Bert in his list but gave him the
cherished next-to-closing spot. The other authority was ac-
tress-playwright June Havoc, who had been a child star in
vaudeville.

So outstanding and varied were the Palace bills of the
twenties that it is next to impossible to single out any special
one. But following is a particularly good example:

The Four Readings (jugglers)

Joe Roberts (banjoist)

Fifty Minutes from Broadway (a one-act musical revue)

Georges Dufranne (concert tenor in his vaudeville debut)

Yvette Rugel (singer)

Vincent Lopez and his Pennsylvania Hotel Orchestra

Moran and Mack, "The Two Black Crows"

and

"As vaudeville's contribution to the Shakespearean revival in America," MISS JULIA ARTHUR as HAMLET.

Who could ask for more variety than those Two Black Crows, so popular with audiences for years to come; Vincent Lopez, his diamond pinky ring sparkling in the spotlight as his nimble fingers danced up and down the keyboard in "Nola" and "Kitten on the Keys"; and the somber, classically beautiful Miss Arthur in the intensely emotional Closet Scene from Shakespeare's greatest tragedy?

Miss Arthur, incidentally, was not the first woman to essay the role of Hamlet. Several actresses had done it before, notably Sarah Bernhardt—in French, of course—and the great star of the mid-1800s, Charlotte Cushman. It had also been played in the 1880s in New York by Anna Dickenson. But never before had a woman attempted the role in a variety theater. By bringing *Hamlet* to vaudeville, Julia Arthur undoubtedly introduced Shakespeare to thousands of people to whom he had been up to then a vaguely disquieting name or a boring subject in high-school English.

117

The Palace continued on the broad highway of success, but even the Palace was not completely immune to the threat of Holy Week, between Palm Sunday and Easter, then as now regarded as one of the two worst weeks in the theatrical year. To guarantee that business that week would be as good as humanly possible, Eddie Darling built a strong bill, including Bard and Pearl ("Vas you dere, Sharlie?") and James Barton, the brilliant comic dancer who later won fame as Jeeter Lester in *Tobacco Road*. The top star was Elsie Janis, who always drew big audiences, regardless of wind, weather, or season.

I mentioned earlier that no star's name, however great, could appear in lights over the marquee. But a few of them had clauses in their contracts allowing them to stretch large banners across the front of the theater. Elsie Janis had such a clause, but for some reason the banner wasn't up for a performance and Elsie's mother served notice to the management that if the banner was not in place by the next day, Elsie wouldn't go on.

The banner was not up and Elsie did not go on. After a series of telephone calls, notes, attacks, and counterattacks, she stayed off the bill. She vowed she would never appear at the Palace again, and Mr. Albee vowed he would never hire her again. But she didn't keep her vow and Mr. Albee didn't keep his. She played the Palace at least once more, in 1928.

Now and then someone quite outside show business would hit the Palace. One such personality was Robert Benchley, the critic and humorous writer. Late in 1924, having scored with his bumbling *Treasurer's Report* at private parties and in revues, he was invited to the Palace, where he shared the bill with Victor Moore and William Courtleigh, capturing new audiences.

A truly fabulous bill of what is still thought of by many as "true vaudeville" opened at the Palace on April 20, 1925. The original headliners, who had been out of circulation for some time, were Weber and Fields. Because of a chance remark by Cissie Loftus, who in earlier days had been part of their company, Eddie Darling decided to put on what he called old-timers' week. For this he gathered such favorites as Marie Cahill, the comedienne; Miss Loftus herself; and Emma Trentini, the operetta star, with her accompanist, Eric Zardo. For a more contemporary touch, he also booked Blossom Seeley with her husband, Benny Fields. Benny's trademark was the sentimental "Melancholy Baby" and Miss Seeley introduced the highly unsentimental "Chicago."

An extra attraction was the wildly funny Dr. Rockwell, who convulsed audiences with his lecture on human anatomy, using a banana stalk as a skeleton. Rockwell was independent, outspoken, and courageous. He refused to join the NVA on the grounds that it meant taxation without representation, and despite this defiance of the front office, he kept on working.

Somewhat to the surprise of the management, the week's business was exceptionally good. Audiences loved the old-timers, and the gross was high. So Darling booked the show for a second week. In his jubilation over the old-timers' success, however, he forgot one thing. Weeks before, he had contracted with Laurette Taylor, then at the peak of her fame as a legitimate star, to appear at the Palace in a French pantomime, *Pierrot the Prodigal,* during the week of

119

April 27. This was to be her vaudeville debut in New York, not counting the time she walked on with Sarah Bernhardt eleven years before. Using all the tact and delicacy he was noted for, Darling went to Miss Taylor and suggested that she postpone her engagement till a later date. It would be more auspicious for her, he said, and (he didn't say) more practical for him.

But the lady was not persuaded. These has-beens, she implied even if she didn't come right out and say it, were no competition for her. She had contracted to play that week. Play that week she would, and did. Her leading man, incidentally, was Clarence Derwent, founder of the Derwent Award for the best supporting actor and actress to appear on Broadway each season in non-featured roles.

That week turned into one of Eddie Darling's greatest headaches. For one thing, it was a ten-act bill. For another, he had to talk the other performers into accepting salary cuts so he wouldn't run over his allotted weekly budget of $8,000. Since he was paying Weber and Fields $3,000 and Miss Taylor even more, he had quite a job. But he managed it.

Again the matter of dressing rooms arose. Nobody, certainly none of the women, wanted to give way to this high-handed lady from the legit who behaved as though they didn't even exist. It was probably this dilemma that inspired Eddie Darling to use his much-talked-of routine of "redecorating" the star dressing room.

At all events, the program was again so successful that he booked a third old-timers' bill a few weeks later. It was substantially the same bill with the omission of Miss Taylor and the addition of another old-time favorite, Fay Templeton. Fay, a contemporary and friend of Lillian Russell, had appeared in the old days with Weber and Fields. By now she was in retirement and enormously fat. But Darling induced her to join her old colleagues, which she did with great success. Almost a decade later she was to win new plaudits when, heavier than ever but still charming, she sang "Yesterdays" in the musical *Roberta,* with that soon-to-be star, Bob Hope. Palace audiences, celebrated for their toughness, could be very sentimental. Cheers and tears flowed freely at Miss Templeton's appearance; the week's business was so good that the whole show was again held over.

In the fall of 1925—October 19, to be specific—the Palace brought together another aggregation of old-timers, all on the distaff side. Repeaters were Cissie Loftus and Marie Cahill; added starters were May Irwin and that very special favorite, Marie Dressler. Joe Laurie says that Weber and Fields had been booked for the week but, claiming illness, walked out when they found themselves billed second to Miss Dressler, who had worked for them in the old days.

Joe Laurie himself was on the bill the following week, for which Miss Dressler was held over. According to Douglas Gilbert in his *American Vaudeville,* it was this Palace engagement that launched her on her second motion-picture career. She had been a pioneer movie actress in such wild comedies as *Tillie's Punctured Romance* with Charlie Chaplin.

The old-timers' bills, successful as they were, naturally did not monopolize the Palace stage. There is just no way to convey the riches of talent that sang and danced and juggled and joked and talked across that stage except to thrust a hand into a giant goldfish bowl and pull out a list at random. In the middle years of the twenties alone there were top-flight performers from all branches of the entertainment world.

From vaudeville and musical comedy: the Four Mortons, Odette Myrtil, Florence Mills, the Six Brown Brothers, Emma Haig, Hazel Dawn of *Pink Lady* fame, Ted and Betty Healey, Lulu McConnell, the Rath Brothers, Charles Withers, Helen Broderick, Vesta Victoria from the London halls, a young man then known as "Rubberlegs" Bolger, and Lewis and Dody, whose fame was based chiefly on a delirious ditty of many verses: "Hello, Hello, Hello." Also there was the extravagantly funny act of Willie West and McGinty, the demon house-wreckers.

From the dramatic stage: Ina Claire, Jacob Ben-Ami, Estelle Winwood, Olga Petrova, Mr. and Mrs. Charles Coburn, Fay Bainter, Helen MacKellar, Louis Mann, Henry Hull, June Walker, Geoffrey Kerr, Ruth Chatterton, and a host of others.

From the movies: Betty Blythe, one of the all-time screen sirens, and Lew Cody, one of the all-time screen villains.

From the world of music: Grace Moore, Robert Chisholm, Orville Harrold and his daughter Patti, Anna Case, Anna Fitziu, and Emma Calvé. Avery Strackosch, writer and member of a famous musical family, remembers sitting in the Palace with Metropolitan Opera star Antonio Scotti when Mme. Calvé, the great Carmen of an earlier day, reappeared at the Palace in 1927. "She was enormous," Avery recalls. "She coquetted with the audience, most of whom had proba-

bly never heard of her, and they just sat there laughing.
Scotti watched, embarrassed for her, and wept. Before it was
over we crept away. It was too heartbreaking.''

By 1927 I had been gone from the Palace for some time
and was working for that charming stage star turned producer, Edgar Selwyn. I remained a fan, however, and almost
never missed a Palace bill. Also, I still saw my friends there
regularly. Oddly enough, I had never met Mr. Albee. Now
and then, while still at the Palace, I would catch a glimpse of
him on the Sixth Floor, and once when I was going out of the
stage door I saw him coming in through the alley. The
doorman, a substitute, failed to recognize him and refused to
let him in until he'd been identified by one of the actors. The
poor doorman was petrified, but Mr. Albee only praised him
for having obeyed instructions.

Not until quite a time after I had left the Palace did I
finally meet Mr. Albee. I had started magazine writing and,
thanks to the information gathered during my tenure, had
done a series on vaudeville for one of the major weeklies. The
first installment had just appeared when I got a call from
Walter Kingsley. Mr. Albee would like to meet me, he said,
and would I please come over to the office.

A few days later I was ushered into that enormous room,
the room so often likened to Mussolini's intimidating office.
The office and the sight of the little man behind the big desk
made me nervous, for the piece I had written disclosed some
of the less admirable business practices I had learned about.
Mr. Albee told me very gently that he wasn't angry, just
terribly, terribly hurt. He didn't deny the accuracy of what

I'd written, but he couldn't see why it was any of the public's business. And he would like to know who had given me the information.

When I said I couldn't tell him that, he suggested that if I could get the rest of the series killed there might be a new and better job for me at the Palace, especially if I could jog my memory about my informants. When I answered that I couldn't get the articles killed, and wouldn't even if I could, he made some vague hints of dire things to come and dismissed me. I wouldn't swear to it, but I have the impression that I backed out of the room. For a while I wondered what malign fate would overtake me, but nothing ever happened. I was not barred from the Palace, and I continued to be a fan.

When people have been international celebrities for decades, it is hard to believe they were once obscure and required years to become thoroughly established. Take the case of Bob Hope. From the numerous claims on record it seems that this worldwide favorite was the most "discovered" talent in the entire history of show business.

According to Stuart Stewart, brother and partner of Rosalie Stewart, it was another member of their family who started Bob on the road to the big time. "My brother Lee," wrote Stuart Stewart, "was the original agent who discovered Bob Hope and brought him to New York. He had been M.C. of a musical troupe playing the small time around Chicago from radio station WLS, and the act's name was *WLS Showboat*. Lee brought him to New York and he opened at the 81st Street Theatre and has been going ever since."

That's one discovery. The next was made by Milton Lewis, brother of Al. Milton has his own version of the Hope beginning. "I handled an act called Hope and Byrne," Milton told me—"a straight singing-and-dancing act—not a word of talk." In Bob Hope's autobiography he says: "Milton Lewis, my New York agent, got a date for me at B. S. Moss' Franklin, a big-time eight-act house."

In a 1929 issue of *Variety* Bob Hope was reviewed under the heading of "New Acts." The theater was Procter's 86th Street, and the brief comment said: "He sings 'True Blue' for laughs, and 'Pagan Love Song' straight—both very good."

Like many another performer, Bob had a long struggle and a series of agents before he hit it big. He had worked on several circuits, small-time and big, before he got a three-year contract with the Keith Circuit. And even then it was quite a while before he got to the Palace. Neither in the Palace record book nor in Bob's own book is there a definite date given for his appearance there as a single. The only reference is to Bob Hope as part of *Antics of 1931*. The *Antics* consisted of four separate acts, Bob's own and three others, plus an afterpiece.

His work in *Antics* brought about Bob's next "discovery." This discoverer was Lewis Gensler, the composer and producer. Lew and Russell Patterson were preparing a revue called *Ballyhoo of 1932*, named after a popular satirical magazine edited by Patterson. In Lew's own words, he saw Bob at the Palace and was so enthusiastic that he brought his partner around and they signed Bob for the show that very night.

After *Ballyhoo* closed, Bob went back into vaudeville and once again he was "discovered." This time it was by Max Gordon, who was seeking a young comedian for *Roberta*. According to Max, he dragged a skeptical Jerome Kern to the theater. Kern, not the easiest man to please, succumbed to Hope's talent and personality.

Quite a few years and several star roles later, Bob Hope was discovered finally and for all time. On this occasion the discoverers were Mitchell Leisen and Harlan Thompson, director and producer, respectively, of an upcoming Paramount musical revue—the kind of movie known in the trade as a clambake. Other Palace alumni were cast in it—W. C. Fields, Ben Blue, and Jack Benny. But something kept Jack Benny out of the picture, and Thompson and Leisen remembered the young man they'd enjoyed so much in a show they had seen in New York. So they persuaded Paramount to send for him. He came, Paramount saw, and Hope conquered. The name of the picture was *The Big Broadcast of 1938*. It was Bob's first picture with Dorothy Lamour, but his love interest in the film was a pretty girl with a sweet voice, Shirley Ross. Toward the end of the picture, after she and Bob Hope had quarreled their way through a dozen reels and one divorce, they met on a transatlantic liner and were reconciled over a few drinks and a rather off-beat song called "Thanks for the Memory." After that he didn't have to be discovered any more.

It has been mentioned earlier that the twenties brought in the era of the big-name band. Paul Whiteman, the big daddy (big in any and every sense of the word), was not the first—

that was Ben Bernie—but he did set a mark for other bands to shoot at. He stayed at the Palace for five consecutive weeks.

In connection with Ben Bernie, a small footnote should be added. When a young violinist from Waukegan, Illinois, first went into vaudeville, he called himself Ben Benny. Some time later he changed the Ben to Jack, in order not to be confused with the "Old Maestro." Another footnote concerns one of the entertainment world's most striking personalities, the wild, witty, wonderful Oscar Levant. Oscar, a friend of George Gershwin and a brilliant interpreter of George's music, was for a time a pianist with Ben Bernie's band, and in that capacity played the Palace.

Other bands made numerous Palace appearances, often playing a week or two, then moving on to other houses in and around New York, returning to the Palace a few weeks later. Besides Ben Bernie with his "Yow-za" trademark and Ted Lewis with his rakishly angled silk hat and his inevitable "Is *ev'*rybody happy?" there were the bands led by Hugo Riesenfeld, Nat Nazzaro, Paul Specht, Abe Lyman, Brooke Johns, and Meyer Davis, then and now the "society" band leader.

There were trick ensembles, like the Mound City Blues Blowers and the House of David Band, a bearded aggregation from a religious sect in the Far West. Once on the Palace bill they were joined by a couple of falsely bearded fellows who proceeded to augment the act with their particular brand of nonsense. Their purpose was to surprise the audience, but before they had a chance to pull off their false beards, the two ringers were recognized by the wise guys out

127

front as Bert Kalmar and Harry Ruby, a team of songwriters and, incidentally, a pair of the nicest men in show business. Bert was an accomplished magician and Harry was—and still is—an equally accomplished raconteur.

Bert and Harry had written many songs for Belle Baker, and later wrote scores for Broadway and Hollywood musicals. Eventually they became famous enough to have a movie written about them. It was called *Three Little Words*, after one of their songs, and it catapulted to film fame a cute little girl named Debbie Reynolds, portraying another cute little girl named Helen Kane, who some time before had been catapulted to fame herself, not by three little words, but by four little syllables: "Boop-boop-a-doop." Helen Kane, who died recently, had been a Palace favorite in her day. She did the singing for Debbie Reynolds in the picture.

Probably the one big band that made the highest Palace score was that of Vincent Lopez. Lopez didn't hold the record for consecutive appearances, but, looking back, it seems that he and his band played the Palace every two or three weeks for several years. Once in the middle twenties he was there four weeks in a row, away for two or three, and then back for five more consecutive weeks.

Lopez not only had a good band; he was a real showman. When he and his men were on stage you not only heard music, you saw it dramatized, whether it was "Waiting for the Robert E. Lee" with miniature side-wheelers racing along the Mississippi on the cyclorama, or Tchaikowsky's "1812 Overture" with realistic-looking flames billowing to the sky as Napoleon's troops made their celebrated retreat from Moscow.

128

CHAPTER SIX

THE PALACE was an impregnable fortress, and Mr. Albee's office on the Sixth Floor was not only a throne room, it was a command post. The fate of thousands hung on his decisions. Anyone who incurred his displeasure was summarily banished, whether performer, office employee, or agent. And he rarely gave reasons for his dismissals beyond the brief comment that this one or that one had been what he considered "disloyal." Disloyalty in these cases usually meant that an act, needing work, had accepted bookings from an opposition circuit, or an agent had procured a few weeks' work elsewhere for one of his clients.

Sometimes, if the culprit crawled enough, he would be reinstated, but only after a period of penitence and idleness. Once in a while someone had the temerity to fight back. Take the case of the agent Max Hart, a rather big man in his field, with a list of clients including such entertainers as Fred Stone, Eddie Cantor, Blossom Seeley, Frank Tinney, the Avon Comedy Four, along with dozens of others. After several alleged infractions of the Albee code, for each one of which he had been "thrown off the floor" for varying periods of time, he was finally disenfranchised permanently early in the twenties. Which meant, as has been noted before, that he could no longer represent his clients for vaudeville.

One day Broadway was electrified to read that Max Hart had brought suit in Federal Court against the B. F. Keith Vaudeville Exchange, E. F. Albee, John J. Murdock, and assorted colleagues. The charge was conspiracy, monopoly in restraint of trade, and violation of the Anti-Trust Law. He claimed damages of one million dollars and punitive damages amounting to another three quarters of a million. His legal battery included one of the greatest and most respected lawyers of the period, Martin Littleton. Hart produced clouds of witnesses, including some of his stellar clients and ex-clients, but his suit was dismissed by Justice Augustus N. Hand. The defendants, the judge said, were definitely not engaged in "Interstate Commerce within the purview of the Anti-Trust Laws."

Hart took his case to the United States Circuit Court of Appeals; the defendants this time had as their chief advocate no less a luminary than Charles Evans Hughes, former governor of New York and unsuccessful presidential candidate. Again the decision went to the defendants. One other agent, Marinelli, the ex-contortionist, was also disenfranchised. He, too, tried to buck the system, and he, too, lost.

The Hart case used up a great deal of money, printer's ink, and paper. It also used up a considerable amount of time. Most of this time, when he wasn't in court or cruising on his yacht or punishing his subjects for their crimes, Albee was building new theaters, studying architects' plans, buying tons of marble and miles of carpet and acres of paintings to go into the creation of such other pleasure domes as the Cleveland Palace, the E. F. Albee Theatre in Brooklyn, and the Keith Memorial in Boston.

Preoccupied with these activities and imperturbably sure of his own supremacy, he scarcely noticed some of the things which were going on in the world outside—such as that elaborate motion-picture theaters were springing up in numbers which, to others, seemed alarming. They had in fact been slowly encroaching on the Palace territory, geographically at least.

First there was the Strand, almost directly across Broadway from the Palace. It had opened in April 1914, only a little more than a year after the Palace. As the Warner Theatre it still stands. Next, in 1916, came the Rialto at Times Square, on the very spot where once Hammerstein's Victoria had reigned supreme, only to die a lingering death at the hands of the Palace. Like the Strand, it was managed by the vigorous, colorful maestro of motion-picture theaters, S. L. Rothafel, better known as Roxy. Musical director of the Rialto was Hugo Riesenfeld, who, ironically enough, had been brought to New York by Oscar Hammerstein as concertmaster of the Manhattan Opera House, and who had appeared at the Palace with his own orchestra on at least one occasion. In 1917 there was the Rivoli. Then came the Capitol, which opened in 1919, also under the direction of Roxy. It was the most ambitious theater up to that time, and it eventually used many old Palace hands for its elaborate stage shows.

Between 1919 and 1926 there was a hiatus, but November of '26 saw the grand opening of Adolph Zukor's Paramount Theatre at Broadway and 43rd Street. Another menacing neighbor was Loew's State, regarded as serious opposition by Mr. Albee, who had issued a Palace ban on any performers who accepted work at the Loew house. Besides their atmosphere of grand luxe, all these temples of the motion picture offered live shows of one sort or another at lower prices than the Palace.

Fred Allen, in his wise and witty autobiography, *Much Ado About Me,* summed up the situation characteristically. Contrasting the vaudeville theaters, including the Palace, with the supercolossal movie houses, he wrote: "The motion picture theaters were cathedrals that made the vaudeville houses look like privies. . . . The big-time vaudeville theaters couldn't stand off this competition."

Just about this time something else quite significant happened. In the spring of 1926 *Variety* moved its vaudeville news section from the front pages (where it had been featured since the very beginning) to the back of the weekly—the section Abel Green calls the balcony—giving films the opening space. Since vaudeville had been Sime Silverman's great love and his reason for starting *Variety,* this switch surely should have been a hint to Mr. Albee. But apparently it wasn't. To paraphrase another comment of Fred Allen's, he had his money stacked up so high he couldn't look over it to see what was happening to the big time, and that included the Palace.

Despite all this, the Palace bills of that late April and early May continued to be top-drawer. The very week that saw the demotion of vaudeville to the back of the book in *Variety*, the bill included Dave Apollon, Eva Tanguay, and Helen Ware, a popular dramatic star. And the following week was even more star-studded, including as it did Charlotte Greenwood, Jack Norworth, Blossom Seeley, Mr. and Mrs. Jimmy Barry (very popular two-a-day standbys), and Charles King from musical comedy, later the star of that pioneer musical movie, *Broadway Melody*.

Eva Tanguay's Palace appearance that spring provided another straw in the wind. One of the strongest of Mr. Albee's taboos, already mentioned, was Loew's State, the combined-movie-and-vaudeville house only a block and a half down the street from the Palace. Yet he booked Tanguay into the Palace at a three-dollar top (Saturdays and Sundays) only a short time after she had played Loew's State, which had a fifty-cent top.

About this time another ban was dropped. Up to then the Palace had had an ironclad rule against performers doubling in night clubs. Sophie Tucker, after a spectacular tour in England earlier that year, had turned down $2,500 a week at the Palace. She was appearing at her own recently opened club, Sophie Tucker's Playground, when Eddie Darling asked her to make a guest appearance at a special NVA benefit performance on the Tuesday afternoon of Easter

133

Week. Because of the exigencies of time—and because she was contributing her services—she was put on just before intermission.

What Sophie apparently didn't know was that the top name on that week's bill was Nora Bayes, and that Nora's act was set for the same spot. This was unusual, because the headliner normally went on next to closing. When Miss Bayes heard that Sophie was being given her spot on the bill, she was outraged. What made it especially touchy was that years before, when Sophie Tucker got her first break in Ziegfeld's *Follies* of 1909, Nora Bayes, the star of that show, had had Sophie's numbers cut down to only one, and very nearly got her fired from the show. Now, almost two decades later, Sophie was getting in Nora's way again, and she wasn't having it.

"I tell you," Nora shouted at Eddie Darling, "she will not go on ahead of me! If she does, I'll walk out of the theater." Sophie went on as planned, and Nora walked out. Whereupon the rule against doubling was abandoned. Sophie, at the salary she demanded, stayed on for the week and was held over for a second.

Nora Bayes was without doubt one of the most beautiful, fascinating, and popular of all the female vaudeville stars, and certainly one of the most gifted. Several critics called her the American Yvette Guilbert. But she was also without doubt one of the most difficult, evidenced by a long series of accompanists. One of these was young George Gershwin. Her walkout from the Palace represented only one example of her constant temperamental outbursts. And her billing while she was teamed with and married to Jack Norworth is a revealing clue to her character. The programs of the period read:

NORA BAYES
Assisted and admired by Jack Norworth

Her marriage to Jack Norworth didn't quite live up to another billing: "The Stage's Happiest Couple." They were divorced after a few years and went their separate ways, professionally and matrimonially. Nora, who had been married once before Norworth, took three more husbands before she was through. Despite a failure at the London Empire during World War I, made all the more galling because of Norworth's simultaneous success at the London Hippodrome, she continued riding high for a considerable time.

After the Empire flop she disappeared, and newspaper stories hinted she had been killed or captured while entertaining Allied troops at the front. But that was not true, and probably just a publicity build-up for her return to the Palace. On this occasion her billing read: "The Greatest Single Woman Comedienne in the World."

She played more vaudeville, and in 1922 starred in *Queen O' Hearts*, with a score by Lewis Gensler, the young Navy lad whose first song she had introduced at the Palace years before. But insidious ill health, creeping up on her without overt symptoms, sapped her strength and diminished her wonderful talent. That, plus her unfortunate reputation for being hard to handle, hurt her badly; as time passed, her salary gradually dropped and her bookings were less frequent.

Then, suddenly, her health improved, and with it her disposition. Her career took an upturn again, and by the time of the Sophie Tucker episode in 1926 she was once more in the big money. But the improvement didn't last, and her final years were heavy with difficulties and sadness. She never played the Palace again, but there is a pathetic little epilogue to that incident. Sophie Tucker tells it in her autobiography as it was told to her by Eddie Darling.

Two years after her willful walkout, Miss Bayes called Darling and asked him to come to see her. Reluctantly, for old times' sake, he did. She begged him to do her a favor. He thought she was going to plead for a booking at the Palace, but that wasn't it. "She wanted Eddie to promise her he'd get out the big photographs of her that used to be in the lobby when she was the headliner," Sophie wrote. "She asked him to put them up in the lobby early next morning 'just as if I were playing the Palace.' He could take them down before the matinee, but she wanted to know, when she drove past the Palace next morning on her way out of town, that her pictures were there."

Darling thought this a very odd request, but she seemed so urgent and looked so ill that he agreed. The pictures of Nora Bayes in her prime went up in the Palace lobby, and presumably Miss Bayes drove by the theater and saw them. Or maybe, as Sophie conjectures, she got out of the car and took a good long look at her handsome old self. A few days later she was dead, a victim of the cancer that had been gnawing at her for years.

Jack Norworth, less flamboyant than Nora, was as talented in his way as she was in hers. Their professional styles had in common complete poise and a refreshing absence of needless gestures and perpetual motion. Jack, like Nora, had perfect articulation. Though his voice couldn't compare with hers, his songs reached the last rows of the balcony in an apparently effortless way. And he never ever moved. Asked once how he managed to hold that one easy, graceful position throughout his entire routine, he said: "I just tell myself I'm standing on a dime and mustn't step off it!"

He wrote a good many songs, including Nora's trademark, "Shine On, Harvest Moon," "Come Along, My Mandy," and "Take Me Out to the Ball Game." So even though he stopped earning big money as a performer and ultimately retired to Southern California, his ASCAP royalties must have kept him comfortable for the rest of his life, which lasted till 1954.

For many years, ever since it had become the lodestar for acts and audiences alike, the Palace had been having trouble with ticket speculators, who did a land-office business on Saturday and Sunday nights, often getting as much as ten dollars a pair for seats. It was such a problem that the management instituted a sidewalk patrol whose function it was to stand outside the theater, spot the speculators, and warn the patrons against them. Then, as now, the warnings accomplished little. People eager to see a show didn't seem to care how much they paid for their tickets, nor how unethical, if not illegal, the practice was. But some time in 1926, a little while after *Variety* had relegated vaudeville to the back pages, the problem dwindled and then ceased. The speculators gradually stopped peddling their illicit wares and disappeared from the beach outside the Palace. Not only that, but for the first time since the very earliest days the Sunday-night shows didn't sell out even at box-office prices.

Now the Palace dropped another long-standing taboo by booking acts that played what were euphemistically called Sunday Night Concerts at the Winter Garden, stronghold of the arch-enemy Shuberts. Next a series of pay cuts began. Salaries of assistant managers and doormen were reduced, and a sizable number of cleaners and porters lost their jobs. Despite the continuing good shows, business fell off noticeably and the blame was placed on the giant movie houses—the Strand, the Rivoli, and the Capitol—all of which afforded live entertainment as well as films.

It is hard to understand why Mr. Albee was not aware of these threats to his castle as well as to his empire, since the same thing was happening all over the country, wherever the new type of motion-picture temple existed. Maybe he *was* aware, but he certainly didn't give any sign of it. There is some indication that one or two of his cohorts, among them J. J. Murdock, tried to persuade him to book films into the Palace along with the vaudeville shows. But he flatly and stubbornly continued along his regal way. One writer (Richard Whalen in *The Founding Father*) said of him, rather grudgingly, that "an impulsive, unshakable trust in a chosen few was Albee's only really endearing quality, and the one which ultimately was his undoing," but the end would be some time off. Meanwhile he was still the absolute monarch.

In March 1927, Rothafel opened his crowning achievement to date, that "cathedral of the motion picture" called the Roxy, with its vast seating capacity, its dazzling décor, its huge orchestra—conducted by Hugo Riesenfeld from the Capitol—rising from hidden depths to stage level, its Roxyettes, and its crops of splendidly uniformed ushers. The stage was so enormous that Joe Frisco offered his fellow performers the following advice: "Don't get lost on the Roxy stage without bread and water."

The opening film was a lurid drama called *The Loves of Sunya*, and its star was glorious Gloria Swanson. The opening night of the Roxy was presented with overwhelming fanfare and publicity. Few events of the sort equaled it until the opening of the new Metropolitan Opera House in 1966. The most sophisticated scribes—even such a non-square writer as Robert E. Sherwood, a movie critic at the time—went into paeans of praise over the new "cathedral."

All this grandeur, with movies to match and elaborate stage shows besides, at a top price of $1.65! The Palace still offered first-rate vaudeville; among its acts during the early days of the Roxy opened were such favorites as Blossom Seeley, Elsie Janis, Jack Norworth, Raymond Hitchcock, Ben Bernie and his orchestra, Burns and Allen, the Four Mortons, and assorted legitimate stars like Leo Carrillo and Lou Tellegen. But these acts were costly and Palace admissions much higher than the Roxy's. The novelty and opulence of the new movie theater made appreciable inroads into Palace business.

It seems that these developments should have been recognized as a cloud not just the size of a man's hand but considerably larger; especially in conjunction with some other portents. But still there was no indication that Mr. Albee, wrapped in his own sense of unassailable power, was

139

aware of the impending danger.

Other changes in the world outside the Palace walls should have cast their shadows before them. There was a little thing called radio, for instance. Starting as far back as 1914, it attracted scant attention from the general public until late 1920, but within a year of that time became a force to contend with. Even then it was regarded by most theater owners as a fad, just as talking pictures and television were to be regarded later. If you just didn't pay attention to it, they believed, it would go away.

Mr. Albee was scornful of radio, but when it showed signs of growing popularity he issued an order not to book any acts that were identified with that medium, on the theory that people were not likely to pay two dollars for something they could hear for nothing. Up to a point he was right, but soon he had to change his tune, because too many Palace favorites were beginning to build up huge followings in radio.

This brings to mind an old show-business classic. A famous producer who had used a certain actor in many plays discovered one day that the actor had done something the producer considered disloyal. He went storming to his stage manager. "That dirty ungrateful monster," he railed. "After all I've done for him! I tell you, I'll never use him in a show of mine again" . . . pause . . . "unless I absolutely need him." The time soon came when Mr. Albee absolutely needed quite a few of the ungrateful wretches who had sold their talents to radio. One of the first was Harry Richman, who had often played the Palace and had made a big hit on radio. So Richman was booked into the Palace with his night-club floor show, scored heavily, and made a lot of money.

Before long the bookers found themselves hard pressed to get the kind of acts they needed to maintain Palace prestige and Palace grosses. The harder it became, the higher the salaries they had to pay; consequently, even when the weekly intake was high, so was the weekly outgo—or higher. Big grosses did not necessarily reflect big profits. The law of diminishing returns had set in.

Just a few of the people assumed by Mr. Albee to have been pretty much his personal property and who were now amassing new fame and fortune on the air were Jack Benny, Fred Allen, Van and Schenck, Ed Wynn, Willie and Eugene Howard, Eddie Cantor, and Paul Whiteman. Recently there came to light a copy of Whiteman's weekly payroll in 1928. Among the names were Bix Beiderbecke, whose salary was listed at $200 a week; Jimmy Dorsey, also $200; and a young vocalist, part of a trio called the Rhythm Boys. His salary amounted to $150 and his name was Bing Crosby.

Another significant development was taking place: pictures with sound. Like radio, the sound screen dealt with an engineering process, and therefore was thoroughly alien to most theater people, who dealt with ideas and flesh. Various scientists had been working on the concept for years. As early as 1913 Thomas Edison had synchronized sound with film, and his invention had even been used occasionally at the Palace, as with the Harry Lauder short and the study of Mayor Gaynor's cabinet. But it was clumsy and didn't catch on, and Edison turned his genius to other things. D. W. Griffith also tried, with a process he called Phonokinema—he

141

even used a few feet of dialogue in one of his otherwise silent pictures. All this went unheeded, if not unnoticed, by those who should have been most on the alert.

By 1925 two sound systems that had been in the works for years came out of their laboratories and on to the motion-picture screen, but in such a limited way as to go relatively unobserved by the very people who had the most to fear—the giant movie companies and the vaudeville tycoons. One system was called Movietone, controlled by William Fox. He used it timidly and reluctantly, mostly to provide canned musical backgrounds for some Fox films and newsreels.

The other was Vitaphone, the rights to which had been acquired by the brothers Warner, then operating a small studio teetering on the brink of collapse. Somehow they found the money to take the gamble. After wiring their own New York theater for sound and persuading other theater owners to do likewise, Warners produced a considerable number of short subjects with sound tracks which they played along with their silent features. Many were musical subjects with luminaries from concert and opera. Others, like one program the Warners offered in their second Vitaphone bill at the old Colony Theatre, were typically vaudeville. A sizable number of top-flight acts, most of whom had been and still were Palace favorites, picked up extra money that way. Among them were the Howard Brothers, Willie and Eugene; Elsie Janis; Joe E. Brown; and George Jessel, who a couple of years before had made a big hit in Samson Raphaelson's play *The Jazz Singer*. Al Jolson, though not a Palace alumnus, was on this same bill of shorts.

If all this vaudeville in the movies caused panic in the

breast of E. F. Albee, he kept it well concealed. The Palace was still his stronghold and its weekly programs continued to be good. During the month of September 1927 the Palace programs sported such names as the Mosconi Brothers, Odette Myrtil, Joe Frisco (who finally got the price he had been holding out for—$1,500), Elizabeth Brice, Jonny Dooley, Blossom Seeley, Brendel and Burt, Benny Rubin, Mme. Nazimova, and Jack Benny. They lasted into the first week of October.

In the middle of that week—October 6—in a theater just four blocks north of the Palace on Broadway, an event took place that revolutionized the entire entertainment industry and ultimately spelled doom for the Palace. The theater— the Warner. The event—the opening of *The Jazz Singer,* a sound movie starring Al Jolson.

Through the years the legend that *The Jazz Singer* burst like a bombshell on Broadway has grown out of all proportion. On the contrary, it was not an overnight sensation. Reviews were less than enthusiastic; Jolson got his usual raves, but the picture itself received cavalier treatment. Curiosity and word of mouth from Jolson fans, however, brought customers flocking to the theater, which did capacity business for many weeks and had a long run at a two-dollar top.

Still it was more than a year before the major studios recognized the inevitability of talkies, and it took the vaudeville magnates at least that long to realize that their supremacy was waning. Even then Mr. Albee did not appear to notice it, despite some disquieting figures. Under a typical

Variety headline, VAUDEFILMS SOAK STRAIGHT VAUDE, the Palace gross a couple of weeks after *The Jazz Singer* opened was reported to have dropped to $20,000 from a former average of $28,000. The weekly overhead of the Palace, *Variety* declared, ran between $17,000 and $18,000. If true, that meant a week's profit of $2,000 or $3,000 against the average net of $10,000 in the past. Not only *The Jazz Singer* and the vaudeville shorts hurt the Palace. The Roxy, since its opening earlier in the year, had been steadily draining away Palace customers.

John Royal of NBC, for years manager of the Cleveland Palace, knew E. F. Albee about as well as anyone could. Recently he theorized why such a shrewd Down-East Yankee businessman could not see what was happening. "Mr. Albee just wasn't concerned with the complexities of bookkeeping," the television executive told me. "All he wanted to know was 'How much did we put out and how much did we take in?'" As long as the balance was favorable, continued Mr. Royal, Albee saw no cause for alarm. Despite his reputation for hardheadedness, Albee was primarily a showman. And at this period of his life he was more interested in establishing himself as an important figure in his home community of Larchmont, New York, where his main preoccupations were his yacht and the Episcopal church.

There may be another explanation of his seeming indifference to what was happening all around him. Why should he worry about Palace finances when vast sums of money were coming in from the Vaudeville Collection Agency? The Agency, still getting 5 percent of the salary paid to performers, plus 2.5 percent of the agents' commission, yielded even now such a golden harvest that when one of its employees embezzled something close to $100,000, no action was taken against him. It was thought better to take the loss than to call public attention to that somewhat unorthodox business practice.

Regardless of what was going on behind his back—or before his very eyes—Mr. Albee could still point to some extraordinarily good bills at the Palace. The Duncan Sisters, Gus Edwards, Clark and Bergman, Irene Bordoni, Eddie Foy, Ruby Norton, and Fanny Brice all appeared during the final weeks of 1927. So did Walter Huston, who after years of playing a sketch with his wife, Bayonne Whipple, had recently emerged as a legitimate star in *Desire Under the Elms* and *The Barker.*

Early 1928 had some good shows, too. Toward the end of January there was an all-English bill, very well received, and among the favorites in the first part of the year were Belle Baker, Fred Waring and his Pennsylvanians, Whiting and Burt, Will Fyffe, Donald Brian (of *Merry Widow* fame), Clark and McCullough, and Trixie Friganza.

But the competition remained fierce, and business fluctuated wildly. One day in February *Variety* called attention to "a line in front of the Palace Monday matinee—*on its way to the Roxy.*" Only a few weeks later, though, the team of Clayton, Jackson and Durante, doubling from a night club, did the season's biggest business, breaking the house record for the year. On the bill with them was Alice Brady, legitimate star and daughter of the producer William A. Brady.

To defend the old Palace tradition against the inroads of

the movie cathedrals with their spectacular films, elaborate presentations, and high salaries, the booking department had to strain every muscle to get shows of the kind for which the theater had become world-famous. Among the many real vaudevillians who appeared there in 1928 were Lou Holtz, Florence Moore—she was the first woman M.C. the Palace ever had—John Steel, Sophie Tucker, Van and Schenck, Will Mahoney, Charlotte Greenwood, Jack Benny, Kitty Doner, George Jessel, Miss Juliet, Harland Dixon, Poodles Hanneford (the wonderful equestrian comic), Elsie Janis, the Watson Sisters, Jimmy Savo, and Burns and Allen.

More than ever before, though, the bills had to be augmented by people from outside the realm of true vaudeville. With varying degrees of critical and box-office success came such luminaries of the legitimate theater as Florence Reed, Nance O'Neill, J. C. Nugent (an ex-vaudevillian turned legit), Lenore Ulric, Taylor Holmes—that same Taylor Holmes who as a monologist had appeared on the first Palace bill—Margaret Anglin, and Eva Le Gallienne. Mme. Nazimova, who had played the Palace many times since her first stormy appearance, returned once more.

Among the men was Lee Tracy, fresh from his triumph as the brash young hoofer in *Broadway*, the play that made him a star and launched the brilliant, controversial career of the saturnine Jed Harris. With Tracy in a sketch appeared Robert Gleckler, a character actor who had scored as the chief heavy in *Broadway*. From the once forbidden night clubs came Moss and Fontana, a marvelously graceful pair of ballroom dancers; Paul Whiteman again, with his Palais Royal Orchestra; and the Jan Garber band. From the ballet came the Albertina Rasch Girls.

There was a trickle—later a flood—of silent-picture stars, already fleeing the terrors of the talkies, and these included the ageless beauty Fannie Ward and her co-star, the Japanese Sessue Hayakawa; also Eugene O'Brien, one of the great heroes of the silent screen and perpetual leading man to Norma Talmadge.

It was perhaps a sign of the changing times that an entirely non-show-business personality appeared on a Palace bill in that year of non-grace, 1928. He was William Tilden, the world's greatest tennis player, handsome, picturesque, and unbeatable for more years than any tennis player up to that time. As head of the United States Davis Cup team, he had led that team to victory every year until 1927. And now he was cashing in on his fame. In the old days, at Hammerstein's, that wouldn't have been unusual, but at the Palace it was startling.

True, top-flight figures from the sports world had occasionally been seen at the Palace, but they were rare indeed, and there was always a special circumstance involved. Rube Marquard, famed baseball pitcher, was married to the star Blossom Seeley. James J. Corbett had been heavyweight champion, and of course Babe Ruth had the status of a folk hero. Big Bill Tilden, great though he was, represented a gentleman's game—tennis in those days had not yet reached a truly mass audience. It was just a case of reaching out for anything that would bring in the diminishing crowds.

Meanwhile in a wide spectrum of other places—executive suites in Boston, mid-town New York oyster bars, Wall

Street board rooms, Hollywood haciendas, even transatlantic liners—other things were happening that would affect the future of vaudeville in general and the Palace in particular.

Through a series of financial maneuvers, one of the great wheelers and dealers of all time, Joseph P. Kennedy (later U.S. Ambassador to England and still later father of a President), had acquired control of a small, struggling motion-picture company, FBO, and built it into a successful operation. Simultaneously he was negotiating with David Sarnoff, head of Radio Corporation of America, for a merger of their mutual interests in the entertainment fields. Only a serpentine mentality could follow the intricacies of these corporate manipulations.

Somewhere along the line Mr. Kennedy made a secret alliance with the one man above all others that E. F. Albee trusted: general manager John J. Murdock, the little white-haired man who looked as if he could be sold the Brooklyn Bridge by any persuasive stranger. The outcome of the game was fairly plain. Early in May of 1928 Joseph Kennedy approached E. F. Albee with an offer to buy 200,000 shares of stock in the recently merged Keith-Albee-Orpheum Circuit, at a figure considerably higher than the market price. Albee hesitated. He certainly didn't need the money, being one of the richest men in show business. But, unable to resist the profits, he changed his mind, and the deal was consummated.

Albee emerged from the deal with something more than four million dollars, and a new junior partner—he thought. On May 17, 1928, *The New York Times* ran a full-column story on its drama page. The lead paragraph said: "E. F. Albee announced yesterday that Joseph P. Kennedy has become associated with him in the management of the Keith-Albee-Orpheum chain of theatres. Mr. Albee took this as an occasion to deny rumors to the effect that he intended to retire from active management of the organization he had been handling for forty years. On the contrary," the story continued, "Mr. Albee is quoted as saying, he and Mr. Kennedy would cooperate fully. Mr. Kennedy would be chairman of the board while Mr. Albee would continue in his present capacity of operating head of the organization, and retain his controlling interest.

"Making it clear that he admired and respected his new partner, who was providing a blood transfusion of money, brains and youthful vigor, Mr. Albee said: 'Mr. Kennedy has shown in a brief but colorful career in pictures such constructive and organizational genius we consider him a tremendous asset to our business. He is energetic, dynamic, and a straight shooter.' "

That was in May of 1928. Not long afterward it became apparent that it was Mr. Kennedy with his 200,000 shares of stock who actually held the controlling interest in the company. Albee's failure to sense this lends credence to John Royal's theory that fundamentally he was not really a businessman. It is hard to accept the fact that he had been so gullible, with all these machinations going on around him, especially since he was supposed to have spies everywhere. All who were then and are still around have substantially the same explanation. He was a dictator, they reiterate, and dictators seldom realize they are being plotted against. They simply cannot recognize the fact that they, too, are human, and therefore vulnerable. Anyone who tries to warn them is not believed and is usually banished.

Things happened fast. One day Mr. Kennedy called a meeting in a conference room on the seventh floor of the Palace. All the bookers and executives were summoned; all, that is, but Mr. Albee. Bill McCaffrey remembers Kennedy telling the assemblage that from here on out he and he alone was boss. He outlined what his plans were and what he expected from each of them; then, without further ado, he turned to Edwin Lauder, Mr. Albee's son-in-law, and said: "Any questions, Ted?" There were no questions. The meeting was over. How much of this was relayed to Mr. Albee nobody seems to know, but both Bill McCaffrey and John Royal have expressed the opinion that even if anyone had had the temerity to tell him of that meeting, he would have been incapable of believing it.

Kennedy did not move into the Palace himself; he put one of his longtime associates, John Ford (not the motion-picture director), in charge of operations, and John J. Murdock, that most trusted henchman of Albee's, stayed on as general manager. After that it was just a matter of time. One morning Mr. Albee came into his throne room on the Sixth Floor to discover that it wasn't his any more. During the night he had been literally kicked upstairs—moved to a small office on the seventh floor.

Bill McCaffrey remembers a day soon after this move when he and a handful of other bookers were sitting in the old throne room, discussing some booking problem. "Suddenly there was a sound at the door," Bill recalls, "and there was the old man, standing in the doorway, and there was I, his former office boy, sitting behind his desk. It was one of the most embarrassing moments of my life." Albee asked, with a trace of his old gruffness, what was going on; then, apparently aware of the situation and not waiting for an answer, he turned and walked away. Not long after that incident Albee's son Reed "resigned," despite a report that he was redecorating the Palace on his father's orders.

When Albee's world finally collapsed, it was not with a whimper but with a bang. And somebody must have been listening at the keyhole. Certainly the incident has been widely disseminated by writers and quoted only recently by both Bill McCaffrey and John Royal.

One day Albee appeared at Joe Kennedy's office with a suggestion about the theater. Kennedy just looked at him with those far-famed steely eyes and hurled a harpoon. "Didn't you know, Ed?" he is quoted as saying. "You're washed up. You're through."

At least one of his bitter survivors, speaking for many others, has said that it couldn't have happened to a more deserving fellow. But Albee still has his defenders, notably John Royal, who contends that, with all his faults, E. F. Albee did a great deal for actors—built them fine theaters to play in, gave them the first decent dressing rooms most of them had ever had. And occasionally, in bursts of sudden generosity, he helped them out financially—like the time he booked Eva Tanguay into the Palace after she had exhausted her millions and her peculiar talents, and the time he sent $1,000 to Jack Norworth, who was out of work and in desperate straits. As Mr. Royal points out, "Albee didn't do anything most of his associates hadn't done. It's just that he always got the blame."

Shortly thereafter E. F. Albee retired, an embittered old man, broken though far from broke. He was listed as the seventh-richest man in show business with a fortune of $14,000,000. There was a certain irony about the situation. His control of the Palace and the theatrical empire he had built had been stealthily though legally taken from him, just as years earlier he had wrested from Martin Beck control of the Palace *he* had built.

On March 11, 1930, in Palm Beach, Florida, E. F. Albee died very suddenly. The official diagnosis was a heart attack. His obituary notices were long and laudatory—in the dailies, at any rate. His body was brought to New York, where services were held in the Cathedral of St. John the Divine, to whose building fund he had willed some $200,000. He left money to the Actors Fund of America, but nothing at all to vaudeville performers. To quote an unidentified quipster of the day: "The funeral played to a small house."

CHAPTER SEVEN

THE PASSING OF E. F. Albee from the scene marked the end of an era at the Palace. Joseph Kennedy did not stick with his vaudeville interests very long. It had never been his intention to do so. After a short interval he sold his stock to David Sarnoff of the Radio Corporation of America, and Sarnoff instituted a new regime with a number of changes.

First was the removal of Albee's name from the electric sign outside the theater. What had for years been blazoned as the corporate title, Keith-Albee, now read Radio-Keith-Orpheum. Just what touch of sentimentality kept the name Keith is hard to figure; Benjamin Keith had been dead since 1914 and had never been active at the Palace.

Next, names of headliners began to light up the marquee. That long-sought and hard-won honor was first awarded to

153

Fanny Brice, who topped the bill of October 29, 1928. Just below her name the lights spelled out the names of Al Trahan, a piano-playing comic, and the dance team of Tamara and Fowler. Trahan was so proud of his Palace booking that he spent a small fortune having it written in the sky by a plane flying over Broadway.

The format of the Palace playbill was changed, enlarged, made into a little magazine of the theater. The name of Albee was removed from its masthead, which for years had read "The Palace Theatre & Realty Co.: E. F. Albee, President." Even the name of Elmer Rogers, gifted and well-liked manager of the theater was dropped. Now it read: "B. F. Keith's PALACE."

To create fresh interest and bring the customers in during the hot weather, a bill called *New Faces Week* was announced. Despite *Variety*'s crack that the only new faces must be the male ushers—the girls having been fired—business seemed pretty good for the week. On the bill were Alan Dinehart, a well-known actor from the legitimate stage; Ethel Waters, then a young singer on her way up; and a pert young boy-and-girl team, each of whom was destined to make theatrical history. The boy was Leonard Sillman, later to win considerable fame and some fortune as the producer of a series of revues called, not entirely coincidentally, *New Faces*. The girl, who appeared in the first of those revues, still later became one of the earliest and most popular of television stars, Imogene Coca. At another time Leonard did a double act with Frances Gershwin, sister of George and Ira.

Performers were cheered by the announcement that the

154

much resented Vaudeville Collection Agency would reduce its take from the agents to one percent; 2.5 percent had been the ironclad rule for years. That gave them reason to hope that the agency might soon give up the old practice of the 5 percent kickback from actors for the privilege of working. Very soon this happened, too. Another hopeful sign appeared when the taboo on *Variety*, which had been barred from the Palace precincts for years, was lifted; hopeful because *Variety*, tough though it could be when judging a show, had always championed the performers' rights.

A third new policy heartened the performers. The feared and hated blacklist had been abandoned, meaning that acts could now appear wherever work was available. A good thing, too, because vaudeville houses all over the country had dwindled, giving way to talking pictures or just closing down. By this time the Palace was one of only two big-time theaters left on the circuit.

Some noteworthy personnel changes occurred in December. After months of floundering and speculation, during which time there was no official head of the circuit, it was announced that the new president of RKO and ruler of Palace destiny would be a Mr. Hiram S. Brown. Invariably Hiram Brown has been referred to by writers and people around the Palace as the president of the U.S. Leather Company. True, but before that he had been a well-known financier, associated for many years with the banking firm of Lehman Brothers, for whom he organized many large companies in a variety of areas. It is therefore not so surprising that he was selected by Mr. Sarnoff to serve as president of RKO, though the fact remains that he didn't know anything about the entertainment business.

Max Gordon, who was then still at the Palace in charge of Orpheum booking and production, tells of going to David Sarnoff and asking why he had chosen Hiram Brown. The answer was short and simple. "A business needs a business-man," he said. Max, never one to muffle his opinions for the sake of expediency, protested with vehemence and choler, not only to Mr. Sarnoff but to anyone within earshot.

It did not take long for the word to reach Mr. Brown. And it did not take him long to react. "After a trip around the circuit," Max tells it, "I walked into my office in the Palace Building and there in the middle of the floor was a barrel of sawdust with a broom leaning on it."

He got the message. Following a brief and highly unpleas-ant encounter with the new boss, he tore up his contract, which still had two years to run, and stalked dramatically out of his office. Max's exit from the Palace wasn't the only one. Gradually most of the old guard left, fired or given the opportunity to walk the plank voluntarily. Among them was Ted Lauder, Mr. Albee's son-in-law, who somehow survived till the end of the year. Another was Bill McCaffrey. Joseph Plunkett, who had managed the Strand Theatre, was ap-pointed operating head of the entire Keith chain. George Godfrey, the former booker who had been gone from the Palace for years, was brought back to succeed Eddie Dar-ling.

The inauguration of a third show on Sunday occurred early in 1929. In addition to the regular matinee and eve-ning performances there was another show at five o'clock. "Same all-star show," read the announcement, "same Sun-

day matinee prices—all seats reserved, buy 'em early." Just
above this ballyhoo was a picture of the Palace with a throng
of people standing outside, presumably storming the box
office. Whatever this extra matinee may have added to the
weekly gross, it did not add anything to the salaries of the
acts involved, and that in turn certainly did not add anything to their happiness.

Throughout this period the printed program sounded a
note of cozy intimacy with the audience, publishing recipes
—one of them was Gilda Gray Chutney—jokes and fashion
hints, and celebrating in flowery prose the recent marriage
of vaudeville and radio. One such piece quoted an editorial
from the *New York Evening Sun,* which read in part: "Vaudeville is on top again. This ever-changing branch of the
theatre seemed a short time ago to have reached its zenith
. . . no new tricks, no new angles and none of its former
resourcefulness. Then suddenly the name Radio appeared as
a prefix to the name of vaudeville's leading exponents,
'Keith-Orpheum' and with a flourish that was almost magical
and certainly masterful, the 'two-a-day' once more became a
powerful influence in the culture and entertainment life of
the nation." Some later events proved this a bit of whistling
in the dark, although the blackest night was still some time
away.

Reflecting the connubial bliss of vaudeville and radio was
a bill that mingled good standard vaudeville acts—Harry
Fox and Beatrice Curtis, for example; Vincent Lopez, who
by now was conducting his orchestra at the St. Regis Hotel
and broadcasting nightly; and Lester Allen, the comedian,

who skipped from revue to book show to two-a-day with ease
—with a radio revue headed by Phillips Carlin, one of the
pioneer announcers. Entitled *On the Air* and produced in
conjunction with NBC, that revue filled the entire second
half of the program.

Another effort to hold on to a diminishing audience and
perhaps enlarge it was the institution of a talent search—always a good gimmick, as movie companies well know. This
particular one, taking advantage of the great number of
amateur theatrical groups all over the country, had started a
campaign to scout the productions and tournaments of Little Theater groups. One show actually got booking. It was a
one-act play called *The Undercurrent,* which had won the
Chicago Little Theatre Tournament, and after a successful
hometown engagement had worked its way east to wind up at
the Palace. No new stars were born, so far as anyone knows,
but the venture provided grist for the publicity mill. Besides,
it didn't cost much.

Still another tie between vaudeville and radio was announced in the Palace playbill. A request-program contest,
to be voted on by audiences at the Palace and in other vaudeville theaters, would result in a special broadcast by NBC,
starring the performers who had won the most votes. Win-
ners of the first contest included many of the outstanding
stars of the two-a-day: Sophie Tucker, Ted Lewis, Ben
Bernie, Van and Schenck, Kate Smith, and Fred Waring's
Pennsylvanians, all of them Palace favorites, and some of
them well known primarily through the radio channels. The
public could hear for nothing a show it had been paying two
or three dollars to see and hear. As much as any single fac-

tor, this sort of thinking contributed to the decline of the Palace and vaudeville everywhere.

At the beginning of 1929, however, there was an atmosphere of general optimism. Even crusty *Variety* said, in a backward glance at the events of the year just ended, that vaudeville "may walk right in between everything, for legit is in bad shape, silent pictures have trouble standing alongside a talker, and one is never certain of a talker, and shorts may whip themselves. . . ." The piece concluded with a prophetic note: "1929 will most likely decide the fate of vaudeville as a business."

That year, as few need to be reminded, decided the fate of much more than the business of vaudeville. It was a year that began happily enough, for the most part. Things were good all over. Herbert Hoover, having defeated Al Smith, was snugly and smugly in the White House, talking about a chicken in every pot and two cars in every garage.

Business in general boomed. Stocks, which had been moving upward for a long time, soared headily to unprecedented heights. Almost everybody was in the market—housewives, telephone operators, shoeshine boys, even actors. After all, playing the market was a form of gambling, and actors by the very nature of their profession and temperament were gambling every day of their lives. Irving Caesar, the talented lyricist, whose shows have included two brands of *Follies* (the *Ziegfeld* and the *Greenwich Village*), *Hit the Deck* and *No, No, Nanette*, with its enduring and endearing "Tea for Two," offers an interesting sidelight on the temper of the times.

159

Irving was on the Palace bill with Lou Holtz one sizzling August week. They were in Holtz's dressing room before the Saturday matinee when Lou's dresser came in with the early-afternoon papers, which listed the closing market prices. In those days the Stock Exchange was open Saturdays till noon. The dresser read the stock reports aloud. Both men had made great gains. Caesar had a profit of $17,000, while Holtz had picked up just twice that amount. Caesar shook his head ruefully. "Lou," he said, "there's something wrong about this. When I can make seventeen grand in half a day and you can double it without either of us doing a lick of work, there's got to be something wrong. Maybe we ought to get out." But they didn't get out. They were still in when the big crash came exactly two months later, on October 29, inspiring the famous *Variety* headline the next day: WALL STREET LAYS AN EGG.

When the market hit bottom on the 13th of November the Palace still offered an assortment of talent guaranteed to bring cheer to any audience—if there was an audience. Headliners were Jimmy Savo, Helen Kane—the boop-a-doop girl—and Clayton, Jackson and Durante.

Though he became a film comedian of note in later years, it was for the Palace that Durante made his first movie appearance. Someone hit upon the idea of having Jimmy arrive at the theater amid a shower of paper, like the Lindbergh ticker-tape parade. Johnny Cassidy of the Palace publicity department hired a cameraman and stationed him on the roof of the building at the corner where Broadway and Seventh Avenue meet. Durante, perched on the back of an open Packard, drove up Broadway; as the car approached the theater, tons of shredded paper and homemade confetti came pouring out of the Palace and neighboring buildings, deluging the apparently bewildered comedian. Arms waving and grin broadening, he dashed out of the car and disappeared into the theater. The film of this stunt was used as the opener for Durante's act throughout the engagement: as the movie sequence came to an end, he would make his entrance from the lobby, dashing down the center aisle of the theater and up onto the stage.

Johnny Cassidy says that Clayton, Jackson and Durante, having been cheated of their salaries by a few unethical night-club owners, insisted, like Sarah Bernhardt, upon being paid in advance at the Palace.

The impact of the market crash didn't hit the Palace all at once. In truth it was only one more element in a combination of events that had started the glorious old theater on its toboggan ride. Abel Green, who probably knows more about show business than any other man in the field, believes the crash was not the greatest contributing factor.

"What really killed the Palace," Abel says, "was the growth of the colossal movie houses. Sime had foreseen that as early as 1926, when he moved the film section to the front pages of *Variety*, relegating vaudeville to the back. The *coup de grâce* was not the market crash. That was a factor, of course, but two years before the crash the movies began to talk, and that further boomed the cinemas. The de-luxers of that period then were able to give the customers big band shows and big stage shows along with their films."

A rumor began circulating that the Palace would soon be wired for sound, but for newsreels only, or maybe just *one* short subject. The rumor was never officially denied; apparently it didn't bother anyone too much. The Palace continued to put on good shows through 1929. Such vaudeville standbys as Will Mahoney, the Marx Brothers, Frances White, Willie and Eugene Howard, Ruby Norton, George Jessel, Lulu McConnell, Harland Dixon, William Gaxton, Pat Rooney, Bill Robinson, Blossom Seeley, Ted Lewis, Bert Wheeler, Jeanette Hackett, and Jack Benny lent their luster to the old place that year.

One of the most amusing and popular of the comedy girl-and-boy acts was the team of Block and Sully. Jesse Block, one of the early Gus Edwards kids, grew up in vaudeville. When he met cute little Eve Sully, they became partners professionally and privately. Privately, they still are. Their formula of the nitwit and the nice guy was similar to that which later made household words of Burns and Allen via the radio. Block and Sully remained vaudeville favorites, and the two couples were fast friends—in fact, became part of a close sextet, the other two being Jack Benny and Mary Livingstone. The intimacy continues to this day, though the death of Gracie Allen a few years ago reduced the group to a quintet.

During World War II, Mr. and Mrs. Block headed USO units overseas; originally they went for three months, but stayed nine. In addition, they engaged in underground activities for the government. Altogether they were in the service for three years. After that, civilian show business seemed anticlimactic, and since then they have devoted much time and energy to entertaining for philanthropic organizations.

Mr. Block switched from stage to stock market, and is

currently an executive of Bache and Company, with an office on Fifth Avenue. But he still enjoys talking about the old days, and remembers the time he and Eve were on the Palace bill with Russ Columbo, the crooning idol of the early thirties, who had a sweet and sentimental but very small voice. "Benny Rubin and Jack Haley were twin M.C.'s," Mr. Block said. "One performance they took the microphone away from Columbo, and the poor guy couldn't be heard past the first row." That was the time Rubin got sick and was replaced by Milton Berle, who scored his first big hit.

One of Mr. Block's fondest memories is of Fanny Brice when she and the Blocks were recalling the great old days. "Actually," as he tells it, "I was doing the recalling. I reminded her of some parties we'd been to. She couldn't remember. I spoke of some old acquaintances. She couldn't remember. I mentioned one week we were all together in Chicago. She couldn't remember."

"You were playing the Oriental," he continued. "You were getting $7,500 a week, and—"

"You're wrong there," Fanny jumped in. "It was $8,000."

Entertainers from other branches of the business made their contributions, too. From the legitimate theater, both dramatic and musical, came such notables as Madge Kennedy, Glenn Hunter, Charles Ruggles, Helen Ford, John Charles Thomas, Claiborne Foster, Jules Bledsoe (the original Joe in *Show Boat*, who rose to fame singing "Ol' Man River"), Beatrice Lillie, and Bert Lytell in the one-act drama that had served him so well for years, *The Valiant*.

With Lytell in the play was an unusual piece of casting. The girl (his sister) was played by Mary Hay, the diminutive dancer who had made her mark in musicals as the dancing partner of Clifton Webb. Miss Hay was married to the silent-movie star Richard Barthelmess.

Horace Heidt brought his orchestra from California. Molly Picon came from the Yiddish theater; Albert Carroll, who had emerged from the Neighborhood Playhouse as a great mimic, did his imitations of stars; and Russell Markert of Roxy fame sent his troupe of sixteen dancing girls.

That year saw a considerable influx of silent-movie stars, fleeing the rigors or indifference of talking pictures but still enjoying great public interest. Among them were Leatrice Joy, Lita Grey Chaplin, Olga Baclanova—the Russian threat to Polish Pola Negri on the Paramount lot—Irene Rich, Esther Ralston, and Carmel Myers. Miss Myers, one of the most beautiful sirens of the silent screen, had made the transition to talkies, and her act at the Palace consisted of songs from some of her pictures.

Another movie star, but one who was not fleeing the rigors or the indifference of talking pictures, was Jackie Coogan. He was cashing in (for his family, it later turned out) on the worldwide acclaim he had received as the pathetic, appealing waif in Chaplin's *The Kid*. And just by way of novelty, as the year neared its close, came another one of the nation's folk heroes, Jack Dempsey.

Despite these valiant efforts to give the public good entertainment, this reaching out in all directions to bring in new talent from other fields, this dreaming up of enticing publicity gimmicks, business at the Palace was just not good

164

enough to carry the burden of mounting costs. Because of the scarcity of star acts, which at long last had several other arenas to perform in, two things happened: management had to pay higher salaries; and they had to keep acts on for several weeks at a time, or bring them back too frequently, which began to irritate the Palace audiences.

Still the whistling in the dark went on. The cozy little human-interest playbill items continued. In the Palace program for Christmas week, 1929—the bill included Ted Lewis, "The High-Hatted Tragedian of Song"; Helen Ford, singing songs from her past shows, *Dearest Enemy* and *Peggy-Ann;* Richard Bennett, the dramatic star, in a one-act play called *A Box of Cigars;* and the old comic favorite Herb Williams—was another hortatory editorial. After extolling the current performers, under the heading RKO LEADS OFF THE "GOOD TIMES" JUBILEE MARCH the article proceeded to the following high-sounding paragraph:

"This program again emphasizes the sequential advance of RKO toward the new nationally dominant idea and plan of making the coming new year the beginning of a permanent 'Good Times' era in harmony with President Hoover's universally approved plan for new activity, more expansion, broader confidence, and more aggressive progress in every line of American industry, commerce and finance."

As 1930 deepened, so did the Depression, and along with it the gloom. The prosperity which was supposed to be just around the corner didn't materialize. Businesses failed, jobs decreased, people began to feel the pinch, and one of the habits they had to start giving up was going to the theater. That included the Palace.

The situation there was complex and contradictory. Although Joe Laurie puts the major share of the blame on Hiram Brown, it doesn't seem to be entirely deserved. RKO was already in a downward spiral when he became president. Because they had been for so long the helpless pawns of management, the vaudeville people leaped at other forms of expression—radio, personal appearances in the movie theaters, and talking pictures. Therefore, to win them back to vaudeville, where working conditions had improved but still left much to be desired, management had to pay more money to headliners who still came to the Palace. And, as they paid more, they took in less.

In the early twenties and even well into the late years of that decade, Palace bills had seldom cost more than $8,000 a week. Now, in 1930, the same bills would cost between $10,000 and $13,000. So the profit was minimal and in many cases nonexistent. According to Abel Green and Joe Laurie, the Palace in those days lost an average of $4,000 a week. "The great showplace," they say in *Show Biz*, "was caught in a web of its own contradictions."

However dark the outlook may have been, the Palace still offered a brave face to the world and ascribed the change in its type of show to a forward-looking attitude on the part of management. Nothing was said about the difficulties of booking the long-time favorites. And a program note in the spring of 1930 gave forth an unmistakable whiff of sour grapes. "Patrons of the Palace," it read, "will have noticed that the current season has brought a giant transformation in the making of programs. The worn-out and so-called time-honored acts have disappeared. . . . Only a few of the

166

perennially popular standard acts—known for their origi-
nality and up-to-dateness—are now seen and heard on the
stage of this theatre."

Just about this time official word went out that the unheeded rumor of a year or so earlier was now an accomplished fact: *the Palace had been wired for sound.* This news
distressed and dismayed the loyal devotees of the Palace, and
they were, despite recent misfortunes, still legion. Exactly
what it presaged nobody was certain. But it boded no good
and was regarded as a shameful humiliation. Was nothing
sacred?

Actually, the installation of sound made no immediate
difference. The Palace remained a vaudeville theater, *the*
vaudeville theater. Despite the rumble of distant drums and
the grumbles of irate patrons who cared less and less for the
shows, the bills throughout that year and a good part of
1931 still featured many of the most cherished names of the
two-a-day: for example, W. C. Fields, Gus Edwards, Irene
Franklin, Jimmy Durante, Rae Samuels—and George Jessel and Eddie Cantor sharing a bill with Burns and Allen.

Helen Morgan, who had burst like a comet on the New
York stage a few years before in *Show Boat* and *Sweet
Adeline* and was the star of her own night club, came to the
Palace during that season. So did Van and Schenck, Harry
Richman, Aunt Jemima, the Rath Brothers, Odette Myrtil,
Karyl Norman, the Creole Fashion Plate (whose real name
was George Paduzzi), Lou Holtz, Smith and Dale, Ted
Healey, Marion Harris, and the perennially popular Owen
McGiveney. *And* Fanny Brice. It was on one of these occa-
sions that she made her memorable crack: "I've been poor

and I've been rich. Rich is better!"

Bands were very numerous during that period: Duke Ellington, Cab Calloway, Abe Lyman, Henry Busse (Paul Whiteman's arranger), Henry King. And people from the legitimate theater—largely operetta and musical comedy—took well-paid flyers into the Palace: people like Vivienne Segal, J. Harold Murray, Norma Terris (the Magnolia of *Show Boat*), and Ethel Merman, hot from her triumphant legit debut in *Girl Crazy*. She had played the Palace earlier, with Clayton, Jackson and Durante, but now she was a top-liner.

The influx of silent-movie stars grew steadily. Among them were Mae Murray, the original Brinkley girl; Ruth Roland, the early serial queen; Ricardo Cortez and his then wife, Alma Rubens; Pola Negri; Lupe Velez; Claire Whitney and her husband, Robert Emmet Keane. And Blanche Sweet, one of the loveliest of the silent stars, who later married the actor Raymond Hackett, brother of Jeanette Hackett, a vaudeville luminary for many years and a particular Palace pet. Ray and Jeanette, now the wife of John Steel, another Palace favorite, were also brother and sister of Albert Hackett, onetime juvenile, now playwright. With his wife, Frances Goodrich, he dramatized *The Diary of Anne Frank*.

Sue Carol, now a successful agent and the widow of Alan Ladd; Fifi D'Orsay, the French firecracker; Fatty Arbuckle; and that star of stars, Rin-Tin-Tin, were a few other film favorites who for one reason or another had fled the Hollywood scene and turned up at the Palace. Another movie star, certainly not a refugee from talking pictures,

168

who came to the Palace during that period was Edward G. Robinson. With a thorough grounding in the legitimate theater, Robinson was one of the first of the film gangsters, and certainly one of the greatest. He had already won lasting fame in *Little Caesar,* and with a string of other pictures to his credit, he was a big box-office draw. He did a monologue kidding Hollywood and the tough guys out there—Cagney, Raft, Muni, etc.—and showed clips from his films. Later he was inveigled into appearing in skits and blackouts with the other acts. Why he wanted to subject himself to the rigors of the two-a-day (with three shows on Sunday) is hard to understand. Probably he missed contact with live audiences. On the bill with him were Dorothy Stone, pretty and talented daughter of Fred Stone, and Kate Smith, who had been making the Palace her personal domain for the past nine weeks.

Many writers on vaudeville, even Palace press agents of later days when looking backward through the years, give Miss Smith the palm for having piled up the longest consecutive run in the theater's history to that date. That claim has been challenged, especially by Madeline Cameron Gaxton, who says that her husband, the late William Gaxton, really had the longest run.

Nobody has a complete collection of Palace programs, and memory is an elusive and sometimes treacherous thing. But there is in existence a complete list of every bill that ever played the Palace, from its beginning in 1913 to its end as a live variety theater forty years later. This list was compiled in a big black book by Sol Schwartz, president of RKO from 1950 to 1961 and more recently a vice-president of Colum-

169

bia Pictures. According to that book, a duplicate of which is in the possession of Thomas J. Crehan, currently vice-president of RKO, Miss Smith and Mr. Gaxton tied for the long-run honors. Each had piled up a record of ten consecutive weeks, though not the same ten.

The big black book shows that Billy Gaxton opened on July 11, 1931, and stayed there continuously until September 18. (On the same bill were Lou Holtz, Lyda Roberti, the little Polish comedienne who died so young only a few years later, and Ethel Merman.)

Again using the Schwartz record book as reference, Kate Smith joined the bill on August 1, which was Gaxton's fourth week, and remained until October 9, three weeks after Gaxton had left to start rehearsing his role of John T. Wintergreen in the greatest success of his long string of successes, *Of Thee I Sing*. But for this interruption, Gaxton could probably have stayed on at the Palace indefinitely.

Many years later Kate Smith, who had zoomed to a top spot in radio almost overnight, told an interviewer that she had absolutely no desire to return to the stage. "And that," she said, "includes the Palace." Referring to Judy Garland's phenomenal engagement in 1951, which was not really vaudeville in its original form, she pointed out, "Judy lasted longer, but I never missed a performance." With Miss Smith during her long run were such people as the above-mentioned Edward G. Robinson, the Boswell Sisters, James Barton, and Jack Benny. Other contenders for long-run honors include the dance team Adelaide and Hughes, favorites of an earlier day.

Quite aside from the movie stars who invaded the Palace, a

curious assortment of outsiders played there during that season. They included Heywood Broun, then at the height of his renown as a columnist, sports authority, and Depression fighter. Broun had once performed in a revue, *Round the Town*, in 1924, and apparently was bitten by the acting bug. He did a monologue at the Palace, and later that season, together with a group of highly talented theater and literary lights, he assembled and appeared in a revue, *Shoot the Works*, for the purpose of providing employment for out-of-work actors and actresses, all too many in that second year of the Depression.

Some other off-beat people found their way to the Palace stage in 1931.

Item: Floyd Gibbons, the radio broadcaster and foreign correspondent, in person and also on the screen in a sports short.

Item: The Siamese Twins—shades of Hammerstein's Victoria.

Item: A pre-Harlow bombshell, Peggy Hopkins Joyce. Although she had appeared on other stages in a variety of roles, she had acquired more public recognition for her skill at collecting millionaire husbands (and other off-stage exploits) than for any conspicuous acting ability.

Item: Harry Hershfield, humorist and cartoonist, creator of the popular comic strip *Abe Kabibble*. Mr. Hershfield later won renown on radio and TV in the comedy panel show *Can You Top This?*, matching wits with Joe Laurie, Jr., and "Senator" Ford.

Edward Hastings Ford, more popularly known as "Senator," is a man of wit, wisdom, and wide knowledge, far removed from the stereotype of vaudevillian. He did not, in fact, start out to be a professional entertainer. His original career was painting, drawing, and sculpture. Some of his figurines of baseball heroes are on display at the Museum of the City of New York.

Having achieved considerable note as an after-dinner speaker, Mr. Ford often found himself on the same program as former Mayor James J. Walker. It was the Mayor who felt that Ford's talent for topical humor would appeal to a wider audience, and he arranged a meeting with the Keith bookers. After listening to one of his monologues, they immediately booked him into a top-flight vaudeville house near New York, and within a few weeks he was playing the Palace, where he made a big hit. His serious, almost solemn face and his deadpan delivery only served to enhance his humor, and he became one of the greatest laugh producers of the genre. One of the few monologists who wrote his own material, he was also one of the few monologists to pay high tribute to another monologist. "Frank Fay," he says, "was the greatest of them all."

That season, too, saw the triumphant return to the Palace of Ed Wynn, who had built his great success in the musicals on that selfsame Fool's character that was so cruelly unappreciated back in 1913 on the very first bill of the Palace. This time, just after a long run in *Simple Simon*, Wynn was a top-liner. The other time he had been, if not a bottom-liner, so near the bottom that he had what was, with cynical humor, referred to as "dog billing." Some performers claimed that this appellation meant their names were so far down on the posters and house boards that only dogs could read them.

172

Others had a less delicate explanation.

One of the biggest things to hit the Palace in its entire history up to that time, coming soon after the Billy Gaxton and Kate Smith long runs, was a bill headed by Eddie Cantor and George Jessel. Cantor and Jessel had been close friends since boyhood, starting with their early appearances in the Gus Edwards revue (one of many) *Kid Kabaret* with a cast that included Georgie Price, Eddie Buzzell, Gregory Kelly (according to Cantor), and the little girl who grew into a lovely silent-movie star, Lila Lee.

Both Cantor and Jessel were experienced showmen—or really, showboys—before they joined Gus Edwards. Eddie, a few years older than George, was still a youngster when he joined a team of comedy jugglers, Bedini and Arthur, in the role we now know as a stooge. Later—according to George Jessel—Eddie yearned to be a single and perform on the real stage a Yiddish monologue he'd been doing at East Side bar mitzvahs.

In those days vaudeville performers had to send pictures ahead to house managers for lobby display. Eddie, having no picture of his own, borrowed some from one of his friends. It happened that the friend did his act in blackface. When young Eddie appeared at the theater in his own guise, the manager would not let him go on until he had made up with burnt cork to match the pictures outside, so the audience wouldn't feel cheated. That's how Eddie became the first (and probably the last) comic to do a Yiddish monologue in blackface. At least, that's the way George tells it, and Eddie, regrettably, is not around to confirm or deny.

Jessel's new professional career began at the Imperial

Theatre on West 116th Street, where his mother was the cashier. Through her he met the house manager, who put him together with two other youngsters to form a singing act elegantly entitled Leonard, Lawrence and McKinley, "The Imperial Trio." The other two boys were really named Jack Weiner and Walter Winchell. The trio didn't last long, and George became a singing single at five dollars a week.

Few things would be more fun than tracing the separate and shared careers of Cantor and Jessel, but that would take too long, and, besides, each one has written about himself and the other. Remarkably, in view of the endless contradictions in all show-business biographies, the Jessel and Cantor accounts pretty well agree. They both became singles, they sometimes worked together, they each played the Palace on and off over the years; Eddie had one marriage and five daughters, George had four marriages—if you count two with his first wife, Florene Courtney—and may well by the time this appears in print have added a fifth. And he has two daughters.

Through it all, though the two men could hardly have been basically more different, they remained close friends. More than friends, George says, they were brothers. The spectacular Palace engagement that brought them together in 1931 grew out of the series of benefits they were constantly called upon to do and always did.

By this time Eddie had been making pictures in Hollywood and also winning great popularity with a radio show, the Chase and Sanborn Hour. Meanwhile George, after his success on the stage in *The Jazz Singer* and his disappointment at not making the picture, had gone through several years of ups and downs, including a frustrating spell in Hollywood.

There have been many versions of *why* he didn't make the picture, but it seems logical to accept George's explanation. The deal was all set, he says, as part of a multiple-picture contract. But when he got to Hollywood and read the script as prepared by Warners, he discovered the ending had been changed. The character he played, instead of going back to the synagogue and replacing his father as cantor, as written and acted in the play, was shown in the last scene back at the Winter Garden, in blackface, his mother applauding frantically from a box. Aghast, George says, he refused to play it that way. And that, he declares, is how Al Jolson became *The Jazz Singer*.

Cantor, arrived in New York from Hollywood and intending to stay there for several months, conceived the notion of putting together the material they had been doing for other people's benefit and doing it this time for their own benefit. After rewriting their material, they laid out the show, which had a prominent place for George Burns and Gracie Allen.

The act, as routined, gave Cantor and Jessel a turn together fairly early in the show. Then, after the act of a beautiful girl named Janet Reade, George came on again and did his own specialty, including the well-known telephone talk to Mama. Just before intermission came Burns and Allen. Cantor, as befitted his pre-eminence, had the next to closing spot. But these distinctions didn't matter so much any more; the stars wandered in and out of the other turns, ad-libbing and enjoying themselves as much as the audiences obviously did. And instead of the usual closing act—acrobat,

175

animal, or such—the whole company came on again and did a grand finale.

The show was a hit from the start. According to Jessel, it was their intention to play only two weeks. But the two weeks grew to four, and the gross on the fourth week was, according to *Variety*, a husky $34,000. George got a $500 raise. This remarkable feat in the midst of the Depression halted the booking office's plan of changing the bill after six weeks. They stayed on for a total of nine weeks and had only one losing stanza—the eighth—just before Christmas, always a tough time in the theater. But the ninth and last—the holiday week—they recouped and closed to the sensational gross of $40,000. Which meant a good profit for a bill that cost the management only $17,000.

George made the first test talking picture, back in 1911, with his pal Eddie Cantor and a then well-known musical-comedy actress named Truly (*really* Truly) Shattuck. It was done for Thomas Edison, and not much good. He also did an early Vitaphone short, his "Hello, Mama" monologue.

George Jessel was, and is, a man of great complexity, enjoying many interests. One of the most consuming of these interests is what used to be called the Opposite Sex. And, while he was capable of carrying on two or three flirtations at the same time, he was also capable of falling deeply and single-mindedly in love. Though a cynic about women, he had a deep streak of romanticism in his nature.

One night during the long run with Eddie Cantor he spotted Norma Talmadge, the great and beautiful silent movie star, in the audience. He persuaded her to come up on the stage, introduced her, and that was the beginning of a great love, one that eventually blossomed into marriage and finally withered into divorce. But it was a wonderful thing while it lasted.

It was during this period that George and Eddie Cantor had the only quarrel of their long and devoted friendship. About what occasioned it, George is rather vague. He attributes it partly, at least, to Eddie's burgeoning success in radio, which made him feel pretty important, but it may also have had its roots in the contrast between Eddie's steady and (to George) stodgy family-man's life and George's playboy activities. At any rate, George says, for several weeks they spoke to each other only on stage; all communication between them was through intermediaries, usually their dressers. But their coolness was soon forgotten and they resumed their Damon and Pythias roles until the end of Eddie's life.

George's penchant for adventure came to a full stop with his marriage to Norma Talmadge. They went so far as to contemplate parenthood. One day Norma, talking to her close friend Jay Brennan, partner and straight man of the late Bert Savoy, told him she was thinking of having a baby. Brennan recoiled in utter horror. "A *baby!* Oh, my darling girl," he exclaimed. "You mustn't have a baby. Babies attract mice!" Now it was Norma's turn to recoil. "What on earth are you talking about?" she demanded. "Don't you see, Norma darling," Jay explained, "babies eat crackers and crackers make crumbs and crumbs spill on the floor. And crumbs attract mice. So, you see, you simply must not have a baby." She didn't.

The last night of the Cantor-Jessel run at the Palace was New Year's Eve of 1931. With the exception of *The Jazz Singer* on the stage, that engagement was the high spot of George Jessel's career for a long time. The same can be said of the Palace.

CHAPTER EIGHT

THE YEAR 1932 was the blackest of the depression. The hopeful sounds coming out of Washington had a hollow tone. Business in general grew weaker, wage cuts and reduced hours were the order of the day. Unemployment rose to twelve million. Men were selling apples on the streets. On Park Avenue, recalls one veteran of this economic war, he was approached four or five times in the space of half a mile by shamefaced citizens asking for money. "Brother, Can You Spare a Dime?" was more than a song. Those spared this tragedy tried to ease their consciences by carrying around pockets full of silver for the less fortunate.

That bleak winter saw evictions, breadlines, and those dismal clusters of shacks known as Hoovervilles. In the midst of all this desolation and fear the entertainment world natu-

179

rally suffered. Business in the legitimate theater was down, vaudeville in general hung on the ropes, but the Palace remained, gallantly trying to hold on by any means.

Although Hiram Brown was president of RKO, Martin Beck had been asked to resume an active role in the theater and the circuit. With his own Martin Beck Theatre under lease to the Theatre Guild, which had Lunt and Fontanne profitably ensconced in *Reunion in Vienna* despite the troubled times, he readily answered the call.

It is interesting to note that the invitation came to Mr. Beck only a few weeks after he had sued the Albee estate and sought, with other stockholders, an examination of the RKO books. News of the suit broke in the press on February 6, and some pretty fast compromises must have been worked out, for on February 24 all the dailies carried an official announcement of Beck's return to the old stand. Despite rumors to the contrary, Hiram Brown stayed on as president; Beck's title was Director of Vaudeville. *Zit's*, a theatrical weekly of the day, editorialized: "With Martin Beck's return the actors will not only have a friend again but a fighter for their rights."

The *New York Times* Sunday drama section carried a front-page interview with the returning executive. "Here is Mr. Beck," the story went, "back in his original calling, this time as adviser and analyst for RKO. The 'O' stands for Orpheum, and Orpheum still stands largely for Mr. Beck." In Beck's words, "The vaudeville that was, was pushed aside by talking pictures, then they drained show business in general amid a good deal of hysteria. . . . There have been too many big presentations. A real vaudeville act never needed

180

scenery. A real vaudeville actor, as I saw him, needed only his personality. . . . I don't object to the high salaries of headliners who are made by the newspapers. I'd rather pay them well if they succeed. But there are never any 'high' salaries in the sense of being too high—where a manager can gauge the draw correctly. The last analysis of show business is made at the box office. It isn't what you take in. It's what you have left over—the profits and their re-investment."

The Palace bill for the week immediately following that interview bore out at least some of Mr. Beck's expressed theories. The number-one headliner was Beatrice Lillie, who immediately before intermission did a skit she had done in *The Third Little Show* and immediately after intermission reappeared in a repertoire of songs she had made famous. She was backed up by an agreeable assortment of talent, including George Olsen and his band; Fifi D'Orsay, the movie comedienne; and Al Siegel with Lillian Slade in a series of Mr. Siegel's songs—Mr. Siegel was the man credited with the original discovery and training of Ethel Merman. Also on the bill were the Mills Brothers, "Radio's New Sensation." That no longer precocious young man Milton Berle wandered through the whole program. The show, favorably reviewed, was held over for three additional weeks. But what was "left over," as Mr. Beck had put it, did not show much profit for the whole four weeks.

The laughter inside the Palace was pretty much quenched by the presence just outside of a soup kitchen operated by Mrs. William Randolph Hearst. A bitter little story was told of house manager Elmer Rogers being called to the telephone by an unidentified woman who asked if he would have her husband paged. "Have you any idea where he's sitting?" asked Rogers. "Oh," said the woman, "he's not in the Palace. He's across the street in the breadline."

There was one moment of brightness. A scrubwoman who had worked at the Palace since its opening in 1913 found a diamond bracelet under a seat and turned it in to Elmer Rogers. Mr. Rogers tracked down its owner, a lady named Du Pont, who reclaimed the bracelet, valued at $3,000, and gave the scrubwoman a $200 reward. That windfall came in handy, for not too long afterward many of the house staff were given pay cuts or fired.

All through those early months of 1932 there were changes and rumors of change, inevitable when a new chief arrives or an old chief returns. Manager Elmer Rogers suddenly found himself director of advertising and publicity. Arnold van Leer, who had been doing that job, was transferred to the Mayfair Theatre and the Brooklyn Albee. Some reports say Rogers stayed on as manager along with his new duties. Whatever the arrangement, it didn't last long. In a couple of weeks Van Leer was back at the Palace and soon Elmer Rogers retired, whether by his own volition or management fiat nobody can or will say. His departure was greatly lamented by hundreds, both on and off the stage. For years his name had been synonymous with the name of the Palace itself.

A vast and complicated set of business moves—the kind that spell panic in high places—dogged the Palace for the rest of that season. Most of them are far too involved for anything but a business trade paper; it is enough to say that scarcely a day passed without some rumor of a change in management or policy, to be followed the next day by a flat denial of same. Lawsuits and threats of lawsuits filled the papers; stock maneuvers abounded. An attempt by the Palace to put film trailers of its forthcoming shows into whatever RKO movie houses remained open was rejected by the house managers.

There were many reasons for the panic that set off all this frenzied activity. One of the principal causes was another onslaught by the Warner Brothers, who had contributed so much to the decline of the Palace when they released *The Jazz Singer* in 1927. Early in February they announced that their Hollywood Theatre (now the Mark Hellinger) would open as a two-a-day variety house, with that old Palace hand Lou Holtz starring in what was called a vaudeville revue. There would be a midnight show every Saturday, and the price scale would be fifty cents to a dollar for matinees, with a two-dollar top at night. Just to rub salt into the wound, some other recent Palace regulars would be on the bill, among them Clark and McCullough, Jay Brennan, Venita Gould, and Vincent Lopez with his Hotel St. Regis Band. Added starters were the Boswell Sisters, the pianist-composer Harold Arlen, a smattering of minor acts, and a dancing chorus of twenty. Lou Holtz and his lavish company opened at the Hollywood in mid-February 1932 to instant success, and the first week's gross was $34,000.

To combat this new threat the Palace had to do some tall talking. On that Monday the papers carried the welcome news that after an absence of three years, during which she had appeared abroad and all over the United States, Sophie Tucker had heeded the booking office's plea to be a one-woman rescue party. Her long absence had been occasioned by a protracted impasse over money. Who finally yielded on that point has never been made public. Only the salary lists for the week would answer that, and they are locked up in a vault far away from New York. But Sophie, being the warm-hearted person she was, probably gave in just for old times' sake.

Backing her up was a strong bill, consisting of Smith and Dale; Jack Whiting, a popular musical juvenile of the period; and Bill Robinson, who filled the entire second half of the show with his *Hot from Harlem Revue*. The ad offered a thousand seats at twenty-five cents to a dollar, afternoon and evening, from Monday through Friday.

Sophie's return was greeted tumultuously. The Monday matinee audience was almost hysterical with joy, and the reviews were ecstatic. Ed Sullivan, covering the show for the *New York Graphic*, said: "She just about tears the roof off the place. . . . This reporter must confess that if Charlie Freeman [chief booker for the whole circuit] had turned her loose for the whole evening it would have been just great."

The entire week turned into a long sentimental reunion between Sophie and her worshipful fans. If any one person could be said to have symbolized the Palace in its greatest days, that person was Sophie Tucker. When she finished her act and the tumult and the shouting died down, she made a brief curtain speech. "I'm glad to be back here," she said simply, tears spoiling her eye make-up. "Returning to this theater is like coming home to me." Then she walked off, the roar of the crowd ringing in her ears. The rest of the bill was well received by all the press and business looked good. Still,

184

with the new low prices and the high salaries involved, profit couldn't have amounted to much, if anything. Nevertheless the bill was held over intact for a second week.

But even that wonderfully nostalgic and sentimental week was not without its traumatic experience. It happened one evening as Sophie was finishing her act, just before intermission. The stage manager was standing in the wings on one side, and Bill Robinson on the other, watching her. Suddenly a tongue of flame appeared on stage left, near the electrician's switchboard, and a second later it shot up the traveling curtain, sending a shower of sparks and smoke onto the stage and over the first few rows of the orchestra. Although she was wearing a highly combustible sequin-trimmed gown, Sophie kept right on belting out her song until a property boy came and pulled her off the stage as the asbestos fire curtain rang down.

In split seconds Elmer Rogers, his staff of ushers, and other personnel were down the aisles, calming the spectators and shepherding them quietly toward the exits. It was this fast and efficient action that prevented panic and a stampede that could have proved disastrous. Within three minutes, seventeen hundred persons had filed out of the theater in orderly fashion. The actors and backstage people kept their heads, too, and got out to the street without major injuries. They also arrived there without much of their clothing, and the crowds that quickly gathered around the scene saw some pretty startling semi-nudity on that cold February evening.

Except for minor scratches and bruises, nobody in the front of the house was hurt. The chief sufferer backstage was Bill Robinson. As he stood in the wings, the smoke got to him and knocked him out. Happily, it was only for a little while; later that night, in true show-business tradition, he made a scheduled appearance at a benefit for disabled veterans. It was, he said, a bit of a problem, since all his dancing shoes had been thoroughly damped down by the firemen's hose. The fire had been quickly extinguished, but not before it had destroyed a great deal of scenery, especially the sets for Robinson's revue, as well as scorching seats in the front rows of the orchestra. The loss to the theater was estimated at $50,000.

The papers next day gave the story a big play, mostly on page one, with Sophie understandably the heroine of the occasion. What copyreader could resist the chance for such a headline as: RED-HOT MAMA BURNS UP PALACE THEATRE or SOPHIE'S SONGS SO HOT, THEATER BURNS UNDER THEM! Thanks to the publicity, the cooperation of the radio stations, and the gallantry of all concerned, the theater didn't miss a single show. The Thursday matinee went on, more or less as usual, without scenery but with extra verve, and played to a virtually sold-out house.

One amusing sidelight to this fire episode is provided by William Liebling, former actor who with Arthur Freed, songwriter and outstanding film producer, appeared in one of Gus Edwards' juvenile revues, *Kids in Candyland*. Liebling later became an actors' agent and the husband of playwright representative Audrey Wood, whose father was manager of the Palace in its early days. Bill, a great Palace fan, and a friend of Smith and Dale, was in their dressing room that evening, watching them rehearse a new bit of business while waiting their turn. Suddenly, he says, Bill

186

Robinson's wife came dashing to the dressing room scream-
ing: "The theater's on fire! Get out, get out!" Believing it to
be a gag, they kept right on calmly rehearsing their act until
firemen came and shooed them out of the building.

In Sophie Tucker's opinion, the event had a symbolic
significance. "The grand and glorious days of the Palace
ended with the fire," she wrote in her autobiography. "The
Palace was never the same again. When it reopened it was on
the four-a-day grind policy." But events did not follow that
literally. Immediately after the fire came a two-week engagement starring Frank Fay and his wife, Barbara Stanwyck,
who by that time was a rising movie star. In line with the
current Palace policy of using the chief comedian to do not
only his own specialty but to serve as master of ceremonies,
Fay M.C.'d the whole bill, which included the piquant Irene
Bordoni, the Ritz Brothers, Gus Van, and Texas Guinan
with her night-club gang.

Fay himself had made a few pictures, but they were not
very successful, and Miss Stanwyck had soon outstripped
him in public acclaim. Not a man to react sunnily to being
downgraded, he was deeply wounded by this situation. He
brooded over it, and the brooding showed in his performance.
Though he was still very funny in his unique fashion, the
wound to his ego added a bitter note to his already misan-
thropic manner. That attitude was to increase with the coming years.

Something was bothering him, and audiences felt it. Miss
Stanwyck, on the whole, received more favorable reviews
than he did, and there was rather too much emphasis on her
present excellence and his former greatness. One reviewer

referred to him as "one of the one-time more engaging and entertaining comedians. . . . There are moments when he recaptures some of his old charm and humor, but for the most part he is neither better nor worse than a lot of other recent masters of ceremony."

As if this were not enough of a putdown, the same critic went on to say: "Miss Stanwyck is altogether too good an actress to be wasted on such an inept and mechanically contrived little sketch such as 'Xmas' [sic] which no less a person than her husband, Mr. Fay, has written for her."

And now, to make matters even more galling, the overlords of the Palace, in another attempt to counter Lou Holtz's success at the Hollywood, decided to introduce—for the first time in the theater's life—a Saturday midnight show. With the Sunday supper show which had been in effect for months, this made a total of sixteen shows a week, and no extra pay for the performers. On the night this policy was inaugurated, Fay, in his wry throwaway style, tossed a little hand grenade at his employers. "We're still enjoying the good old two-a-day," he told the audience with a bittersweet smile. "Yes. Two a day and two a night."

His fellow actors and the audience enjoyed the crack, which naturally didn't go down so well with the gentlemen at the top. They were further alienated by the sudden non-appearance of Mr. Fay during the second week, leaving the show without a master of ceremonies. This lack was later filled by Ross Brown or Gus Van, depending on what paper you read.

The official reason for Fay's absence, given by Miss Stanwyck, was a very bad cold. Management made a discreet

188

statement, saying only that he was not expected back. The press, however, especially the theatrical press, regarded this explanation with some skepticism. "The facile comedian," said the *Morning Telegraph* of Thursday, March 10, "was overtaken by obscure demons of misery over the week-end and could not rally his recuperative powers sufficiently to resume his co-starring with Barbara Stanwyck, his wife."

An item in the *New York American* hinted that Fay's indisposition had been caused by his distress over a suit brought by his first wife, Frances White (the "M-i-s-s-i-s-s-i-p-p-i" girl), for what she claimed was thirteen years' worth of back alimony.

An unhappy time was had by all. Lou Holtz's revue at the Hollywood was still outgrossing the Palace, a situation that brought about an agonizing reappraisal of future activities. For one thing, negotiations which had been under way to bring Marilyn Miller to the Palace as co-headliner with Paul Whiteman for the week of March 19 were hastily dropped. With Whiteman's $7,500 and Miss Miller's $5,000 a week there wouldn't have been enough left to pay the balance of the program and keep within the newly re-established limit of $15,000 a week for the whole show.

Another new policy, announced during this troubled time, was the elimination of long-run shows at the Palace. Since the long runs of the Cantor-Jessel, Lou Holtz, William Gaxton, and Kate Smith shows had been the most profitable weeks of the season, it is not entirely clear why this decision was made. But, as in most businesses when things are going wrong, people tend to make hasty decisions, and that's what they were doing at the Palace. It must have been especially maddening to realize that only a few months earlier Holtz had drawn great crowds to the Palace, and that now he was accomplishing the same thing for the rival Hollywood Theatre.

No matter what the management tried, business was just not good enough. Even with magnets like Benny Rubin, Jack Haley, a Gus Edwards revue, and the tremendously popular Russ Columbo, the Palace couldn't keep pace with the Lou Holtz show at the Hollywood.

In the executive offices things were topsy-turvy. Notes in the press reversed themselves with dizzying frequency: *Beck in full command . . . Beck tired of it all . . . Beck reorganizes entire booking system, breaks down barriers between bookers and agents, announces he will be available to all comers . . . will hold open house at least one hour a day in the interest of improving future shows . . . may start production units again, possibly under the direction of Max Gordon, who has been seen around the Palace frequently since Beck took command.*

More reports and/or rumors: *Van Leer will be out again as press agent, with Richard Maney* (later to become as famous as the people he publicized) *predicted as P.A. of the Palace. Bookers constantly shifted from one theatre to another . . . Haley and Rubin, originally booked in for two weeks, canceled because management refused to keep the rest of the acts for the second week . . . except Columbo, who stays on for upcoming bill which is topped by Paul Whiteman.*

The Whiteman engagement at $7,500 brought a flood of reminiscences. Jim Gillespie in the *Evening Graphic* wrote:

190

"In 1920, when Whiteman's band was booked into the Palace at an experimental $900 a week, Broadway was skeptical. Did Albee expect the Palace audience to listen to a dance orchestra for twenty minutes, and no place to dance?"

That week, with the added attractions of Jay C. Flippen, the Albertina Rasch Ballet, and the reunion and return after seven years of the beloved Weber and Fields, the Palace grossed $30,000—particularly good since it was Holy Week. But—and it was a maddening but—the Lou Holtz show at the Hollywood beat that figure by $2,000.

Still, if the salary limit was really held down to $15,000, it seems there should have been *some* profit on the week, though neither Russ Columbo nor Weber and Fields could have been cheap. To balance those salaries, according to *Variety*, one turn on the bill, a "flash act" called *Glad Rags* with a cast of ten, was paid a total of $100; this breaks down to fifty-six cents per person per performance. A great many incredible things were going on during those dolorous days, but that seems almost too bad to be true.

The next week was a calamity for the Palace, which grossed only $21,000. Up the street the Hollywood, where Lou Holtz was well into his second month, took in $30,000. Desperate, the Palace cast its net in all directions, bringing in for the next couple of weeks such an assortment of big fish as the Pat Rooneys, Senior and Junior; Julia Sanderson; Frank Crumit; Pola Negri; and Will Mahoney, as well as a lot of little fish.

But April was the cruelest month. For, despite a really tremendous array of talent—James Barton, Ethel Merman, the Yacht Club Boys, Milton Berle, Moran and Mack, Mary

Brian and Ken Murray (from the movies), the Albertina Rasch Ballet, two Metropolitan Opera stars—the young Nanette Guilford and the veteran Mme. Frances Alda—and Eddie Leonard, the Palace just couldn't keep pace with Warners' Hollywood. While the latter showed a consistent profit, the former showed almost equally consistent losses. According to *Variety*, the Palace had been in the red since the Ides of March.

One more step along the downward path was the engagement of Nils T. Granlund, a well-known Broadway character who had parlayed a loud voice and a penchant for displaying nudes or near nudes on the night-club floor into a successful career. He appeared in what was billed as "The Biggest Act in Vaudeville":

N.T.G.

with his sensational

HOLLYWOOD GIRL REVUE

60 in company *60*

including

40 World's Loveliest Girls *40*

Not only that, but for a couple of days before the opening of this extravaganza the Palace lobby was adorned with portraits of undraped young ladies, advance heralds for the proffered goodies. Shades of the decency bulletin! Mr. Albee must have been whirling in his grave. After an outcry, paint was applied in strategic places and the girls stayed on in the lobby, more or less clad. But the degradation was like the blood on Lady Macbeth's hands—it couldn't be washed away.

The reviewers were enthusiastic about Will Mahoney, friendly toward the Rooneys and Herman Timberg and *his* son, but either ignored the N.T.G. revue or denounced it as vulgar, inept, and downright deplorable. The *Times* man said: "While it is an entertainment not entirely at home within the confines of even so elastic a stage as the Palace's, it does present, in varying degrees of undress, an assortment of Times Square eyefuls. Accordingly, in one way and another, yesterday's Sabbath concert managed to be quite an affair."

Speaking favorably of Fifi D'Orsay, the *Sun* reviewer wrote: "Unfortunately the same cannot be said of Nils T. Granlund's revue of forty beautiful girls. They come on with little more than their strings of beads for display through a long and tiresome act of mediocre material amateurishly executed."

How did this bit of booking ever get by the keen eye and good taste of Martin Beck? Whatever the reason, it was useless, though the whistling in the dark continued.

On the last Sunday in April, Mr. Beck was interviewed by Howard Barnes of the *Herald Tribune*. "In his spacious office high in the Palace Theatre building," wrote Barnes, "he [Mr. Beck] is plotting great things for the two-a-day these spring days and getting a tremendous kick out of it. 'The younger generation [Barnes quoted Beck] hasn't had any real vaudeville. The talking sketch, which used to be the mainstay of variety, has virtually become extinct. In its place you have crooners and singers, leading to a terrible sameness.' . . . In place of the crooners and singers Mr. Beck will bring back novelty to the Palace (and other vaudeville theaters): jugglers, acrobats, sleight-of-hand artists, animal acts, that gave vaudeville its zest in its heyday. That these performers will be good is no idle speculation on Mr. Beck's part. He leaves for Europe at the end of this week to inspect them, in company with Roxy."

The Palace bill that week included Dave Apollon, the mandolinist-revue producer, Moran and Mack, Mme. Frances Alda, Ethel Merman, Mitchell and Durant, and four other acts. The first week in May had several holdovers, plus Rosetta of the Duncan Sisters, Floyd Gibbons, and William Demarest.

It was a grim week for the Palace. Elmer Rogers' rumored retirement from the theater he had managed so long and so well became a fact. Lou Holtz was concluding his Hollywood Theatre engagement after a run of eleven big weeks. *Variety* ran an item claiming that "more people were standing on the beach outside the Palace than were sitting inside, and management was threatening to call the police to shoo away homeless actors." Most significantly for the future, *Variety* also reported a $5,000 loss at the Palace every week since the previous January 1.

And that week the Palace, after rumors and denials, finally admitted the dreaded truth: beginning May 14, it would no longer be a two-a-day (a three-a-day with a midnight show on Saturdays) but a four-a-day. LAST BIG TIME QUITS, ran the headlines. "Five thousand weekly loss since January 1 sends ace vaudeville theatre to 10-act grind with shorts. The change was ordered by the theatre department with Beck *not in accord*. Scale to be 50¢ to $1.00, no reserved seats, and $7000 top for bills."

When the official word came, it was announced as a summer policy only, but nobody believed that. Everyone had been expecting it, yet the blow struck just as hard as if it had been a total surprise. It *couldn't* have been a surprise, considering the competition. At the Paramount: the feature film and a tabloid version of *The Band Wagon,* a big hit of the previous Broadway season, with Fred Astaire in his original role. . . . At the Capitol: the movie plus personal appearances by Edmund Lowe, Victor McLaglen, Fifi D'Orsay, Cab Calloway's band, Burns and Allen, and Arthur Tracy, "The Street Singer." . . . At Loew's State: in addition to the picture, a cut-down version of *Girl Crazy,* another recent Broadway hit, plus a vaudeville bill including Smith and Dale.

The unhappy honor of headlining the first grind bill at the Palace fell to Phil Baker, which may account for his wistful expression on the cover of that week's program, with its "continuous from 11:00 a.m. to 11:30 p.m., plus a midnight performance every Saturday." Among those supporting Baker were Joe Laurie, Jr.; a Gus Edwards revue with Hildegarde and the Keating Twins; Eddie Garr, the impersonator; and Ethelind Terry, star of *Rio Rita.*

A photograph of the theater for the second grind week shows the marquee featuring Milton Berle, Queenie Smith, Harry Puck, the Colleano Family, Grace Hayes, Jack Whiting, and Roscoe (Fatty) Arbuckle. Above the marquee was a huge sign saying: CONTINUOUS PERFORMANCE, and floating from the third-floor terrace were two banners proclaiming, "10 Real Star Acts," with Arbuckle's name glittering from three different locations. Considering the nature

195

of the scandal that had rocked the country and ruined his film career more than a decade earlier, this engagement could hardly have been considered appropriate for the entire family. It must have caused at least another whirl or two in the Albee grave.

One performer whose name was not on the marquee, but who later rose to fame and fortune in pictures, theater, radio, and television, was a young man who appeared with his mother, a well-known belter of songs. She was Grace Hayes, and he is widely known today as Peter Lind Hayes. With his charming and beautiful wife, Mary Healy, he has a very popular breakfast radio conversation show Monday through Friday.

Peter Lind Hayes had what he accurately refers to as a bloody debut at the Palace. He was sixteen at the time and not too interested in his great opportunity. His mother, affectionately known as Hazy, was far more nervous than he as they stood in the wings ready to go on. The act immediately ahead of them was a brother-and-sister team named Fritz and Jean Hubert. Fritz finished with a knockabout comedy fall that propelled him clear across the stage. "To break the fall," Peter remembers, "Fritz hurled himself headlong into the main curtain, where Hazy's minipiano was waiting to be pushed on stage." Result: an unconscious and badly bleeding comedian and a hysterical sister.

Grace Hayes, the consummate pro, immediately went into her act, singing a hit song of that year, "Lovable," parading across the stage in a trailing white organdy gown. "It was white at the start," Peter says, "but by the time she had crossed the stage twice it was knee deep in gore." Nothing

daunted, Hazy introduced her new partner, then called
Peter Lind because her agent thought it unwise for her to
admit having a sixteen-year-old son.

Meanwhile Peter, more nervous than he had thought, had
cut his finger to the bone on a prop he used in the act.
Unaware of this, Grace proudly announced that young Mr.
Lind would do his impression of Cab Calloway. "I started
trucking to the microphone," Peter says. "There was a new
spurt of blood—only this time it was mine—splashing like a
fountain over my brand-new white suit."

Despite all this, they were a big hit, and as they stepped
down to make a thank-you speech, Lynne Cantor, one of
Hazy's close friends, stood up in her box and, mascara
streaming down her face, shrieked, "I knew you'd do it!" and
promptly fell out of the box. "As they carried her from the
theater," Peter recalls, "we retired to our dressing room and
started a partnership that was destined to have many a
rough row to hoe."

Despite a great deal of publicity and a bill that by almost
any standard was quite good, business remained bad. And it
continued to be. George Godfrey, who had been called back
from limbo by Martin Beck and was now booking the grind
shows, got his notice, and Arthur Willi, one of the veteran
Palace bookers, was slated to replace him. This switch turned
out to be brief, however; Martin Beck, still abroad scouting
new acts, cabled his objection, whereupon Godfrey's notice
was tabled pending Mr. Beck's return.

June 1932 proved a nightmare. Even with such sure-fire
draws as Harland Dixon, Kitty Donor, Toto the clown,

Buddy Rogers (still a movie idol), Lulu McConnell, Herb Williams, and the never-failing Sophie Tucker, plus a goodly throng from the once-despised radio medium, the Palace couldn't get out of the red. Things were bad all over. Of the Broadway shows that opened that month, only one lasted more than twenty performances. Reports were rife that the Roxy, too, was in trouble, and that it would close down for an indefinite period at the end of the month. Martin Beck took the fastest boat back from Europe, but it was too late. In its June 28 issue, *Variety* front-paged the following headline: SIX ACTS, FILMS IN N.Y. PALACE JULY 9.

The story explained that the theater had dropped about $30,000 in six weeks, that the current bill was the cheapest in the nineteen years of the theater's history, with a total salary list of $5,200 for nine acts. The prediction followed that the total vaudeville budget for the new vaude-pix policy would run between $5,000 and $6,000 weekly, and that the opening picture of the new set-up would be *Bring 'Em Back Alive,* the Frank Buck animal film, which had finished a first-run engagement at the neighboring Mayfair Theatre.

Everything about that story proved to be correct except for the date. July 9 was not the first week of the vaudeville-cum-film policy. It was the *last* week of straight vaudeville. The new combination show would begin on the 16th. Included on that final straight bill were Fred Keating the magician, Leon Janney (now a well-known figure in legit and TV), and Louis Sobol, the Broadway columnist.

A *Times* review said: "After almost twenty years of straight vaudeville, the Palace is saying goodbye to all that with its current show. On Saturday a program combining variety acts and feature motion pictures will take over the stage of what until recently was the proudest and most em-purpled of all the country's former big-time music halls, the goal of vaudevillians everywhere."

During that sizzling summer the distinguished actor Den-nis King headlined at the Palace, after a smashing success in *The Three Musketeers.* The week's take was a total of $8,000, a thousand less than the theater had ever made before. Mr. King, currently president of The Players, recalls that after his final monologue he thanked his handful of spectators for coming to the theater. "I told them," he reminisced not long ago, "that I had the honor of playing to the lowest gross in the history of the Palace."

In times like these, when people in the hundreds of thou-sands are dying of misery, of famine, of war, of man's inhu-manity to man, it seems frivolous to wail over the downfall of a theater, the death of a tradition. But to those who were around at the time, to the performers who lost their liveli-hood when the Palace assumed that semi-picture policy, and to those who had been loyal and loving patrons of the Palace for almost two decades, its degradation was a legitimate cause for sorrow.

The opening week of pictures at the Palace, with *Bring 'Em Back Alive* and six acts of vaudeville including Russ Columbo and Hobart Bosworth, had a new low scale of prices: 30 to 65 cents weekdays, 40 to 85 cents Saturdays, and 55 to 85 cents Sundays. It was the first profitable week the theater had seen in four months, with a gross of $16,000. The net profit was $2,500, a sad figure compared with the days when the Palace had often shown a clear profit of half a

199

million dollars a year.

"You wouldn't recognize the old Palace this week," said the *Times*. "Its screen is given over to the first full-length film ever to play there . . . the excellent animal film *Bring 'Em Back Alive* . . . and on its stage are only six acts. . . . Among the Tories who have been addicts of the Palace's straight vaudeville, this bow to the necessities of the moment is a matter of regret."

From that July date until mid-November the situation remained static: four, five, or six vaudeville acts with one headliner, and a picture, usually a second-run though now and then a first-run film thought not important enough to show in the regular first-run houses. Kate Smith came back during that period, with her *Swanee Revue;* so did Bill Robinson, Olsen and Johnson, Fred Waring's Pennsylvanians, Eddie Dowling and Ray Dooley, Gus Edwards, and a few other big names from the old days. Miss Smith did $19,000 on the week and that was regarded as outstanding. But with a picture—*Congorilla* and *The White Zombie*, to name a couple—and four shows a day, five on Saturdays, it was on the whole a losing gambit. The flesh might have been willing, but the spirit was weak. Even the strong and shining spirit of Franklin Delano Roosevelt, who was elected so overwhelmingly in November and whose very existence brought new life to the sluggish country, couldn't quite reach the Palace.

November 12 saw the opening of the final vaudeville-and-picture combination. The film, *Once in a Lifetime*, seems appropriate to the circumstances. The live show consisted of Sid Marion, Nick Lucas, Ross and Edwards, Ola Lillity, the

Honey Family, Giovanni, and Hal LeRoy.

"Vaudeville is singing its swan song at the Palace this week," said the *Times*, "prior to the defection of the time-honored variety house to motion pictures." In conclusion, the review said: ". . . the Honey Family are swinging the old Palace trapeze for what may be the last time. *Sic transit gloria mundi.*"

That bill lasted five days. Then came what Abel Green and Joe Laurie, in *Show Biz*, call the official kiss of death. The Palace turned into a straight picture house with Eddie Cantor in *The Kid from Spain*. The top was two dollars. The *Times* review was good, the first week's business was encouraging, and it was believed the picture would run eight weeks.

About this time the vaudeville section in *Variety* was moved still farther back in the paper—now behind radio. The weekly also took occasion to point out that "vaudeville never knew what the Palace meant to it, until the Palace passed and newspapers all over the country wrote farewell tributes."

There was just a chance that the straight picture policy might work out well financially, no matter how deeply it grieved the old Palace fans; but even that was destined to defeat. As *The Kid from Spain* went into its fifth week, a new theater opened just three blocks north and one block east of the Palace. To call it simply a new theater is a considerable understatement, since it happened to be Radio City Music Hall.

What very few people remember is that the Music Hall, when it made its debut on November 27, 1932, "under the personal direction of Samuel L. Rothafel," was only that—a music hall along European lines. No motion picture. To give some idea of the scope of Roxy's soaring ambition for his new cathedral, here follows a part of the vast and varied inaugural program which the display ad modestly described as "the supreme stage entertainment of all time":

Taylor Holmes, impersonating Francis Scott Key and declaiming the words of "The Star-Spangled Banner"

Impressions of a Music Hall by the Wallendas and the Kiutas

In the Spotlight, a radio act with the "Sisters of the Skillet"

Dr. Rockwell, the monologist

The Radio City Ballet, Patricia Bowman, prima ballerina

Vera Schwarz of the State Opera of Berlin

The Tuskegee Choir

Ray Bolger

Harald Kreuzberg

Martha Graham

The Roxyettes [later the Rockettes], under the direction of Russell Markert

Tita Ruffo of the Metropolitan Opera, singing excerpts from *Carmen*

Finale by the whole company, headed by DeWolf Hopper and Weber and Fields

The opening was deemed worthy of a front-page story in the *Times*, with an extravagant account of the grandeur of the theater and the elegance of its accoutrements and service. However, a review by no less a personage than Brooks At-

kinson was something else again. "Size is no friend of merriment and no great breeder of hospitality," wrote Atkinson,
"and the truth seems to be that Maestro Rothafel has opened
his caravansery with entertainment which, on the whole, does
not provide much enthusiasm. It is more a product of a radio
and motion-picture mind than of a genius for the short turns
and encores of the music hall stage." Mr. Atkinson was not
alone in his estimate, and ten days later the following announcement appeared in all the papers: RADIO CITY MUSIC
HALL TO BE MOVIE HOUSE—6200 SEAT THEATRE TO GO ON
POPULAR PRICE BASIS WITH FILM AND STAGE SHOW.

Two days later the Music Hall announced that it had
adopted a policy of combining outstanding films with gigantic Roxy-produced stage shows. "Now," it continued, "*all*
can enjoy the wonders of the world's largest and finest theater, with hundreds of performers, the Roxyettes, a mighty
orchestra, plus one of the year's most thrilling motion pictures." That picture was *The Bitter Tea of General Yen*. It
starred Barbara Stanwyck, with Nils Asther and Walter
Connolly in important supporting roles.

General Yen's tea was bitter for every competing theater,
and especially bitter for the Palace, because the only two live
holdovers from the Music Hall's first unfortunate stage show
were Dr. Rockwell and Ray Bolger, both popular Palace
alumni. Back in 1926 Bolger had been one of the many Gus
Edwards kids who later became famous.

Once the Music Hall was established—and at low prices
—as the magnetic attraction it has remained to this day, it
seriously damaged the other film-plus-stage-show houses and
even the few legitimate plays on Broadway. The Palace,

which had confidently expected to run *The Kid from Spain* eight weeks, had to take it off at the end of six.

After this, confusion followed upon confusion. For the next five weeks, from January 7, 1933, through February 4, the Palace reverted to its previously tried and discarded movie-and-vaudeville policy. The final bill of this brief interlude featured the delightful birdmen Arnaut Brothers; Maria Gambarelli, premiere danseuse of the Capitol and Roxy; and Benny Leonard, the undefeated lightweight champion of the world. The film was *The Bitter Tea of General Yen*, in its second run after the Music Hall showing. On February 11 the theater went back to a straight picture policy.

On April 29 the theater made still another turnabout, combining a motion picture with a few acts of vaudeville on a continuous-performance basis. This policy lasted two and a half years, until September 30, 1935. The names on the bill during that period, with few exceptions, ring only the faintest bell these days. Among the memorable ones are Frances Langford, Venita Gould, the Runaway Four, Jay C. Flippen, Lulu McConnell, Lanny Ross, the Pickens Sisters, George Givot, Molly Picon, Shaw and Lee, Gertrude Niesen, Joe Penner, Yorke and King, Ben Blue, Bert Lahr, Buck and Bubbles, Gus Van, Jack Whiting, the Colleano Family of superb aerialists, Janette Hackett (who had changed the spelling of her first name), Owen McGiveney, Eleanor Holm, the Mandel Brothers, Buster West, Alf Loyal's Dogs, and the Honey Family, who, after all, did get another chance to swing on that old Palace trapeze. And, oh yes, Bob Hope.

* * *

Between April 1933 and September 1935 a number of important events were happening in the world outside. President Roosevelt reminded us that we had nothing to fear but fear itself; he closed the banks for a few days, established the CCC, the NRA, the WPA, and a host of other monogrammed projects which restored confidence and helped get the country back on its feet. A clownish fellow named Hitler was stirring things up in Germany, but nobody here paid much attention to the ranting brownshirt or his followers. More interesting was the legalizing of three-percent beer and the repeal of Prohibition, which came on the 6th of December 1933.

By the fall of 1935 things were looking up in most parts of the country and F.D.R. was getting ready to run for his second term. That autumn the Palace had given up—apparently forever—the idea of live shows. The last vaudeville-and-film bill was presented during the week of September 20, 1935. Not a name on the bill stirs memory today. The picture, with more than a touch of irony, was *Page Miss Glory.*

Sometime during this era the booking office, that arena where so much Palace history had been made, left the once sacrosanct Sixth Floor and moved to new quarters on Sixth Avenue and 50th Street, which just happened to be the office building connected with Radio City Music Hall. Despite this move, the motley throng of agents, tipsters, hangers-on, curbside comedians, and actors, mostly layoffs by now, continued to gather daily "on the beach." What made them do it? one wonders. Habit? Nowhere else to go? The hope that springs eternal? Who knows?

In the fall of 1935 the Palace once more turned to a

straight film policy, running on a continuous basis from early morning until late at night. The opening picture was the Astaire-Rogers hit *Top Hat*, moved over from the Music Hall, at popular prices. Though most of the pictures shown during this period were second runs, a conspicuous exception was *Citizen Kane*, that brilliant and controversial *chef d'oeuvre* of Orson Wells, which opened May 1, 1941, on a reserved-seat, two-a-day basis at a $2.20 top.

Four years after the return to a straight picture policy, the *Daily News* said that the Palace was holding its own funeral, and all Dream Street mourned. "Yesterday," ran the lead paragraph (bylined by Robert Sylvester), "they started to tear down and 'streamline' the old-fashioned marquee and lobby, with its twinkling little electric bulbs and displays that once were as bitterly contested for as the favors of a great beauty.

"The marquee still reads B. F. Keith's Palace," the story continued, "having ignored the changes and mergers of the years. But inside the 25-year-old theater a double feature film bill was the attraction on the stage where Sarah Bernhardt once played *Camille*, dragging her wooden leg from stage to dressing room over a long white bearskin rug."

The renovation, carried on at night, was completed late in August. In addition to the new marquee, the Palace now sported an outer lobby done in granite, with a black base and white walls. The walls of the inner lobby were of zebra wood with a black marble base. Cost of alterations, exclusive of the new marquee and an outdoor box office, was estimated at $25,000.

For fourteen uninterrupted years, from 1935 to 1949, no living performer set foot on the Palace stage. It was a sleeping beauty.

During those years Hitler rose to power, bringing tragedy and war in his train. Mussolini became more bombastic than ever after the Axis was formed. World War II broke out in 1939 and the United States, after staying uneasily "neutral," as it had done through the rape of Ethiopia and the Spanish civil conflict, had a shattering awakening on December 7, 1941, that "Day of Infamy" so eloquently described by President Roosevelt, then in his third term. We were in the war. That fact brought unity to the country and sorrow to many. It also brought an almost unparalleled prosperity.

Everybody was in service, if not in the armed forces, then in war plants or other fields that contributed to the war effort. The theater boomed, "movies were better than ever" (and bigger), the USO sent units of actors and actresses overseas to entertain the troops. Among them were many ex-vaudevillians, most notably Bob Hope. Those were the days of *Oklahoma!*, Frank Fay's triumph in *Harvey*, and *The Voice of the Turtle*.

Then at last the war was over. But not in time for President Roosevelt to see the fruits of his efforts. He died on April 12, 1945, only a few months after starting his fourth term, only a few weeks before V-E Day. By 1949, with President Truman in his fourth year, the U.N. had been formed, business was still booming, and the theater was having a banner year. In the spring of 1949 vaudeville returned to the Palace. The man responsible for that return was Sol Schwartz.

Mr. Schwartz, a seasoned, thoroughly experienced showman and a most amiable gentleman, was a sort of twentieth-century Alger hero. He wasn't exactly *Paul the Peddler* or *Phil the Fiddler*, but he did move from a toehold on the lowest rung of the Keith-Albee ladder to the very top after that ladder had been taken over by Radio-Keith-Orpheum.

Mr. Schwartz began his theatrical career as a stenographer at the Alhambra Theatre, Seventh Avenue and 125th Street, one of the circuit's important houses in the New York area. "I had a dull daytime job," Mr. Schwartz said recently, "and I'd been studying stenography at night. When I thought I was good enough I wrote to every theater manager in New York offering my services as a part-time stenographer. The only answer I got was from the Alhambra, so that's where I went." Pretty soon he gave up his dull daytime job and from then on was part of show biz.

Although totally ignorant of theater practices, he must have been an apt pupil and a quick study, for soon he was promoted and transferred to another Keith house, a process that continued through the years until, after having served as house manager, district manager, etc., he was named vice-president and general manager of the RKO Theatres. Only a year later he became president, a post he held through 1961. When he left RKO to join Columbia Pictures as a vice-president, he was succeeded by Harry Mandel, who had been part of that Mark Luescher miniature city room back in the twenties.

208

In addition to his other attributes, Mr. Schwartz had a flair for exploitation; when he got the idea of reviving vaudeville at the Palace he built up a tremendous advance interest. Everything was planned to work on the emotions of people who had long mourned the passing of live shows from the Palace. To give the event additional prestige, it was described as the 36th Anniversary Program, and did win considerable advance attention. In an interview with J. P. Shanley of the *Times* Sunday drama section, Mr. Schwartz expounded his theories about reviving vaudeville.

"I think the time is ripe for a little change," he said. "Many people haven't seen 'round' actors perform on a stage for more than fifteen years. Some of the men who were in the service during the war were seeing live talent for the first time when USO shows played for them. They liked it and I think they want more."

Asked what would be the difference between vaudeville at the Palace and the stage shows at the local cinemas, Mr. Schwartz's answer was summed up in one word: intimacy. "The Palace was built as a vaudeville house," he continued. "You can sit in the second balcony and feel you're part of what's going on onstage. We'll have the orchestra down in the pit where it belongs. Our acts will be announced by old-time annunciators, not by a master of ceremonies."

The *Times* ran not only the Shanley interview, but an editorial about the new move. While pointing out that eight acts of vaudeville plus a motion picture were not exactly a return to the old Palace days and ways, it did say by way of welcome: "It is heartening to know that 'round' actors are coming back to the Palace, where such artists as W. C.

Fields, Joe Frisco, Miller & Lyles, Moran & Mack, Van & Schenck, Julian Eltinge, Sophie Tucker and hundreds of others once made it a household word throughout the nation."

The new bill opened in the afternoon, as in the old days, but it was on a Thursday, not the traditional Monday. The theater had been scrubbed and polished till it shone. New seats, new carpets, scenery, and other accoutrements had been installed at a cost of some $60,000. The audience included countless show-business people, among them Florence Moore, Will Morrissey, Lillian Shaw, and Tom Patricola. And there were numerous old Palace fans, as well as reporters, radio commentators, and columnists from far and near; even theater critics of note, including Brooks Atkinson.

To stir the audience, which hardly needed stirring, Mr. Schwartz had twisted the arm of Milton Berle and enlisted his unreluctant help. During the show, Milton leaped "spontaneously" from his seat in the orchestra, ran down the aisle to the stage and served, not as an M.C. in the usual fashion, but simply to introduce some special events.

One of those events was the appearance of the old-time singer Bessie Wynn, that same Bessie Wynn who, thirty-six years before, had had the misfortune to follow Sarah Bernhardt's *Camille* at the Palace. Mr. Schwartz had persuaded her to be guest of honor. Specially gowned by the management, she was introduced by Berle with a tear-jerking flourish and given an armload of long-stemmed roses. Thirty-six roses, to be exact. Another touch of nostalgia was the introduction of eighty-two-year-old William Clark, who had been stage manager of the Palace on its opening day and for ten years thereafter. A third extra, carefully arranged in advance, was the "surprise" appearance of old Pat Rooney, always a Palace darling. When he executed a few steps of his famous waltz clog, the house went into a frenzy of sentimental delight.

Whipping up additional emotion, the orchestra under the direction of Don Albert, a veteran Palace musical conductor, played "There's No Business Like Show Business" followed by "Strike Up the Band." When the curtain went up, the audience responded with hysterical applause and cheers, so overwhelming that the feminine half of a dance team which opened the bill was terrified into a state of paralysis. Moments passed before she could unfreeze enough to go into her number.

Next day Brooks Atkinson, writing in the *Times*, referred to ". . . choked and appreciative people who were determined to see a glorious past reborn and who fervently applauded Pat Rooney's fatherly blessing at the end. . ." Sad to relate, however, Mr. Atkinson was regretfully unimpressed by the show as a whole. "If wishes could make vaudeville shows," he said, "the bill that opened the Palace yesterday would have been overflowing with enjoyment." The feature picture was *Canadian Pacific*, starring Randolph Scott. Bosley Crowther, the *Times* movie critic, didn't like it.

Nevertheless, the opening week was a great success, and Sol Schwartz was hailed as a hero, a role he was disinclined to accept. "Let's wait and see," he said with what appears to have been characteristic modesty. "We'll know better the second week." The second week, with a bill of bright newcomers and a couple of standards from earlier days—the Arnauts and Aunt Jemima (Tess Gardella)—did even better business than the first, playing to standees at some performances. Indeed, with a top talent budget of $4,000 and the picture rental a slim $3,000, the week's gross of $28,000 was highly satisfactory. For the first time in many months the Palace had two profitable weeks in a row.

Though it wasn't vaudeville in the great two-a-day Palace tradition, it obviously pleased enough people to keep the theater going successfully for something more than two years. And it did give an impetus to vaudeville all over the country. Units went out intact from their engagements at 47th Street and Broadway and played in many cities with the Palace name once again working its old magic.

Most of the acts were new and young, recruited from radio, night clubs, and TV. A few, like Kaye Ballard, Johnny Downs, Dorothy Loudon, and Art Lund, went on to success in the theater and/or films, but nothing truly tremendous emerged from this revival. However, quite a number of old favorites showed up on the bills from time to time to serve as reminders of the late great days. The Watson Sisters, for example, and John Steel; Frances Williams, Irene Bordoni, Shaw and Lee, and Gus Van; Buck and Bubbles; and Will Mahoney, still dancing on that xylophone.

Joe Jackson did the tramp bicycle act in July 1950, but this time around it was Joe Jackson, Jr. Pat Rooney (Senior) came back to the Palace once more that same July, just a few months before he scored his heartwarming hit in *Guys and Dolls*. There was a second anniversary program, with less fanfare this time, but with the one and only Belle Baker and the indestructible team of Smith and Dale.

Smith and Dale, by any count, probably played the Palace as often as any act that ever trod those boards. And, one way or another, they were involved in several history-making events there, among them the Palace fire of 1932. Later they shared the bill with a young woman, the doomed bearer of a great theatrical name, making her only appearance at the Palace some thirty years after her illustrious aunt had played her last engagement there. The family name was Barrymore, the young woman's name was Diana; she was the daughter of John.

On the 4th of October 1951, after a week of undistinguished vaudeville (there was a man on the bill with the curious name of Alfredo Landon) and a picture, *The Tall Target*, starring Dick Powell, the Palace went dark . . . but only for two weeks.

CHAPTER NINE

ON THE 16th of October 1951 the sleeping beauty was *really* awakened. Only it wasn't a prince who woke her, and it wasn't with a kiss. It was a princess named Judy Garland, and she did it with a song, a whole trunkful of songs. What is there to say about Judy Garland that hasn't been said before, and how to tell it without turning admiration into idolatry, enthusiasm into hysteria, sympathy into bathos?

It is virtually impossible, but it can be summed up in the words of a nine-year-old who was taken to hear her. He had seen *The Wizard of Oz*, but this was his first visit to a live theater. At the end of the show, Judy sat down on the stage, her feet dangling over the footlights, and sang "Over the Rainbow." After the applause and cheering had died down, it was hard to rouse the boy from the spell she had cast, hard to get him out of the theater. All the way home he was silent, silent and contemplative. He didn't hear what was said to him; he seemed to be in some other place, somewhere far away, lost in a dream. Then at last he spoke: "You know," he said with a deep sigh, "this has been the greatest experience of my life."

The facts are simple. Beset by troubles, private and professional, the little girl whose wistful face and wonderful voice had won the whole world's love departed from MGM and Hollywood and embarked upon a four-month tour of Europe, ending with a spectacular engagement at the London Palladium. It was this engagement with its international headlines that brought her the invitation to come to the Palace. Sol Schwartz was responsible for that invitation.

There was some something particularly right about Judy playing the Palace. Some ten years earlier, in the film *For Me and My Gal* (with Gene Kelly), she had portrayed a girl whose one great dream was to play the Palace. And before that, when hardly more than a child, she had sung a duet in a musical film with Sophie Tucker, the *grande dame* of all Palace dames. Even earlier, as a small child, she had been a vaudevillian singing in a trio as Frances Gumm of the Gumm Sisters, when George Jessel, on the same bill, gave her the name of Judy Garland.

After several weeks of darkness the Palace was ready for Judy. The theater had been refurbished, dressing rooms redecorated, crystal chandeliers restored, even some of the old Albee art collection brought back from other theaters to decorate the lobby. Her act was staged by Charles Walters, costumes designed by Irene Sharaff and Pierre Balmain.

Max Meth was the musical director and Hugh Martin (who with Ralph Blaine had written one of her greatest hits, "The Trolley Song,") was at the piano. Sid Luft, her manager and later her husband, supervised the entire production.

The first half of her Palace program was a typical bigtime vaudeville bill, the kind that had brought the Palace its years of fame and fortune. On that bill were the Langs, an acrobatic act; Doodles and Spider, who silently acted out popular records; the European dancers, Giselle and Francis Szony (who later appeared with Ed Wynn in his award-winning TV show); Max Bygraves, a clever English comedian in his American debut; a group of young men collectively billed as Judy's Boy Friends; and the grand old team of Smith and Dale, already marking a half-century together.

On the 16th of October 1951, the big night arrived. The red carpet was literally rolled out for a distinguished and eager audience. The reception overwhelmed her; the house cheered and wept and overflowed with joy for the little girl who had overcome so many tribulations, as if this were happening to one of their own—a little sister or, even more, a child. That was one of the secrets of Judy's appeal. No matter what she did, she was everybody's darling.

Buoyed by the reviews and the response of her audiences, she worked too hard, gave too much of herself for even that strong little body to bear. And during the Sunday matinee of her fourth week she collapsed on stage and couldn't continue. Vivian Blaine, then starring as the pathetically funny Miss Adelaide in *Guys and Dolls*, left her seat in the orchestra, took the stage, and proceeded to hold the audience for a full twenty minutes. When she had finished, comedian Jan

Murray took her place for another twenty minutes.

For a few days after that the Palace went dark again and rumors were rife, but the following Friday Judy came back, rested, restored, and more loved than ever. Her entrance was greeted by a tremendous ovation. The interruption and its consequent publicity had only whetted the public's appetite for Judy. Though her original booking had been for just four weeks, the run was extended twice, until it piled up a total of nineteen weeks, almost twice as long as that reached by any previous performer. Some old-time vaudevillians and their fans, of course, refused to count this long-run record, not regarding the show as true vaudeville.

The business for those nineteen weeks was about $750,000—that is, the actual Palace business. Top at the time was a reasonable $4.80, but ticket speculators were getting as high as $30 a pair. Sol Schwartz, reminiscing, says ruefully, "We didn't know what we had in advance, and didn't want to raise prices after the smash reviews."

During Judy's run, there were a few changes in the supporting company. The Langs gave way to another acrobatic act, the Christianis. Along about the eighth week Max Bygraves was replaced by Señor Wences, the brilliant Spanish ventriloquist, who painted an entracing little dummy on his hand in full view of the audience. Still later Doodles and Spider left, to be followed by the Nicholas Brothers, a highly gifted pair of dancers. One more change was the replacement of the Christianis by an act called the Shyrettos.

The final night of the Garland run at the Palace occasioned an almost unprecedented emotional experience. *Almost* unprecedented, because people with long enough memories can recall the emotional binge that accompanied every one of Al Jolson's closing nights, or the wildly hysterical salute given Geraldine Farrar after her farewell appearance at the Met. One special thing these three had in common, separate from and perhaps even greater than their unquestioned talent, was the gift of capturing the imagination of the audience as human beings. Their quality of personal radiance embraced each and every person in the house as if nothing in the world existed but that collection of people.

That final night, the 24th of February, saw a tremendous outpouring of love from the girl on the stage to the people who jammed the house. And when, exhausted by her generous encores and her overstrung emotions, she begged them to let her go, they answered by singing "Auld Lang Syne." Sentimental? Schmaltzy? Corny? Of course. But what a lovely night!

After Judy's record-breaking run, the Palace went back to its original two-a-day straight vaudeville policy. The first bill was topped by such disparate headliners as Lauritz Melchior, the great Metropolitan Opera tenor, and Ben Blue, the pixie-like comic with the sly eyes and the slippery feet. Melchior's singing ranged from Wagnerian arias to semipop standards. Imposing in white tie and tails and an impressive array of decorations, he "radiated conviviality, dignity and charm," in the words of one reviewer. Supporting acts included Leo de Lyon, a budding comedian; Jean Carroll, a ditto comedienne; the Chandra Kaly Dancers; and Les Compagnons de la Chanson, a collection of young male singers who had come to this country with Edith Piaf. A soap-opera sketch called *Long Distance* was dropped after the first performance. With that deletion, reviews were good, the bill seemed well balanced, but it just didn't draw. "Head-line-wise," *Variety* said, "the parlay had plenty and yet it was a loser."

Next came those wild old knockabout zanies Olsen and Johnson, in a cut-down version of their stage revue *Hellza-poppin'* with a company of thirty-four. José Greco and his ballet troupe headlined the first half of the bill, with Rudy Cardenas, Bunin's Puppets, and comedian Jackie Miles rounding out the show. It should have worked—certainly Olsen and Johnson were long-time favorites and Greco had built up a strong following—but again it didn't. *Variety*, in a characteristic headline, said: FROM TOUR JETÉ TO "IRISH JUSTICE" AT PALACE, BUT IS THIS VAUDEVILLE?

Judy Garland's sensational run had changed the habits of audiences and the history of the Palace. From that moment on, audiences would not be satisfied with anything less than a blockbuster. And following three weeks of Palace darkness, a blockbuster was what they got: Betty Hutton, the young tornado from Paramount Pictures, who had just ended a tour of army bases in Korea. Betty, who had inherited Jean Harlow's sobriquet "The Blonde Bombshell," was really more reminiscent of that earlier tornado, Eva Tanguay.

Betty's Palace show, which opened on April 12 with a $40,000 advance sale, was a walloping success. For fifty minutes she held the stage—singing, dancing, clowning, and doing imitations of former Palace stars, among them Blossom Seeley, around whose life she had made a picture, *Somebody Loves Me*.

Covering her act for the *Times*, Lewis Funke wrote: "If

219

she stops bouncing for sixty seconds in the entire fifty minutes, it isn't clear to the naked eye." He added that thus far
lexicographers had failed to come up with an adequate de-
scription of her energy. Supporting acts included the Sky-
larks, a popular recording quintet; Herb Shriner, the ra-
dio-TV monologist; and Borrah Minevitch's Harmonica
Rascals. A few days after her opening, *Variety* summed up
the situation in a headline: PALACE TWO-A-DAY NEEDS A
HUTTON OR GARLAND TO MAKE POLICY STICK. Acknowl-
edging that the routine shows had been pretty good, the
story went on to say that they exerted no magnetism. "It has
to be a headliner—there is no in between seemingly."

There just weren't enough headliners of the Garland/
Hutton caliber to provide constant booking for that kind
of show. Where were the stars of yesteryear? Two of them
were dead—W. C. Fields and Fanny Brice. Sophie Tucker
stuck to the night clubs. The rest—Eddie Cantor, Jack
Benny, Ed Wynn, Burns and Allen, Jimmy Durante, Bob
Hope—were in Hollywood working in movies, radio, television, or all three. They were older now, and enjoying the
comforts of their attractive homes, swimming pools, big cars,
and large staffs of servants. They had the glory and they
didn't need the money. Besides, they could reach more people
in one hour, or maybe only one half-hour, than they could
possibly reach in a year at the Palace.

Only two kinds of stars were receptive to the Palace lure
—the ones who had spent not wisely but too well, and the
ones with an insatiable need for a live audience to play to.
And there were only a few of those. So, when Betty Hutton
ended her four-week engagement, the Palace once more went

back to the Schwartz 1949 policy of eight vaudeville acts and a movie. And that policy prevailed, with a few notable but intermittent exceptions, for a long time.

The first exception was Danny Kaye, who opened at the Palace on Sunday night, January 18, 1953. His brilliant gifts and quicksilver charm had long since established him as one of the outstanding personalities as well as one of the truly great performers of his own or any other time. He, too, had behind him a series of successful movies, the latest of which was *Hans Christian Andersen*. He, like Judy Garland, had recently returned from a sensational engagement at the London Palladium. He had given a command performance for King George VI and had formed friendships with the younger and livelier members of the royal family, giving rise to the quip that he made good at the palace even before he made good at the Palace.

Like Judy Garland, he ended his act sitting on the edge of the stage, long legs dangling, talking and joking as though the audience was one big happy family, which indeed it was. Unlike Judy, Danny had nothing of the waif about him, nothing to tug at the heartstrings, no implicit history of sorrow and pain—it was all pure joy. He simply made people feel *good*. That was *his* special secret.

It was Brooks Atkinson himself who covered the Kaye opening for the *Times*. "For an hour and three quarters," wrote Mr. Atkinson, "everybody, including Danny, was having a wonderful time. He was all amiability, with no suggestion of patronage or unction in his manner. His whole act seemed like pure improvisation."

Variety's tone was more exuberant. "An atomic bomb

struck New York over the weekend," said the review. "But there were no casualties. There was no panic. Just an audienc bewitched and held spellbound by a blond blockbuster named Danny Kaye. For one hour and forty minutes Kaye held a gala opening night audience at the Palace in a vise-like grip that was in the finest tradition of this famed playhouse of the two-a-day era."

All this was straight Kaye. No production, no extravagant scenery, no high-style attire. Kaye worked the whole show in a sports jacket and slacks against a black backdrop. With him was a first-rate collection of performers including Darvas and Julia, European dancers; the singer Fran Warren; and that marvelous Marquis family of comic monkeys who later appeared on television with Jack Benny and Ed Sullivan.

The Kaye show ran fourteen weeks at the Palace and set a record for Palace grosses over that period of time— $893,630 and a few cents, for anyone interested in figures. Danny gave 135 performances and played to 243,250 people.

His closing performance on April 26 was not an occasion for tears and sentimental sighs. The audience simply loved him, and most of them, it was said, had come just for a second helping. The only note of sentiment was the gift of a gold bracelet from the usherettes and the other front-of-the-house employees.

The next big show didn't come along till fall, when Betty Hutton returned for an engagement limited to four weeks. She opened on the evening of October 14 with a $50,000 advance sale after only thirteen days' notice of her forthcoming appearance. The show was what is known as a boffo and its greatest surprise, an attraction equaling Miss Hutton herself, appeared in the person of a new young comic named Dick Shawn. He went on before the act that closed the first half of the bill and the lobby buzzed with excitement during intermission.

"For the history books," wrote Abel Green, "young Mr. Shawn will go down in the decadent vaudeville annals as being one act who was 'made' in a straight vaudeville theatre as late as the fall of 1953. He is a personable young man destined for the heights. The records may well prove that a star was born at Betty Hutton's comeback to the Palace, October 14, 1953."

And that is exactly what the records do prove. His Palace appearance with Betty Hutton indeed made a star of Dick Shawn. Before the opening he had very modest billing— small letters on the same line as Bil and Cora Baird and their Marionettes. He didn't even, as comedians usually do, have the spot next to intermission—that was given to the Chavalos. But next day, as in all the trite but often true stories, his name went up in lights along with Miss Hutton's.

"And it was Betty who made them put it there," he said. "If it hadn't been for that engagement I might still be playing small cafés like the Village Barn, where I had worked just a year before at $125 a week. I only got on that bill by accident. The William Morris office needed someone to go on for fifteen minutes in the first half, and for some reason or other they picked me."

Asked if he had been nervous on opening night, he said no. "At first I didn't have sense enough to be nervous—the

Palace tradition meant nothing to me; I didn't grow up in New York and I'd never been on a stage before. Then, when I heard the roars of laughter, I was too stunned to be nervous. For the rest of the run I kept on being stunned."

Among the celebrities in the house that night was Marlene Dietrich, shortly to do her first night-club act at the Sahara in Las Vegas. At a party after the show she came to Shawn and asked him to be on the bill with her. P.S., he took the job, and his salary jumped from $1,500 to $7,500 per week.

He was as big a hit in Las Vegas as he had been at the Palace, and since then his career has been an almost unbroken succession of hits: in night clubs, television, and on Broadway in both musicals and straight comedies. He replaced Zero Mostel in *A Funny Thing Happened on the Way to the Forum*. As of this writing he is again a big hit as the hillbilly Hitler in Mel Brooks' wild movie comedy *The Producers*, which also stars Mostel.

Now and then during the ensuing few years, while the Palace waited for another blockbuster, there was a break in the eight-acts-and-picture routine. For example, one week in August 1955 the whole show was taken over by Phil Spitalny and his All Girl Orchestra, a popular radio and television group of the period, featuring the lady known as Evelyn and Her Magic Violin.

The following November, country music invaded the Palace; *The Grand Ole Opry* replaced the regular acts. Starring were such country favorites as Roy Acuff, Pap and His Jug Band, the Tennessee Mountain Boys, Cedar Hill Square Dancers, the Smokey Mountain Boys, and a particular favorite of country-music addicts (who by that time were numerous), Kitty Wells, the top female vocalist in that field. About Miss Wells, the liner note on one of her albums says: "Kitty has another first that will stand for all time. She was the first female Country and Western singer to play that high court of the entertainment world—the Palace."

It was during this interim period that one of the Palace's former favorites, who had fallen upon evil times, made a remarkable and happy comeback. That was Lillian Roth, whose book *I'll Cry Tomorrow* gave an honest and moving account of her struggle to overcome alcoholism.

But it was three years, less three weeks, after Betty Hutton's second engagement before a blockbuster hit the Palace again. On November 26, 1956, after a tremendous advance build-up and an enormous advance sale, Judy Garland came back. Since her first triumphant appearance there in 1951, Judy had had more than her share of notoriety and disasters, which seemed only to consolidate her hold upon the public imagination.

This time there was not only a red carpet outside the Palace, but police barricades to keep the frenetic fans under control. The ovation that greeted her entrance outdid anything that had gone before; the critics brought out all their superlatives. If Alexander Woollcott had lived to see the day, he most certainly would have danced in the aisles and thrown his hat in the air. Walter Kerr said: "Last night at the Palace it was perfect." John McClain: "You can kick a thesaurus around the evening long for a word to describe that peculiar magic peddled by Judy." Abel Green wrote: "She makes a Brill Building lyric sound like a Shakespeare sonnet." The Brill Building, it should be explained, was—

and still is—HQ for that nonexistent street known as Tin Pan Alley. Whitney Bolton rhapsodized: "When she starts to sing, the larks pack up and move away."

The first half of the bill included the Amin Brothers, acrobats; Bob Williams, a young man whose limp and listless dog refused to do any of the tricks his hapless master demanded of him; Kovach and Rabovsky, a team of Hungarian dancers; Judy's Twelve Boy Friends; and Alan King.

Those two somewhat different critics, Brooks Atkinson and Abel Green, each commented favorably not only on Judy but on the entire show. "Since vaudeville is officially dead," wrote Mr. Atkinson, "it is astonishing to find five excellent acts flourishing as though nothing grim had ever happened."

And speaking of the then little-known comic Alan King, who was the featured act in the first half of the bill, the *Times* man said: "He delivers an uproarious polemic against the insanity of life in the suburbs." He did indeed, establishing an immediate empathy with all the men in the audience while at the same time creating a sense of recognition among the women.

Abel Green wrote: "The first half of the bill is as solid a chunk of big-time vaudeville as the history of the medium in its most halcyon days would want. . . . The first-half comedy surprise was a stand-up comedian, Alan King. King has been around, but he has never clicked as resoundingly as here."

Like his colleague Dick Shawn, Alan King was "born" at the Palace. He had started in the Catskills at fifteen and never got beyond small night clubs until his agent (Larry

Barnett of MCA) and Sol Schwartz sold him sight unseen to Judy and Sid Luft. "I didn't meet them until rehearsals began," he said recently, "and even then there was practically no communication. I was pretty unhappy about the whole thing, especially when I found I was billed under the Hungarian dance team. Not only that, but I didn't get the next-to-closing spot in the first half. I almost quit, but Mr. Schwartz and my agent talked me into staying."

It would be mock modesty on Alan King's part to put on the cloak of humility. The roars of the audience told him he was a hit. "I went to my dressing room," he said, "proud, but pretty mad. I was sitting there brooding over it when there was a sudden knock on the door." It was Judy, in make-up and bathrobe, almost ready to go on. "You can close my show any time you like," she said, and vanished. From the next day on he did. And, naturally, he was no longer billed below the dancers.

Alan King has nothing but praise for Judy Garland, not only because she started him on the road to his present eminence but also because of her kindness, especially to performers. "For instance, when an old pro on that bill stayed on too long and held up the running time, they were going to give him his notice," recalled King. "But Judy heard about it and insisted on keeping him."

Today the name of Alan King is tops in practically every branch of show business: television, night clubs, legitimate theater, both as actor—he had a big success in 1965–66 in the comedy *The Impossible Years*—and as a producer. During that same season Mr. King was co-producer of *The Lion in Winter*, a drama about King Henry II of England, robustly played on the stage by Robert Preston. He is also the author of a couple of highly entertaining books.

After Judy had been at the Palace a few weeks during her 1956 run, Sol Schwartz gave her a gold key to the star dressing room, henceforth to be known as the Judy Garland Room. For a while all went beautifully, but by mid-November Judy began to be plagued by laryngitis and had to miss several performances. On December 12 it was announced that she would take a week's vacation between the 19th and 26th; actually, she did three shows that week but had to give up. This started a new crop of rumors about the true nature of her illness; considerable doubt was expressed in the columns and on Broadway that she would return to the show at all.

Return she did, however. The box office, which had slipped considerably during her absence, climbed back to $50,000, which at a $7.50 top was just about capacity. Her second Palace engagement ended on Tuesday evening, January 8, 1957, giving her a total of fifteen weeks.

The next big explosion was Jerry Lewis. Having recently, with deplorable bitterness and widespread publicity, broken off his longtime night-club and film partnership with Dean Martin, the madcap Lewis came in to the Palace on February 8, 1957. His booking was limited to four weeks and the advance sale was a phenomenal $90,000, with a top ticket set at $6.00.

Surprisingly, in view of his customary brashness, Jerry had a noticeable attack of opening-night nerves. Maybe not so surprising, since it was his debut as a solo turn and there had been more than a little wondering whether either he or Dean Martin could go it alone successfully. He met that unspoken but strongly felt challenge right off the bat. "I used to double," he said, "but"—gesturing to the Aristocrats, an octet of young male singers and dancers who backed him up—"now I've cut it down to eight."

That broke the ice; the audience roared approval and Lewis leaped vigorously into his familiar zany antics. He sang, he danced, he cavorted, he did the monkey bit, he slipped in his false buck teeth and went into his Japanese routine. He even coaxed his audience into joining him in a chorus of "Shine On, Harvest Moon," and when one recalcitrant gentleman failed to sing along, Jerry clambered up the proscenium into a box and tried persuasion by methods something less than orthodox. In other words, he acted like Jerry Lewis.

Though a few reviewers took exception to some slightly off-color material and felt the act was more suited to a night club than to the Palace, the critical consensus was favorable. "Ninety minutes of Jerry Lewis," wrote Abel Green, "with his great versatility, makes this Palace excursion very worth while. That Lewis had first-night jitters is incidental, because despite the somewhat uphill struggle, it cannot be denied that he has nothing but talent and is as potent a comic as there is to be found in front of a mike—electronic, saloon or podium. *Vaudeville is not dead.*"

The first half of the Lewis show attested strongly to the accuracy of that statement. Among the acts were two particularly outstanding turns. The first was a Continental trio, the Wiere Brothers, who sang, danced, clowned, mimed, and played the fiddle with consummate skill. They were not new to vaudeville, but they had never had the kind of exposure given them at the Palace. They were a solid click.

So was the other newcomer—Eydie Gormé, a pert little brunette with a big voice, who had won quite a following as a recording artist and as a steady performer on the Steve Allen TV show. Her Palace appearance was her first on any stage. She scored an unqualified hit, and without a doubt provided one answer to the oft-repeated cliché: "Where's the new talent coming from?"

Taking her final bow on that exciting night, Miss Gormé with charm and grace dealt a blow—and one could wish it had been a knockout blow—to another oft-repeated cliché. "It's difficult to be humble," she said, beaming with well-earned pleasure, "when I feel so proud." What a relief to hear just one performer not protesting humility!

From that moment on, Eydie Gormé's career moved straight and steadily upward. Now she is the happy wife of Steve Lawrence, the recording, night-club, and TV singer and the Sammy of *What Makes Sammy Run?* They have two children, and at this writing are co-starring in the Broadway musical *Golden Rainbow*.

Jerry Lewis's first week hit $61,500, a new high for the Palace. From the demand for tickets it looked as if he could have remained there at least six weeks longer; unfortunately he had an unbreakable film commitment and could stay only a few days past his original booking, which took in more than $275,000.

On his closing night, March 13, Lewis was the recipient of two gifts, one silver, the other gold. Sol Schwartz on behalf of the management gave him a silver tray, engraved with the front of the Palace. And Steve Allen presented him with a gold platter of his "Rockabye Your Baby" recording, which had sold a million copies.

The ensuing weeks made it ever more apparent that eight acts of routine vaudeville and a motion picture were simply not good enough. Palace patrons, conditioned now to the high-powered entertainment of a Garland, a Hutton, a Kaye, or a Lewis, couldn't settle for anything as modest as the ordinary bill. It was like offering people rice pudding and milk after caviar and champagne.

The big question was where to get the great entertainers, the magnetic attractions that had put the Palace back on the big-time map after years in the doldrums. It is ironic that the big-star factor which had restored the famous theater to its old-time glory was responsible for still another downhill slide.

The fact is, there were simply not enough stellar attractions available to keep the Palace running on the glamour basis. Management made repeated efforts to acquire the big names and finally came up with a notion that seemed little short of genius. Having failed to make much of a dent on the younger set with a series of "diskers" (pop recording stars), someone had the brilliant idea of offering the Palace to that curly-haired, dimpled, be-sequined darling of the rocking-chair set, Liberace. After weeks of negotiation, that much derided and much adored virtuoso of the piano was booked into the Palace for an engagement of four weeks, starting April 20, 1957.

The scene outside the Palace at Liberace's opening performance was as close to a riot as it was possible to get. Hordes of the faithful, largely blue-haired, flower-hatted ladies of a certain age, milled around the entrance. Ticket holders had to fight their way in with the strength and agility of a broken-field runner in a game between the Green Bay Packers and the New York Giants.

Once within, they swarmed down the aisles like a cloud of brightly colored dragonflies, buzzing with happy anticipation. To be perfectly fair, there were a few younger women in the audience and even a smattering of men, but the Liberace idolators were predominantly middle- or very aged matrons, come to watch and worship the ideal son they'd always longed for, whether they had sons of their own or not.

Restively they sat through the first half of the show, but when at last their idol made his entrance the buzz rose to a composite squeal of ecstasy probably never equaled till the Beatles came along a generation later.

The full Liberace regalia graced the stage: the brilliant, glittering evening clothes, which he changed seven or eight times during the course of his performance; the candelabra atop the gleaming piano, the equally gleaming toothpaste-ad smile, the winsome ways, the ever deepening dimples.

His performance held no surprises. It was exactly what he had been doing on television and in personal appearances when, to the gibes of his critics and the joy of his fans, he had been "crying all the way to the bank." He trotted out his whole routine: played the piano with the usual trills and arpeggios, essayed a soft-shoe dance in which he was likened by one observer to an overweight burlesque chorus girl, told a few not very funny jokes, and smiled with an air of modesty that entranced his worshipers.

The audience on the whole responded with delirious joy. The press, on the whole, responded with what at best can be called modified rapture. The only real praise went to Mitzi Green, the former child vaudevillian, now grown up and doing her imitations of famous old-timers; and a skillful juggler named Francis Brunn.

It had long been a favorite sport to kid Liberace, who managed to take everything with good humor, reminding his baiters from time to time that nobody liked him but the public. Repeating the panning administered to him is like shooting a sitting duck, but a couple of comments from those who felt that his charm somehow eluded them may be worth noting briefly.

"He opened at variety's sacred citadel," wrote Lewis Funke in the *Times*, "supported by brother George, the Liberace Symphony Orchestra . . . and a double dose of treacle and honey." And a long magazine review was written by a man who by some freak of fortune had never seen him before. The magazine was *Cue* and the man, John Keating. "His lengthy act," wrote Mr. Keating, "is a tasteless mélange of mediocrity sicklied over by the cloying sweetness of the Liberace personality. . . . He will try anything and isn't at all deterred by the fact that he has no talent for any of the things attempted. Even his piano playing is a fraud, a thing of runs and flourishes, as flashy and meretricious as his 'showmanship.' "

Tough-minded *Variety*, however, ran a good review and predicted big business. Liberace was, the reviewer wrote, "a versatile performer with a highly developed sense of show-manship able to deliver in several directions. He will please the bulk of the audiences that come to hear him, especially the distaff side."

For some reason never exactly determined, Liberace did not do well at the box office. In truth, although business was bad all over Broadway, the Palace suffered the most. The first week's business was a small $34,000 and the second week dropped $10,000 from that low gross. The show, originally booked for four weeks, lasted only two, and the Candelabra Kid, as he was being called by his detractors, was said to have lost a healthy wad. It was reported that he paid for the whole show and had the theater on a 65/35-percent basis, so it seems probable that if he cried all the way to the bank, it was to take some money out.

After the closing was announced, an interesting phenomenon occurred. "The show is not dying peaceably," *Variety* said. "Howls from all segments of society are flooding newspapers. Many critics are getting letters from both men and women for having rapped their idol and contributed to his demise . . . and those who bravoed the show were kudoed by fans with kind letters." But outraged letters to unkind critics were not backed up by lines at the box office, and that marked the end of Liberace at the Palace.

For a short time after Liberace's departure and an unsuccessful attempt to get Noel Coward for an engagement, the Palace management once again fell back on its eight-vaude-ville-acts-and-a-movie policy, but it was just no go. On August 13, 1957, vaudeville gave up the ghost, and the theater went into a straight picture policy, opening with *Man of a Thousand Faces,* starring James Cagney, and based on the life of Lon Chaney.

The straight picture policy lasted about eight years, making the Palace just one more Broadway movie theater and a rather seedy one at that. Only once was this policy abandoned, for the Harry Belafonte engagement.

From the overpowering sweetness and light of Liberace to the cool, almost remote presence of Belafonte, from the calculated boyishness and sugary sentimentality of the one to the taut, take-it-or-leave-it attitude of the other, the distance was immeasurable, even without consideration of their respective talents. Liberace was unabashedly Mother's Boy. Belafonte was unquestionably nobody's boy but his own.

While the Garland, Hutton, Kaye, and Lewis shows all carried on the vaudeville tradition, even though departing somewhat from what the purists call true vaudeville format, Belafonte's show could not under any possible definition be called vaudeville.

His performance was in essence a recital, a one-man show. He brought to the Palace what he had been doing in theaters all over the world since his great success in *Three for Tonight,* a 1955 revue in which he co-starred with Marge and Gower Champion. Even before that he had built up a strong core of followers among record collectors and what might be described as the intellectual night spots.

Attempting the Palace was a tough decision for him to make. As a youth from Harlem he had haunted the Palace the way his schoolmates had haunted the ball parks, never dreaming that someday he would walk through the stage door as a star instead of sneaking in through the side entrance as an uninvited guest. It worried him when Sol Schwartz, still president of RKO, offered him an eight-week booking with options for an indefinite stay.

Could his type of program succeed at the Palace? he asked Mr. Schwartz. He had no comics on the bill to precede him, no acrobats, no famous old vaudeville names. He had only himself, backed up by a male quartet, a couple of guitarists, a drummer, and a bass violin, with a very small orchestra in the pit. He would be onstage the whole evening except for intermission. What should he do? "Just do the same things you're doing now," Mr. Schwartz assured him, "and you won't have a single problem."

Mr. Schwartz was right. From that day in September 1959 when the Belafonte show was announced until the opening night, December 15, and after, the line at the box office was endless. The advance sale rang up a staggering $200,000 with tickets ranging from a top of $7.50 to the lowest price in years for a stellar show—$1.75—this at the insistence of Belafonte, who wanted in his audience people who couldn't afford to pay more.

Despite the tremendous advance sale, Belafonte opened scared. "I don't think," he wrote in *The Theatre* of April 1960, "I've ever been so nervous or filled with anxiety as I was that night. It wasn't like opening at just any theatre—it was not only the Palace, it was *A* Palace, the fabulous place where great names had appeared and created a legend . . . names like Eddie Cantor, Ethel Barrymore, Jack Benny, Frank Fay, Billy Gaxton, Pat Rooney, Sarah Bernhardt and hundreds of others had contributed to that legend. And

236

now it was my turn; would I become part of that legend?"

It didn't take long to get the answer. He came on quietly, with no fanfare, no manufactured build-up, wearing the black breeches, the wide-ringed belt, and the open shirt that had become his trademark. There was no set, just two large screens flanking the stage, designed by Ralph Alswang, one of the theater's most gifted scenic and lighting artists. On these screens shifting shadows played a visual accompaniment to Belafonte's singing. Unobtrusively behind him were his quartet and instrumentalists, who sometimes joined him, sometimes not. Either way it was his evening, and his alone.

He made no pitch to the audience. In fact, there were moments when his concentration was so intense that he seemed to be looking past the audience into some faraway place of his own. It was almost as if he were in a hypnotic trance, a trance that hypnotized his audience along with himself. He sang the songs people had come to associate with him—"John Henry," the moving "Take My Mother Home," the lilting "Matilda," and many others, including an Israeli folk song called "Havah Nageelah."

Only once in the course of the evening did he make any direct contact with the audience; that was when he did "The Saints Go Marching In" and coaxed the people out front to join him. The audience loved it, though some of the critics felt it would have been better for him to keep his emotional distance all the way. Everyone agreed, however, that he had a quality that was both earthy and mystical, always magical.

John McClain, writing in the *Journal-American*, referred

to his unpretentious sex appeal. Unpretentious it may have
been but not uncalculated. Any man who wears tight pants
and a shirt open all the way down cannot be totally unaware
of the sex appeal of such a costume covering a slim and
handsome body.

"What emerges as an informal evening with Mr. Belafonte," McClain went on, "is as uncontrived as a General
Motors Board Meeting, but as with GM it pays off." Pay off
it most assuredly did. For the first week, six performances
—Tuesday through Saturday evenings and a Sunday matinee—Belafonte played to standing room only and the house
grossed $45,000.

During the course of his engagement Belafonte reached
his thirty-third birthday, and at the end of the show the
Palace staff surprised him by wheeling a huge birthday cake
on stage. After the excitement had died down, the audience
called for more, and he went into an encore. Suddenly the
audience burst into howls of laughter, which surprised him
even more, because he wasn't singing a funny song. Looking
around, he discovered that Pat Boone and Bobby Darin, who
had been in the audience, had appeared on stage from opposite wings, dressed in Belafonte costumes and mimicking his
characteristic mannerisms. At this point Belafonte lost what
would now be called his cool, and joined his audience in
hysterical laughter.

By the next night he had resumed his controlled perfection, that tense and electrifying quality, the air of a man
with a mission and a message, that zeal which caused *Variety*
to say: "It's this added air that sets Belafonte apart." Long

before his original eight weeks were up, his options had been lifted, and he stayed at the Palace more than three months, with almost all of them capacity. So his anxiety had been unnecessary. Belafonte had made his own contribution to the Palace legend, and had joined the Palace immortals.

CHAPTER TEN

A WISE MAN once said, "Happy is the country that has no history." Conversely it might be said, "Unhappy is the Palace that has no history." And from that raw March in 1960 when Harry Belafonte walked off the stage of the Palace, the Palace had no history—at any rate, not for five years.

During that period the Palace was just one more movie house in the growing clutter of movie houses, some of them former legitimate theaters, strung along Broadway between 42nd to 51st Streets; an undistinguished movie house, operating on a grind basis from early morning till late at night, at popular prices. The first picture following Belafonte was a reissue of *The Glenn Miller Story*, starring James Stewart and June Allyson. After that came a steady stream of routine movies, from absurdities like *Hercules Unchained* to

240

romantic dramas like Edna Ferber's *Ice Palace* to psycho-
logical thrillers like *Portrait in Black*. Once in a while there
would be a special event, such as *Sunrise at Campobello*,
Dore Schary's film based on his play about F.D.R., which
played on a reserved-seat basis at a two-dollar top.

It is interesting to note that those cathedrals of the motion
picture which had hurt the legitimate theaters of the thirties
and forties, and very nearly destroyed the Palace, were now
succumbing to a decay of their own. No more were the
mighty Wurlitzers and colossal stage shows offered to the
public at bargain prices. The splendiferous interiors were
gone; so too were the baroque ornaments, the sweeping stair-
ways, the gallant ushers in military gear. The originally
gaudy walls were hidden by acres of fiberglas hangings, and
the seating capacities drastically cut down by closing off the
back rows of the orchestra and the upper balcony. The
Strand, the Capitol, Loew's State, all of which had contributed to the decline of the Palace a couple of decades before,
were themselves victims of television, the rapacious monster
that ate up entertainment faster than it could be created.

The crowning blow came in the summer of 1960, only a
short time after the Palace's conversion to pictures, when the
Roxy, that ambitious dream of S. L. Rothafel, fell to the
wrecking crews, making way for one more midtown office
building. Lucky Roxy—he had not lived to see this happen.
Now there was only one colossus left, Radio City Music
Hall, regal and majestic on its crowded corner, a corner very
nearly replacing Times Square as the Crossroads of the
World.

The last movie shown at the Roxy was an unremembered

item called *The Wind Cannot Read*. Still remembered by
many, though, is a newspaper photograph of Gloria Swanson, stunning and stylish as ever, standing in the rubble on
the day the Roxy's last walls came tumbling down. Resplendent in evening gown, arms outflung, smiling a brave,
compassionate smile, and trailing a feather boa, she made a
dramatic contrast to the surrounding dust and destruction.
There was something both poignant and appropriate about
her presence there. It had been a Swanson film that marked
the beginning of the Roxy. Now a Swanson picture of another sort marked its end.

If the opening of the Roxy had seriously hurt the Palace,
its closing came too late to help. No more crowds milled
around the theater, no more actors lounged along the beach.
Most of its audiences went there because they had missed a
picture during its first run or because it was cheap or because their feet were tired or because they had nowhere else
to go. Its lost existence as *The Palace* could have been
summed up by an old Irving Berlin song: "Nobody Knows
and Nobody Seems to Care."

But that was not quite true. At least two people knew and
cared very much—a young man named Paul Vroom and
another young man named Jack Perlman. Vroom, born to
theatrical tradition, was manager of the Lunt-Fontanne
Theatre, an aristocrat of the legitimate playhouses. Jack
Perlman was a lawyer with a considerable theatrical clien-
tele. The two young men were friends; they both loved the
theater. Paul remembered the Palace with nostalgia, and
Perlman cherished an urge to represent a theater. Both recognized an existing problem: the lack of legitimate theaters

to house the plays hovering out of town like planes stacked
up over Kennedy Airport on a busy Sunday. There were
rumors that the Palace, sinking further and further into
obsolescence, was doomed to destruction as wrecking balls
hurled themselves about all over town. The Palace might be
the next to go. So—why not find a purchaser for the Palace?
They tried. They tried and tried and tried. There was no
trouble lining up the financing. The trouble lay with the
owner, RKO.

By this time RKO was a subsidiary of a giant company,
Glen Alden. Glen Alden had bought the theater chain from
Howard Hughes, who had acquired it, along with the RKO
Studios in Hollywood, somewhere along the way. Hughes
kept the studio, but divested himself of the theaters, including the Palace. The rumors that the Palace was facing destruction were false, Vroom and Perlman had been told. The
Palace was making money. Sol Schwartz, still president,
scoffed at the idea of selling.

"He still clung to the idea of reviving vaudeville," Paul
Vroom said later, "and while he was president there was no
chance of the theater being sold." But rumors of doom still
persisted, and so did Vroom and Perlman. Though not an
official New York landmark, the Palace was a landmark
nevertheless, important and precious to many people. Also
its strategic location with frontage on Broadway appealed to
the practical Mr. Perlman. "After all," he said, "the theater
would never have to be dark. You could always show movies
during the summer, an advantage not enjoyed by theaters on
the side streets."

In 1961 Sol Schwartz resigned as president of RKO, to be

succeeded by Harry Mandel. Encouraged by a shift in attitude by the new management, the two young men renewed their efforts. During the next few years negotiations with a variety of people came frequently to the very edge of consummation and then broke down. Prospective buyers, eager at first, would find the stage too shallow, the price too high, the remodeling job too big, the storage space too small. "At least six times we thought we had that theater bought," Jack Perlman said recently, "but at the last minute the deal would collapse."

Then one day things began to fall into place. During World War II, Paul Vroom had been company manager of *Winged Victory*, Moss Hart's answer to Irving Berlin's *This Is the Army*. In the box office was a young airman named James Nederlander, one of five sons of David Nederlander, a Detroit jeweler who had formed a partnership with the Shuberts back in 1912, just as the Palace was being built. His first theater was the Detroit Opera House. Later he acquired other theaters in Detroit, and eventually parted from the Shuberts. His latest Detroit house was the resplendent Fisher, and he had acquired several Chicago houses as well.

The family had long wanted to own a theater in New York, and one day in 1964 James Nederlander learned that the Palace might be available. There is nothing noticeably sentimental about James Nederlander, but his instinctive showmanship told him that the acquisition of the Palace would bring the kind of publicity money alone couldn't buy.

Some time later Nederlander, his wartime colleague Paul

Vroom, and attorney Jack Perlman held a meeting. Then followed a series of negotiations with RKO, and on August 19, 1965, James Nederlander, representing his family, took title to the Palace. Paul Vroom was named general manager and Jack Perlman legal counsel. Though never officially stated, the purchase price was $1,600,000. That was for the theater building alone. The ground would rent for $63,000 a year—and up—until Martin Beck's original lease expired on January 1, 2017. The plan was to restore the Palace to its original Edwardian elegance and convert it into a legitimate theater for musicals; with its seating capacity of nearly two thousand, it would be much too big for straight plays.

Because there had been so many false alarms, negotiations had been kept fairly quiet: the announcement of the purchase was greeted with cries of joy and a good deal of space in the press. The Palace would be the first addition to the list of Broadway's legitimate theaters since the Ethel Barrymore opened in 1928. A few diehards mourned the final sealing of vaudeville's fate, but that was strictly academic. Vaudeville no longer existed; what passed for it could be seen only on television.

The restoration of the Palace was done under the watchful eye of James Nederlander. To redesign the theater, strip away the gimcrack accretion of years, and uncover its original beauty, Mr. Nederlander acquired the talents of the brilliant Ralph Alswang. Like Nederlander and Vroom, Alswang was an alumnus of *Winged Victory*. A man of great gifts and enormous energy, he had been associated with the Nederlanders in previous theater projects.

In August 1965 the Palace ran its last movie, *Harlow*—a

tawdry affair based on a tawdry book that purported to be
the life of the sex symbol of the 1930s. Reclamation began
immediately thereafter. If there were ghosts of old-time Palace greats still lingering around the premises, they soon
found themselves homeless. Before the theater could be built
up, it had to be virtually torn down. Restoring the Palace to
its former beauty would require demolition of nearly everything but the foundation and the four walls.

"What we want," Jimmy Nederlander told reporters, "is
plush, not plastic." And his brother Joseph, interviewed
back home in Detroit, declared: "We bought the Palace
because it was there. Buying it was to us what scaling the
highest peak is to a mountain climber."

The first few weeks were bedlam. Saws and hammers, chis-
els and drills, shouts of workmen, made an ungodly racket.
Outside changes were comparatively simple. Inside, the theater faced radical reconstruction. The star dressing room on
the stage floor, for which all those great ladies of the Palace
past had fought and bled and walked out, was demolished to
clear space for the deeper backstage area now needed for big
musicals. A new star dressing room was in the process of
construction in the basement for the use of Gwen Verdon,
who—it was presently announced—would open the new Palace in the title role of *Sweet Charity*, a musical by Neil
Simon, Cy Coleman, and Dorothy Fields. The show was
based on Fellini's touching film *Nights of Cabiria*.

If the first few weeks had been bedlam, the next few were
chaos. It hardly seemed possible that the theater would be
ready for the show, whose opening date had been announced

as January 25. Besides new dressing rooms and the enlarged stage, a whole new electrical and lighting system was installed. Every conceivable mechanical improvement was made. Only the old backstage elevator, allegedly installed for Sarah Bernhardt, remained untouched. That tiny cage, with its scruffy walls, worn carpet, and creaky machinery, survived, for reasons either of sentiment or economy. Or maybe it was just an oversight in the reigning hysteria.

Amid the chaos, work somehow progressed. Out front, the seats were ripped from their moorings. Sections of the orchestra pit were hewn away to make room for additional musicians. Ugly false fronts, now torn out, revealed for the first time in years the original stage boxes, the beautiful painted ceiling, the annunciators on either side of the proscenium arch, still lettered with the name of some long-forgotten act.

Ralph Alswang seemed to be everywhere at the same time. Exploring the basement, he uncovered a large, handsomely paneled room with twin marble mantels, originally a gentlemen's lounge, but for many years sealed up. In this room— now restored—he also found several crystal chandeliers that had graced the theater and lobby in days gone by. In a corner was a vintage safe which turned out to be the repository for Mme. Bernhardt's nightly shower of gold.

Where pieces of old paneling were missing, Alswang had them reproduced by the finest artisans. Where sections of the old chandeliers were lost, he had them copied. The walls were paneled in crimson and gold. The new seats, far more comfortable than the old ones, were upholstered in matching red plush. And the new Palace would have one thing the old Palace never had—a bar running the whole length of the outer lobby.

The blank walls of the inner lobby and the mezzanine presented a problem. Through the solving of this problem I found myself once again involved in Palace activities. Back in New York after a long Hollywood spell, I was working part time at the Museum of the City of New York. There, in the Theater Collection, was an enormous file of Palace portraits. Sam Pearce, the Curator of the Collection, decided to put on a retrospective exhibit to coincide with the reopening of the theater. It was my happy task to help him organize it.

James Nederlander, told about the forthcoming exhibit, came up to the Museum with Ralph Alswang and persuaded Mr. Pearce to put on a larger display of Palace performers in the theater itself. So some two hundred paintings, drawings, and caricatures were transferred from Fifth Avenue and 103rd Street to 47th Street and Broadway. For a couple of delightful weeks I spent long hours in the theater, helping Mr. Pearce and Ralph Alswang with the job of hanging the pictures. It wasn't exactly like old times, but for that little while I felt a part of the Palace again.

Ralph Alswang was the guiding spirit of the theater's reincarnation. The new Palace, he felt, should have the ambience of the old one. "It will not be a slavish copy of the old theater," he explained. "What we want to do is to re-create the look and the atmosphere of the old Palace, but with greater convenience and comfort. We want people to feel as if they were coming to the Palace with the same sense of anticipation that brought them there in the old days."

Accomplishing all this took infinite pains, infinite patience, a great deal of time, and a great deal of money—outrageously more, stormed Mr. Nederlander at one point, than the original budget. So much more, in fact, that for several days it seemed likely that the ladies' lounge would look the same in 1966 as it had in 1913.

There were the usual delays—rainstorms, blizzards, material that didn't arrive, fabrics that didn't match, bouts of influenza. And then there was the one great *un*usual delay, caused by the paralyzing transportation strike that hit New York on New Year's Day of 1966 and practically immobilized the whole town for twelve nightmarish days.

Somehow, through it all, the work went ahead. And somehow, despite the lack of transportation, the box office, presided over by still another *Winged Victory* veteran, George Handy, did a rushing business. Lines formed early and stayed late. Curious members of the public sneaked into the theater, mingling with the workmen and the newspapermen who came round in ever increasing numbers as the opening date of January 25 grew closer. But the closer it came, the further away it seemed. At last, and reluctantly, that opening date was postponed to the 29th, a Saturday. All tickets dated January 29, read the announcement of the delay, must be presented at the box office for exchange or refund. Only tickets marked Opening Night would be honored on Saturday.

That brought forth a storm of protests. One outraged ticket holder for the Saturday-night performance made dire threats of everything from lawsuits to mayhem if his tickets were not honored. Only the imperturbable Mr. Vroom knows how that was settled.

Saturday, January 29, was cold and clear. At the Palace scores of people worked feverishly all through the day. On stage the cast of *Sweet Charity* rehearsed almost until curtain time. Out front and in the lobbies, up in the balcony and down in the depths, workmen and artisans struggled to bring the final touch of perfection to the reclaimed theater. At the box office, lines of people waited patiently and vainly to buy seats for what they knew would be a night to remember.

Long before the scheduled seven-o'clock curtain, long before the earliest first-nighters began to arrive, the curious and the celebrity seekers gathered on the once famous Palace beach, undeterred by the snow that had started falling late in the afternoon. Television cameras, radio announcers, and newspaper people from near and far were at their posts, ready to record one of the most important events in recent theatrical history.

For this event was more, much more, than the opening of a new show. It was the reopening of a fabled place, the realization of one man's dream, a theater that had first opened its doors more than half a century ago. This theater, scorned in its earliest days, had overcome its original handicaps, confounded its critics, burgeoned into worldwide fame, sunk into near oblivion, and survived a series of vicissitudes that had come close to destroying it. Somehow it had not only endured but been restored, when many theaters and other landmarks of 1913 had been demolished or debased in the name of progress.

250

The Republic Theatre, where I had seen *A Good Little Devil* that Easter Saturday afternoon so long ago, was still standing, surrounded now by cheapjack shops and orange-drink stands on the ruined block that is 42nd Street west of Broadway. But not the Republic any more; the Victory.

Directly opposite, the New Amsterdam, for decades the beautiful home of beautiful girls and fabulous funmakers of the *Ziegfeld Follies*, also remained, much of its charming exterior obscured by billboards, playing second-run movies almost around the clock. A bit farther down, another haven for late-night moviegoers, was the Eltinge—now, by an ironic twist, renamed the Empire.

On the northwest corner of 42nd Street and Broadway, Hammerstein's Victoria, so long the undisputed queen of vaudeville houses, had been for many years the Rialto, once specializing in horror films, recently another home of sex pictures. On the southeast corner stood the building that had been the Knickerbocker Hotel, a shabby ghost of its former self. On the ground level were a chain drugstore, a cheap jewelry mart, and a bookshop catering to "mature readers." Across the street, what used to be the Times Tower had become the Allied Chemical Tower. Its skeleton remained the same, but its face had gone modern.

Down Broadway, at 40th Street, where the original, beautiful Empire had proudly stood, one could still see the Metropolitan Opera House, silent, grimy, and waiting for the executioner. A few blocks north, where Rector's had once reigned supreme, were a shoe store, a souvenir shop, and an eatery named Hector's. Directly opposite, the once beautiful Hotel Astor was in its death throes. Gone, all of them. Gone, or going, or changed past enduring. But the Palace was still there, and still beautiful.

Well before the announced seven-o'clock opening the audience began to arrive, stepping out of town cars and taxis onto the carpet spread from the street to the lobby, treading carefully through the falling snow and the jostling crowd, glowing with anticipation. In furs and jewels and evening gowns, in black ties and white, through the ooohs and ahs and the "Who's she?" of the onlookers and the whirring of the TV cameras, the first-nighters made their way into the theater. The outer lobby, its bar stretching the full length of the south wall, blazed with light from the crystal chandeliers. And from the brocade walls of the inner lobby the stars looked down.

Palace stars they were, old and young, living and dead. Bernhardt was there, the Divine Sarah, who had brought the Palace its first success. Ed Wynn and Sophie Tucker; Judy Garland and Alan King; Will Rogers and Fanny Brice; Ethel Barrymore and Eddie Cantor and W. C. Fields and Elsie Janis and the Marx Brothers and Nora Bayes and hundreds more who had helped make the Palace what it was. Looking down, they seemed to be remembering the old and giving their blessing to the new. Many of them were gone forever, others too ill or too far away to be there in person. Among those who did come that night were Ethel Merman and Milton Berle. Peter Lind Hayes, who had played the Palace with his famous mother, Grace Hayes, was there, too, covering the opening for the radio show he does with his beautiful wife, Mary Healy.

252

The murmurs of delight at the beauty of the theater, regal in its crimson and gold, sank to a whisper and then died down as the house lights dimmed and the overture began. The golden curtain began its slow, suspenseful rise.

It was a night of triumph for Gwen Verdon, a dazzling step upward in the already sparkling career of a young star who had now earned her place among the Palace immortals, with whose portraits her own hung in a place of honor. But it was a night of triumph for the Palace, too; another star whose light, once so brilliant, had often flickered and almost gone out since the long-ago dream of Martin Beck. Now, thanks to new dreams and the imagination and hard work of a handful of men, that star shone with even greater luster than before. "That theatre of much legend and weepy remembrance," as one reporter put it, was The Palace once again.

TEN DREAM BILLS

Because many Palace fans, after all these years, feel so strongly about their personal favorites, the author of this book has included here a sampling of ideal programs contributed by some of those who remember. How visionary these passions may be is shown in a note from Abel Green of *Variety*, which accompanied his own choice: "Ideal vaudeville bills are unrealistic, since even in that era the Big Time could not afford them. Keep in mind that a $10,000 to $12,000 budget for a Palace bill that probably grossed $22,000 was disproportionate. Obviously if they paid that thousand a day (in gold yet!) to Sarah Bernhardt, they had to cheat on the rest of the show; that is, cool it on the lesser acts but still make the show appear costly. Nevertheless my ideal bill does illustrate how a typical show would be laid out—that is, the dumb show for opener, and usually a flash act for closer. A No. 2 act would be a so-called 'polite' turn, but by then the audience should have been seated. It was kind of chic to walk in on the first act; hence it had to be silent—animal or pantomimic. The same planning would apply to the final act, which, unless it was a big band and held them seated, they would start walking out on."

ABEL GREEN
(EDITOR OF *Variety*)

Toto the Clown
George Whiting and Sadie Burt
Julius Tannen
Irene Bordoni
INTERMISSION
Lou Holtz
Belle Baker
Will Rogers
Willie West and McGinty

JOHN BYRAM
(former publicity man at the Palace and a drama editor of
The New York Times)

Willie West and McGinty
Rastelli (great juggler)
Phil Baker and Sid Silvers
Savoy and Brennan
Nora Bayes
INTERMISSION
Maurice and Florence Walton
Frank Fay (the act he did with Patsy Kelly and
Willie Haggerty)
Jack Donahue
Marx Brothers
Afterpiece, using most of acts

255

ANDREW A. PONARAS
(former owner of Gus and Andy's restaurant, close to the Palace stage door)

The Albins (acrobatic adagio team)
King, King and King (tap dancers)
Peter Higgins (Irish tenor)
Yorke and Allen (Bert Yorke and Fred Allen, comedy)
The De Marcos (ballroom dancers)
INTERMISSION
Buck and Bubbles (comedy and dancing)
James Barton in *Mad Dog*
Willie West and McGinty

MAX GORDON
(theatrical producer, formerly associated with the Palace)

Gillette's Monkeys
Williams and Wolfus
Frank Keenan and Co.
Mr. and Mrs. Vernon Castle
INTERMISSION
Avon Comedy Four
Frank Tinney
Robert Emmet Keane and Co. in *The Faker*
Nora Bayes
Willie West and McGinty

WILLIAM McCAFFREY
(former Palace booker)

The Bracks (acrobats)
Doyle and Dixon
Avon Comedy Four
Harry Carroll and Anna Wheaton
Ethel Barrymore
INTERMISSION
Bert and Betty Wheeler
Elsie Janis
Ted Healey and Stooges
Fink's Mules

LOUIS SOBOL
(theatrical columnist)

Joe Jackson
Jimmy Hussey
Eva Tanguay
Jack Donahue
Ethel Barrymore in *The Twelve Pound Look*
INTERMISSION
Clayton, Jackson and Durante
Sarah Bernhardt
Nora Bayes
Willie West and McGinty

ARTHUR WILLI
(former Palace booker)

Long Tack Sam (magic)
Step Brothers (tap dancers)
William Gaxton in *Kisses*
Burns and Allen
Fanny Brice
INTERMISSION
Harriet Hoctor
Clayton, Jackson and Durante
Frank Fay
Rath Brothers (acrobats)

GEORGE OPPENHEIMER
(playwright, author and dramatic critic of *Newsday*)

Charles Withers in *Grand Old Opry*
Clark and McCullough
Blanche Ring
Doyle and Dixon
Fanny Brice
INTERMISSION
Ethel Barrymore in *The Twelve Pound Look*
Joe Jackson
Annette Kellerman
George Jessel

SAM PEARCE
(curator, Theatre and Music Collection, Museum of the City
of New York)

A. Robins
Savoy and Brennan
Fanny Brice
Ted Lewis and His Orchestra, with Bobbe Arnst
INTERMISSION
Mr. and Mrs. Vernon Castle
Ethel Barrymore in *The Twelve Pound Look*
Sophie Tucker
Willie West and McGinty

BROOKS ATKINSON
(theater critic)

"My ideal Palace bill would be composed of the clowns. Here
are my favorite buffoons":

Marx Brothers	Joe Jackson
Ed Wynn	Bert Lahr
Smith and Dale	Jimmy Savo
Willie West and McGinty	W. C. Fields
Ben Blue	Phil Silvers
A. Robins	Lou Holtz
INTERMISSION	

INDEX

261

264

INDEX

Ulric, Lenore, 146

Van, Billy B., 49
Van, Gus, 45, 187, 188, 204, 212
Van and Schenck, 45, 141, 146, 158, 167, 210
Van Hoven, 109–11
Vannis, Four, 4
Velez, Lupe, 168
Verdon, Gwen, 246, 253
Victoria, Vesta, 122
Vroom, Paul, 242–3, 244–5

Walker, Charlotte, 44
Walker, June, 122
Wallendas, 202
Walsh, Blanche, 32, 47
Walters, Charles, 215
Walters, Gustave, 8
Walton, Florence, 53–54; see also Maurice and Walton
Ward, Fannie, 147
Ware, Helen, 133
Waring, Fred, 145, 158, 200
Warner Brothers, 183
Warren, Fran, 222
Water Rats, 70
Waters, Ethel, 154
Watson Sisters, 48, 146, 212
Webb, Clifton, 32–3, 164
Weber, Joe, 70; see also Weber and Fields
Weber and Fields, 48, 102, 119, 121, 202
Weiner, Jack, 174
Welch, Joe, 41
Welles, Orson, 47, 206
Wells, Kitty, 225
Welsh, Charles, 105
Wences, Señor, 217
West, Buster, 204

West, Mae, 50
Whalen, Richard, 138
Wheeler, Bert, 115–16, 162
Wheeler, Betty, 115
Whiffen, Mrs. Thomas, 52
Whipple, Bayonne, 145
White, Frances, 49, 52, 162, 189
White, George, 32
Whiteman, Paul, 78, 115, 126, 141, 146, 168, 189, 190–1
Whiting, Jack, 184, 195, 204
Whiting and Burt, 18, 48, 145
Whitney, Claire, 168
Wiere Brothers, 229–30
Willi, Arthur, 65–6, 197
Williams, Bert, 30, 88
Williams, Bob, 226
Williams, Frances, 212
Williams, Herb, 48, 165, 198
Williams, Percy, 9
Willie West and McGinty, 122
Wills, Nat, 18
Winchell, Walter, 27, 72, 174
Winwood, Estelle, 122
Wirth, May, 30, 95
Withers, Charles, 122
Wolfus, Hilda, 48
Wood, Audrey, 186
Woolf, Edgar Allan, 81
Wynn, Bessie, 21, 210
Wynn, Ed, 4–5, 6, 17, 141, 172, 216, 252
Wynn, Keenan, 5, 17

Yacht Club Boys, 191
Yorke and King, 84, 204
Yorke and King, 84, 204

Zardo, Eric, 119
Ziegfeld, Florenz, 32, 68–9, 115–16

267

MARIAN SPITZER

Marian Spitzer is a New Yorker by birth, education, and temperament. After graduation from New York University she was a reporter for metropolitan newspapers, while contributing stories and articles to major national magazines ranging from the *American Mercury* to the *Saturday Evening Post*. Her early passion for the theater was fed by her publicity chores at the Palace, described in this book, and a hitch on the staff of *Variety*. With her husband, the late playwright and film producer Harlan Thompson, she spent many years in Hollywood, where her work included screenplays for *The Dolly Sisters* and *Look for the Silver Lining*. She also has written two novels, as well as numerous radio and television scripts. Returning to New York with Mr. Thompson, she wrote the James Cagney movie *Shake Hands with the Devil* and worked two years for the New York City Office of Cultural Affairs. Today, when not writing, she devotes her time to the Theatre Collection of the Museum of the City of New York.

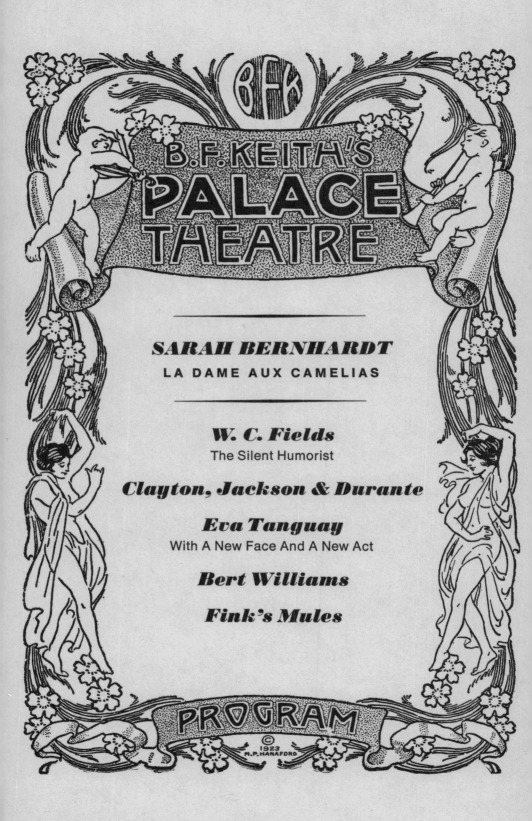

B.F. KEITH'S PALACE THEATRE

SARAH BERNHARDT
LA DAME AUX CAMELIAS

W. C. Fields
The Silent Humorist

Clayton, Jackson & Durante

Eva Tanguay
With A New Face And A New Act

Bert Williams

Fink's Mules

PROGRAM
© 1923
M. P. HANAFORD